ITALY
IN COLOR

Bonechi Edizioni • Firenze

Front cover: San Giulio Isle, Lake d'Orta, in Piedmont

Pubbli Aer Foto, conc. S.M.A. n. 534 del 27/12/1977

© Copyright 1972 by Bonechi - Edizioni «Il Turismo»
© Copyright 1985 by Bonechi - Edizioni «Il Turismo» S.r.l.
© Copyright 1991 by Bonechi - Edizioni «Il Turismo» S.r.l.
Via dei Rustici, 5 - 50122 Firenze
Tel. 055/2398224-5 - Telefax 055/216366

ISBN 88-7204-023-X

Text, layout, and editing: *Paolo Mazzoni* and *Claudio Pescio*
Translation: *Merry Orling*
Maps: *Studio Grafico Biagi & Capaccioli*, Firenze
Typesetting: *Leadercomp*, Firenze
Offset: *La Fotolitografia*, Firenze
Printing: *Lito Terrazzi* Firenze
Printed in Italy

NEW EDITION

CONTENTS

OUTLINE OF ITALIAN ART

GREEK

Starting from the 8th century B.C., the spread of Greek art and culture in the Mediterranean basin went hand in hand with the political expansion of the Greek city-states. While contacts with local civilizations sparked the birth of hybrid art forms, the presence of their original prototypes was always plainly discernible. In Italy, Greek influence was not confined to Greek-founded cities, spilling far beyond the borders of Magna Grecia northward to the Italic tribes, Etruscans, and eventually to the Latins inhabiting North and Central Italy. Indeed, its effect would endure for centuries. In ARCHITECTURE, three styles (or orders) developed in Greece between the 7th and 4th centuries. The same progression took place in Italy, albeit at a somwhat slower pace. A case in point is the *Doric* style, which was still being widely used in the Magna Grecia provinces, while *Ionic* was already giving way to *Corinthian* in Athens. Essential features of *Doric* columns (superb examples of which are to be found in the Paestum, Selinunte, and Agrigento temples) are a fluted shaft, tapered and resting on the ground, with éntasis to set off the unadorn capital. The columns sustained an architrave above which ran a frieze alternating sculpted and fluted metope panels. Gable-shaped tympanums adorned the sides of the temple, inside of which was a pronaos leading to the cella The *Ionic* order differed in three main respects: less bulk in the shaft, a base (plinth) inserted between the shaft and the ground, and volute ornamentation added to the capital. In the *Corinthian* order, the plinth became higher, the shaft even slimmer, and more elaborate ornamentation (acanthus-leaf motifs) was used to adorn the capital. Widespread use of the Ionic and Corinthian orders did not really come about until the Roman period, remaining, aside from brief intervals, constants in Italian architecture up to recent times. Greek theaters were also of prime importance as prototypes for Roman architecture. Semicircular in shape, they were in most cases incorporated into pre-existing natural slopes. Greek SCULPTURE, whose subjects mainly revolved around myths, may be divided into three major periods: Archaic, Classical, and Hellenistic. The *Archaic* (mid 7th century B.C.) produced smiling male (*kouros*) and female (*kore*) figures rendered in a rather abstract style. During the *Classical* period (mid 5th-mid 6th centuries B.C.), masters of the ilk of **Phidias**, **Polycletus**, **Myron**, and **Praxiteles** attained the ideal of equilibrium between nature and the divine toward which Greek art had been striving from the outset — thereby setting the esthetic canons that would govern the entire art world for over two millennia. In the *Hellenistic* period, the last and the longest (mid 4th century B.C. - 1st century A.D.), important schools (e.g., Pergamon) grew up in Asia Minor, while the Classical heritage split into a myriad of diverse styles whose only common trait was a marked trend toward realism. Greek PAINTING, reflections of which may be gleaned from Etruscan and Roman frescoes, has come down to us through vase painting. Three periods are distinguishable: *Geometric* (9th-8th centuries B.C.), *Corinthian* (8th-7th centuries B.C.), and *Attic* (after 7th century B.C.). Black figure decoration (black designs on light ground) preceded red figure (red designs on dark ground).

ETRUSCAN

Around the 9th century B.C., Etruscan civilization gradually began to fan out from Tuscany northward to the Po Valley in Emilia and southward into Campania, only to disappear completely in the 2nd century B.C. No unified Etruscan state ever existed, but rather confederations of cities ruled by a king (*lucumone*), the most prominent of which were Tarquinia, Cerveteri, Arezzo, Fiesole, Cortona, and Chiusi. Of Etruscan art, only tombs and tomb fittings have survived. The works that have come down to us comprise paintings, urns, votive statues, and inscriptions — in a language that to this day has not been wholly deciphered. Stylistically, Etruscan art was primarily oriented to naturalism, shunning the idealistic strivings of the Greek masters. The little we know about Etruscan ARCHITECTURE comes from Roman sources. Scholars believe that the Etruscan temple (of which there are no examples extant) consisted of two sections, one porticoed and one roofed in, with terracotta sculpture adorning the roofing. The smooth columns of the portico were girthed by protective walls interpersed with gates. Two of the building techniques used in the walls, i.e., the *arch* and the *vault* would later be widely adopted by the Romans. Tombs, mainly concentrated in the major necropolises of Cerveteri, Populonia, and Tarquinia, were mostly underground, either surmounted by a *tumulus* mound or else by a *tholos* (i.e., a circular structure preceded by an entrance hall). The earliest examples of Etruscan SCULPTURE that have come down to us, urns with lids in the shape of human figures (*canopi*) unearthed in Chiusi, date from the 7th century B.C. In the 6th century the school of Veii (whose greatest exponent, **Vulca**, was active in Rome) turned out works such as the *Villa Giulia Apollo* (Rome) in a style that recalls the Greek *kouros*. Two bronzes, the *Capitoline She-Wolf* (Rome, Palazzo dei Conservatori) and the *Chimera* (Florence, Museo Archeologico), date from slightly later. Sarcophagi with portraits of the deceased on the lid, e.g., the 6th century *Sarcofago degli Sposi* (Rome, Villa Giulia) are typical of Etruscan sculpure. The naturalistic treatment of the tomb figures became more and more marked, culminating in the incredibile realism of the 2nd century B.C. lifesize bronze figure called the *Haranger* (Florence, Museo Archeologico). Surviving Etruscan PAINTING consists mostly of tomb frescoes (the finest of which in Tarquinia). Their strikingly bright color schemes were evidently influenced by Greek mosaics. The most popular subjects, scenes from everyday life, include festivals, religious rites, banquets, deities, and battle scenes.

Detail of Statue A, one of the celebrated Bronze Warriors of Riace. The two masterpieces of 5th century B.C. Greek sculpture were discovered by a skindiver in 1972 off the coast of the Calabrian village of Riace and restored in Florence. They are now the pride of Reggio Calabria's Museo Nazionale.

Left: Mater Matuta, Etruscan funerary urn from Chianciano (Florence, Museo Archeologico).

Detail of the Acilia Sarcophagus, a fine example of 3rd century A.D. Roman sculpture. (Rome, Museo Nazionale Romano).

ROMAN

Prior to the conquest of Greece, Roman art was primarily the result of the Greek influxes it received via the Etruscans (afterward assimilated directly). As a result, for centuries it was impossible to speak of Roman art in the real sense of the term — still another reason being that, since Roman citizens considered artistic activities beneath their dignity, they left such piddling matters to foreigners. In addition, a distinction must be made between the official artistic output of the capital and that of the provinces and outlying regions of the Empire. The Romans made their greatest contributions in ARCHITECTURE (and engineering), mainly in the public works they left wherever they set foot. Among their innovations: the basilica, the commemorative column with relief scenes, and the arch of triumph. The *Colosseum* and the *Amphitheater* of Pozzuoli are examples of the Romans' inimitable skill at exploiting their taste for the gigantic as propaganda for their own grandeur. Roman baths and temples were a fusion of diverse styles (i.e., the *composite order* combining the Ionic and Corinthian). Like the commemorative columns of Trajan and Hadrian, the triumphal arches in the major cities recall the military victories of the emperors, while the Oriental style mausoleums evoke their personal glory. The palace complexes the emperors built themselves were so huge that even the scarce surviving remains (e.g., the *Domus Aurea* and *Palatine*) well suffice to convey an idea of their incredible size. Non as huge, but equally impressive is *Hadrian's Villa* at Tivoli. Two mainstreams run through Roman SCULPTURE: Etruscan-Hellenistic Greek realism and Classical Greek idealism. Both tendencies appear in official portraiture (e.g., the *Augustus*

of Prima Porta in the Musei Vaticani in Rome). Two of the most revealing examples are Augustus' *Ara Pacis* in Rome, whose procession reliefs typify the rhythmic Classical style, and *Trajan's Column*, whose spiraling reliefs of the Emperor's military achievements are executed in a much less Classical manner, clearly imbued with the expressionism typical of provincial art (and indeed they have been attributed to a foreigner, *Apollodurus of Damascus*). Nevertheless, the Classical style continued to prevail under Hadrian, but, by the end of the 2nd century A.D., the provincial style, notably abstract and symbolic, had become firmly entrenched (e.g., *Marcus Aurelius' Column* in Rome). Such tendencies grew more and more marked in the 3rd and 4th centuries (see sarcophagi and decorative reliefs such as those on the *Arch of Constantine*). Late Roman sculptors looked eastward — even imperial power was conceived in Oriental terms, with the emperor representing an abstract deity outside the bounds of history or even reality. Most of the Roman PAINTING that has come down to us consists of the 2nd-1st century style (i.e., rapid brush stroke and patches of color conveying a great sense of immediacy and vitality), then widespread throughout the Hellenistic world.

EARLY CHRISTIAN

Christianity's earliest years were spent in alternating periods of tolerance and persecution, depending on the moods and whims of the emperor who happened to be on the throne at the time. Only in the 4th century, under Constantine, could the new religion come out into the open and monotheism replace the gods of pagan Olympus. However, newborn Christian art, aside from its subject matter, was very much

8

Left: Equestrian Statue of Marcus Aurelius, 1st century B.C. bronze (Rome).

Christ with Archangels, St. Vitale, and Bishop Ecclesius, 5th century mosaic in the church of San Vitale, Ravenna.

part of its times in terms of technique. In ARCHITECTURE, the Christians utilized the Roman aisled basilica for their churches, adapting it to their liturgical requirements and later adding transepts (that incidentally created a cross-shaped plan in keeping with Christian symbolism). One of the earliest examples of the basilican church, *San Giovanni in Laterano* in Rome, was built in the 4th century, about the same time that another type of building, the round baptistry, was developing. In SCULPTURE, carved sarcophagi continued to be the major form of expression. In PAINTING, right from the time of the catacombs, Christianity developed its own iconography, endowing conventional Classical motifs with new symbolic meanings. For instance, Christ was representend as Orpheus, but divested of Orpheus' pagan attributes, thus becoming an allegory for the souls in Limbo. This process continued for some centuries until assimilation of everything the Classical repertory could offer in terms of Christianity's message and correspondingly, the Church's teachings, was completed. Numerous examples of frescoes dating from the 1st through 4th centuries (after which time mosaic supplanted fresco as the main form of church decoration) are visible on the catacomb walls. Between the 4th and 6th centuries, the overriding influence was Byzantine, i.e., abstraction, gold grounds, and profusion of ornamental motifs, as evidenced in the mosaics of Milan (*Sant'Ambrogio*), Rome (*Santa Costanza*), and Ravenna (*San Vitale*). At the outset of the Middle Ages, the center of the art world was no longer, as in the Imperial Age, Rome. The splintering of the Classical heritage into a host of little rivulets was reflected in both political and economic spheres, as well as in language itself (i.e., Latin slowly dissolved into

dialect and then developed into the separate Romance tongues). During this time, all phases of culture became the exclusive dominion of the monasteries, whose main output consisted of illustrated (illuminated) manuscripts.

ROMANESQUE

Pre-Romanesque art (8th-10th centuries) had two distinct facets: the art of the Northern European courts (Carolingian and Ottonian) which, in a certain sense, was a continuation of the Classical tradition, and provincial art which followed in the direction taken by the Late Roman schools. Both of these co-existed in feudal Italy, that had gradually become a land of fiefs, each of which a separate entity. The Romanesque period did not really begin until the 11th century with the renewed upsurge of the cities , which led to the construction of the first great cathedrals. The architecture of the period was characterized by massive, thick-walled buildings covered with cross vaults or exposed beam ceilings, and sustained by round arches. Decorative motifs were inspired by local art with occasional Classical influxes. The main artistic centers were cities, i.e., Milan, Pavia, Modena, Venice, Florence, Pisa, Rome, Bari, and Monreale, but abbeys and monasteries were active all over the Italian countryside. Influences from Northern Europe were considerable. The typical church plan entailed a raised choir over a corresponding sunken crypt. The buildings were faced in stone (marble, whenever available), often in striped geometric patterns. SCULPTURE served mainly as church decoration (e.g., on portal jambs, architraves, capitals, and altars). Romanesque art, concrete and solid, showed little interest in proper proportions or accurate perspective.

9

Interior of the Romanesque church of San Miniato characterized by great round arches and ornamentation of colored marbles.

Facing page: rose window and Gothic portal of the Upper Church of the Basilica di San Francesco, Assisi.

Legends, Biblical stories, and scenes from life in the fields were among its most popular subjects. Several masters emerged in this period, e.g., **Wiligelmus** (bronze doors with *Genesis scenes* for the Duomo of Modena), **Gruamonte** (active in Pistoia), and **Bonanno** (*bronze doors* of the Pisa and Monreale cathedrals). In PAINTING, the most widespread forms of expression were illuminated manuscripts, frescoes, and mosaics (Monreale, Rome, and Venice). The impressive mosaics were mostly hieratic and abstract in style, revealing unsevered ties with the Byzantine tradition.

GOTHIC
The Gothic style, which originated in France around the end of the 12th century, began to exert its influence on Italian art in the 1200s. Its impact, due to strong local Romanesque undercurrents constantly present, differed from town to town. In Italy, Gothic was the art of the new social class, the bourgeoisie, accompanied by the re-emergence of the cities and the renewal of trade. In ARCHITECTURE, the cathedral represented a collective project, i.e., the house of worship of citizens often associated in guilds (*Arti*). The main features of this style, i.e., pointed arches and use of stained glass and rose windows to convey a sense of airiness, emphasize a strictly upward thrust (in contrast to the earthbound Romanesque churches). Some notable examples are the Parma *Baptistry*, *San Francesco* in Assisi, *Santa Chiara* in Naples, and the cathedrals of Pisa, Florence, Siena, Orvieto, and Milan. Civic architecture, mainly in the form of *palazzi pubblici* (town halls), also enjoyed a boom. Among the great achievements in this sector were *Palazzo Vecchio* in Florence, *Palazzo Pubblico* in Siena, and the

Doge's Palace in Venice. SCULPTURE, primarily commissioned to adorn churches, took on a more graceful look, adding sinuous curving lines to the geometric patterns favored in the Romanesque period. Some outstanding works were produced by **Benedetto Antelami** (Baptistry and Cathedral of Parma doors), **Nicola Pisano** (whose *pulpit* in the Pisa Baptistry reveals a prediliction for Classical art), and Nicola's son, **Giovanni** (who masterfully fused the Classical and Gothic in his *pulpit* in the Pisa Cathedral). Later **Arnolfo**, the Pisanos' pupil, spread their style throughout Italy, while the **Bon** and **Dalle Masegne** families worked in Venice and the **Cosmati** school was active in Rome. In PAINTING, altarpieces became just as important as frescoes in church decoration. The Byzantine tradition remained strong, however, even in innovative painters such as **Cimabue** until the late 13th century when the Florentine master, **Giotto** came along. In his Assisi, Padua, and Florence frescoes, he endowed the human figure — no longer rendered in abstract forms — with a new psychological insight, placing them in believable, rather than symbolic, settings. The more courtly school that was developing around **Simone Martini**, the **Lorenzettis**, and their followers about the same time in Siena never lost its ties with the contemporary Northern European school known as the International Style. Although Florence and Siena dominated 14th century painting, other schools started to emerge: **Tommaso da Modena** and **Giovanni da Milano** in the north, **Traini** in Pisa, and **Jacobello del Fiore** in Venice. Non-Tuscan International Style painters such as **Gentile da Fabriano**, **Jacopo Bellini**, and the **Vivarinis** were the major exponents of late 14th century painting.

The Burning of Borgo, one of Raphael's frescoes in the Vatican Stanze, Rome (1514-1517).

RENAISSANCE

Much has been said and written about what the *Renaissance* (literally, rebirth) was and just when it took place: by the term, people generally refer to the unequalled artistic outpouring that originated in 15th century Florence from whence it spread to all of Europe. A major factor in its development was *Humanism*, i.e., the rediscovery of the Classical world by 14th and 15th century scholars who viewed man at the center of the universe — as opposed to medieval philosophers to whom man was a subordinate component in the organization of the cosmos. Anatomy, perspective, and foreshortening were thoroughly investigated. In ARCHITECTURE, the greatest contribution was made by **Filippo Brunelleschi** whose daring projects such as the Florence Cathedral *dome* and *Pazzi Chapel* changed the course of 15th century art. Research along similar lines was pursued by **Leon Battista Alberti**, both in theoretic terms (a treatise, *De Re Aedificatoria*) and concretely (a church, *Sant'Andrea* in Mantua). The Renaissance innovations rapidly spread throughout Italy, in part thanks to the patronage of the *Signori*. The enlightened dukes commissioned, among others, **Laurana** to design *Palazzo Ducale* in Urbino, **Rossetti** to transform Ferrara's townplan, and **Rossellino** to rebuild an entire city (Pienza). In the 1500s, the spatial investigations initiated in the previous century reached their culmination in Rome where **Bramante** designed his *Tempietto in San Pietro in Montorio*, and **Michelangelo** the *dome* of St. Peter's. At the same time, Sansovino was constructing the *Libreria Marciana* in Venice, **Vasari** the *Uffizi* in Florence, and **Palladio** villas in the Venetian countryside. In SCULPTURE, the first great

master of the 15th century, **Donatello** invented a new relief technique (the flat *"stiacciato"* of the *St. George* predella in the Bargello) while, at the same time, endowing his sculpture with new naturalism and emphasis on three-dimensionality. The great sculptors who followed him, **Jacopo della Quercia**, the **Della Robbias**, and **Verrocchio**, continued along these same lines. The end of the 15th century and most of the next were dominated by the gigantic figure of **Michelangelo**, whose works span the *St. Peter's Pietà* of 1499 to the *Rondanini Pietà* he was still working on at his death in 1564 (Milan, Castello Sforzesco). The great contributions of 15th-16th century PAINTING consisted essentially in the mastery of perspective, foreshortening, and light-shade effects, plus addition of new (more wordly) themes to the already numerous religious subjects. Chronologically, the major names of the early 15th century after **Masaccio** (frescoes in the Carmine Church *Brancacci Chapel* in Florence) were **Piero della Francesca** (frescoes in San Francesco in Arezzo) and **Fra Angelico** (frescoes and altarpieces in the San Marco Museum in Florence). The second half of the century was dominated by Lorenzo the Magnificent: **Paolo Uccello** (*Battle of San Romano* in the Uffizi) and **Sandro Botticelli** (*Allegory of Spring* and *Birth of Venus* in the Uffizi) were two of the outstanding artists who worked under his patronage. At the same time, **Giovanni Bellini**, Jacopo's son, was painting his warm-hued *Virgins* and *Pietàs* in Venice, laying the foundations for several generations of Venetian masters, and **Carpaccio** was creating his charming illustrations of Venetian life. They were followed by the great 16th century colorists: **Giorgione** (*The Tempest* in the Accademia in Venice), **Titian** (*Sacred*

Triumph of St. Ignatius, grandiose Baroque fresco painted by Andrea Pozzo (1685) on the ceiling of the church of Sant'Ignazio in Rome.

and *Profane Love* in the Galleria Borghese in Rome), **Tintoretto** (*Miracle of the Slave* in the Accademia in Venice), and **Veronese** (frescoes in the Villa di Maser near Treviso). Elsewhere, around the late 15th-early 16th centuries, **Leonardo da Vinci** carried out his Milan fresco experiment (*Last Supper* in the church of Santa Maria delle Grazie) while his fellow Tuscan, **Michelangelo**, was working on the Sistine Chapel ceiling in the Vatican. **Raphael,** who favored clear, bright color schemes and perfectly balanced compositions, was Michelagelo's chief rival. Among the most celebrated Raphaels are the *Vatican Stanze*, the *Marriage of the Virgin* in the Brera Museum in Milan, and the *Transfiguration* in the Musei Vaticani in Rome. Some outstanding artists were active outside the major centers: **Mantegna** (Mantua), **Correggio** (Parma), **Lorenzo Lotto** (Lombardy), and **Antonello da Messina** (an inveterate wanderer). *Mannerism*, a style which grew out of the enormous influence wielded by Michelangelo and Raphael on their contemporaries, originated around the middle of the 16th century. Its main exponents were **Rosso Fiorentino, Pontormo, Andrea del Sarto**, and **Parmigianino**.

BAROQUE

A prime factor in promoting Baroque religious art was the Catholic church's response to the rise of Protestantism in the form of the Counter-Reformation. The church, especially the Jesuit order, was instrumental in commissioning works aimed at instilling rigorous Catholicism in the viewers. The Jesuits sponsored many prominent works of ARCHITECT-URE, including the church of *Gesù* in Rome, the forerunner of scores of flamboyant creations that soon mushroomed all over Europe, which was designed by **Vignola** in 1568. The outstanding figure of the period was undoubtedly the architect-sculptor **Gian Lorenzo Bernini** whose overpowering buildings, fountains, and sculptures changed the face of Rome. His main rival, **Borromini** *(Sant'Ivo alla Sapienza)* favored a less theatrical Baroque. Outside Rome, the major names were **Guarini** (dome of the *Cappella della Sindone* in Turin) and **Zimbalo**, the principal exponent of the flamboyant Baroque school of Lecce (church of *Santa Croce*). **Bernini** was also the dominant figure in Baroque SCULP-TURE, aiming to fuse dynamic three-dimensional masses into the architecture itself. Proof of the emotional effect he attained can be seen in works such as the *Ecstasy of St. Theresa* in Santa Maria della Vittoria in Rome. Two widely different mainstreams co-existed in PAINTING: on one hand, a return to Classical models championed by the **Carracci** workshop (active in Rome and Bologna), and, on the other, harsh realism emphasized by intense light-shade contrasts developed by **Caravaggio**. Other important facets of Baroque painting are the huge murals and ceiling frescoes painted by **Pietro da Cortona, Maratta**, and **Luca Giordano** to decorate the grandiose Baroque palaces, and the new subjects which achieved great popularity such as landscapes, still-lifes, views of Roman ruins, and the like.

18th CENTURY

In the 18th century, Italy relinquished its its primary position in the European art world, as Italian Baroque gradually shed its religious content, turning into the flouncy ornamental style known as *Rococo*.Nevertheless, the birth of Illuminism had a positive effect on all sectors of artistic endeavor. In

Two Mothers, by Giovanni Segantini (1889), from the collection of the Galleria d'Arte Moderna in Milan.

ARCHITECTURE, the most important names were **Filippo Juvara** in Turin (*Basilica di Superga*, 1717-1730), **Fuga** in Rome (facade of *Santa Maria Maggiore*, 1743), **Vaccaro** in Naples (*cloister* of Santa Chiara), and **Vanvitelli** in Naples and Caserta (*Reggia* of Caserta). Outstanding works of SCULPTURE were produced by **Serpotta** (in Palermo) and **Morlaiter** (in Venice). In PAINTING, **Solimena** continued Luca Giordano's decorative tradition in Naples, although the fulcrum of the painting world had in the meantime shifted back to Venice. Among the Venetian masters active during the 1700s, the most prominent were the landscapists **Canaletto, Guardi**, and **Bellotto**, the frescoist **Tiepolo**, the genre painter **Longhi**, and the woman portrait painter, **Rosalba Carriera**.

19th CENTURY

At the end of the 18th century with the birth of *neo-Classicism*, Rome once more ranked as a major art center. In ARCHITECTURE, scores of Classical-style palaces and churches were built all over Rome, Venice, and Milan (where **Piermarini** designed the *Teatro della Scala* at the turn of the century). Not long afterward, new technologies and building techniques allowed experimenting new architectural forms such as the *Mole Antonelliana* in Turin (1863) and the *Gallerie* of Milan and Naples. The most prominent figure in SCULPTURE was **Antonio Canova** (*Paolina Borghese* in the Galleria Borghese in Rome). Two mainstreams ran through 19th century PAINTING. At the beginning of the century, the neo-Classical school, mainly focusing on historical subjects, predominated, although it was soon supplanted by the *Romantic school* whose subjects dwelled on every form of human sentiment as well as the picturesque quality of places and things. The major Italian exponents of this school were **Cremona** and **Hayez**. Around the mid-1800s, the Tuscan *Macchiaioli* (e.g., **Lega, Fattori,** et al) reacted to traditional schemes, aiming instead to duplicate what the eye perceives through the juxtaposition of patches (= *macchie*) of paint. Some years later, the innovations of the French Pointillists and Impressionists exerted considerable influence on the Italian art world, especially on artists such as **Segantini, Previati**, and **Pellizza da Volpedo**.

20th CENTURY

There have been so many schools and currents in 20th century art — most of them on an international scale — that it would be impossible to sort them out. In ARCHITECTURE (as well as several other artistic fields), the dominant style at the turn of the century was *Art Nouveau*, the flowery ornamental style of curving lines and flourishes that soon became popular with architects and designers all over Italy. Thereafter, Italian architects, like those elsewhere for that matter, designed buildings to fit the changing times — industrial plants, high-rise housing, and skyscrapers. The most prominent include **Nervi, Ponti**, and **Michelucci**. In PAINTING and SCULPTURE, *Futurism* (**Balla, Boccioni**) was the first major art movement of the 20th century. Among the mainstreams that have played, or are playing, a significant role in Italian art of the 20th century, we might mention *Cubism, abstract art, metaphysical art* (**De Chirico**), *Surrealism, neo-Realism, Op, Pop, hyper-Realism...* but, of course, the list will not stop here.

VALLE D'AOSTA

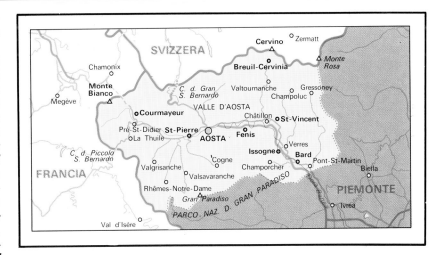

The Valle d'Aosta, the alpine region par excellence, occupies the whole northern section of the Graie Alps, the western Pennine Alps, and whole group of little valleys situated in the vicinity of the Vallata della Dora Baltea, the "backbone" of the region. The tallest peaks in Europe are all to be found in this area: Gran Paradiso (4061 m), Mont Blanc (4810 m), Cervino (4478 m), and Monte Rosa (4638 m). (Monte Rosa is partly in Aosta, partly in Piedmont.) The landscape of the region is typically alpine: the valleys are farmlands and, as altitude increases, you encounter pasture lands, forests, glaciers, alpine rocks, and sheer cliffs. Aosta's economic resources comprise cattle-raising, mining, steel mills, hydroelectric power, textiles, and crafts (furniture and embroidery), but tourism is the most important of all, especially in winter when the region is a skier's paradise. The climate is milder in the valleys, with very little rainfall, and very cold in the upper reaches of the mountains.

HISTORY AND ART - The Ligurian tribe of the Libui were the first to settle the region. They were succeeded by the Salassi, of Ligurian and Celtic background, who in turn were succeeded by the Romans in the 1st century B.C. after long, bloody battling. There are still extensive remains of the Roman period all over the region, especially in the capital. During the Middle Ages, Valle d'Aosta, first a Frankish territory, was chopped into tiny fiefdoms. (Evidence of this is visible today in the numerous castles dotting the region.) In the 11th century it passed under the jurisdiction of the House of the Savoy. In the 12th century the Valdostani obtained a constitution, the Magna Carta, from Duke Tomaso I of Savoy that allowed them a certain amount of autonomy. This marked the beginning of one of the best periods in their history: churches and castles were built and all the arts, including the so-called minor arts, flourished. The region's autonomy was officially sanctioned by the Italian government in 1948.

Mt. Cervino viewed from Lake Bleu in the Breuil Valley. One of the most scenic in the Alps the 4478-meter peak was climbed for the first time in 1865.

AOSTA

Located at the confluence of the Buthier and Dora Baltea rivers, right where the roads to Mont Blanc and the Gran San Bernardo intersect, Aosta is an important industrial and artistic center. It was settled by the Salassi in the pre-Roman period. When it was conquered by the Romans in 25 B.C. it was made capital of the region and christened *Augusta Praetoria*. Under the Romans, building activity was intense: bridges, aqueducts, and public and private buildings were erected. Today, echoes of Aosta's Roman past are still visible in the city walls, the grid townplan, and several important monuments. During the Middle Ages, it was conquered first by the Goths, Franks, and Saracens, be-fore succumbing to the Savoys in 1025. From then on it remained under the Savoy monarchy, without, however, completely losing its political and administrative autonomy. It also achieved notable economic well-being and a prominent standing as an artistic center. Modern-day Aosta a major tourist center, extends way beyond the old Roman city walls. Its best-loved festivity is the Fair of Sant'Orso, held annually on January 31.

ARCO DI AUGUSTO - The Arch of Augustus, erected by the Romans when they founded the city of Aosta in 25 B.C., consists of a single arch framed by four semicolumns on the sides. The slate roofing was added in the 18th century, while the wooden *Crucifix* in the middle of the archway dates from the 1400s.

COLLEGIATA DI SANT'ORSO - Early medieval church buildings once rose in the area around the Collegiata. The present-day church, founded in the 10th century, was altered in the Renaissance period and once again in the 18th century. The facade, with its pointed-arch portal and two huge windows, dates from the 15th century. The massive belltower is Romanesque. Pillars set off the single-aisle interior. The nave and apse are adorned with late 15th century paintings. The wooden *choir stalls* were carved by local craftsmen in the 16th century. The subjects of this remarkable work include saints, animals, and hunting scenes. In the *Treasury* are goblets, illuminated manuscripts, and ecclesiastical garments, as well as the so-called *Reliquary of Sant'Orso*. Another interesting feature of the church is the 11th century *crypt* and the remains of frescoes — also 11th century — below the church roofing (reached by the stairs in the left aisle). The 12th century Romanesque *cloister* contains superb *capitals* sculpted in a style very reminiscent of the French Romanesque. Their subjects range from Biblical scenes, prophets, and animals, to episodes from the life of St. Orso.

ROMAN THEATER - All that remains of what was once a huge Roman theater are sections of the cavea, stage, and the huge outer walls. Rusticated stone arches are cut into the ground floor and single arch openings into the upper floor walls. Not far from the theater, where the monastery of Santa Caterina now stands, are sections of the Roman *amphitheater* characterized by wide-span archways.

FENIS - (14 km). Situated on a hill in the Valley of the Dora River, the *Castle of Fénis* is one of the most beautiful, picturesque, and best-preserved in all of Europe. It was built in 1340 by Ajmone di Challant, descendant of one of the oldest and most renowned of the Valle d'Aosta noble families. Despite 19th century restoration, its original appearance is virtually intact: it is a perfect medieval castle with both cylindrical and squared-off towers, crenelation, and window slits. Inside is a courtyard with a staircase leading to picturesque loggias. Upstairs are 15th century frescoes by Jacopo Jacquerio depicting *St. George and the Dragon* and a cycle of *Sages from Antiquity*. Inside is the *Museo dell'Arredamento Valdostano*, with exhibits covering various periods of furnishings from the Valle d'Aosta region.

COURMAYEUR - (30 km). Courmayeur, situated 1224 meters above sea level below the peak of Mont Blanc, is one of the most famous ski resorts in the world. The town has superb hotels, restaurants, and skiing facilities, as well as lifts giving access to the peaks. Nearby are sights of extraordinary historical interest. First a Salassan, and then Roman city, it soon became a popular resort. The British, pioneers of

17

alpine tourism, have been coming here since the 18th century. In 1965 its importance was enhanced by the opening of the eleven-kilometer-long *Mont Blanc Tunnel* which from Courmayeur, Italy, goes to Chamonix, France. In the central square called Piazza Abate Henry are two noteworthy buildings, the 18th century church of *SS. Pantaleone e Valentino* and the *Museo Alpino* with exhibits relating to mountaineering. *Mont Blanc*, Europe's tallest mountain (4810 meters), is a

Entrance to the Mont Blanc tunnel.

spectacular sight. The first climbers to reach its peak were Michel Paccard and Jacques Balmat on August 8, 1786.

PIEDMONT

Piedmont, located in the westernmost corner of Italy, is bordered by mountains on three sides; on the south by the Maritime Alps, on the west by the Cozie and Graie Alps, and on the north by the Pennines. The region's eastern border, on the other hand, is the great Padana plain which comprises the Po, Italy's longest river (652 km), and its numerous affluents.

HISTORY - Settled in pre-Roman times Piedmont only reached prominence when Augustus' veterans founded cities all over the region. After the fall of the Roman Empire, it was conquered first by the Longobards and then by the Franks. During these troubled times, it broke up into a myriad of bickering fiefdoms, Turin and Ivrea ranking among the most powerful. The importance of Turin steadily increased throughout the 10th and 11th centuries, along with that of its rulers, the counts of Savoy, and that of the marquis of Monferrato. In the 14th century the Savoys, led by Amedeo VI (called the Green Count) and Amedeo VII (called the Red Count), successfully thwarted the expansionist aims of the Viscontis, lords of Milan, and proceeded to unify the entire region. At the outset of the 15th century, the Savoys obtained the title of dukes and extended their territory even further. This period of grace did not, however, last long, and soon Piedmont succumbed to the French king, Charles III. In the 16th century the region was swept by the winds of Protestantism, which arrived in the form of the converted Valdese sect (Pietro Valdo was a 12th century preacher from Lyon) and spread throughout the alpine valleys. In 1559 Emanuele Filiberto managed to restore Piedmont's autonomy from the French. Only a few decades later, in the early 1600s, a new threat arose, this time from Spain bent on annexing Monferrato to her territories.

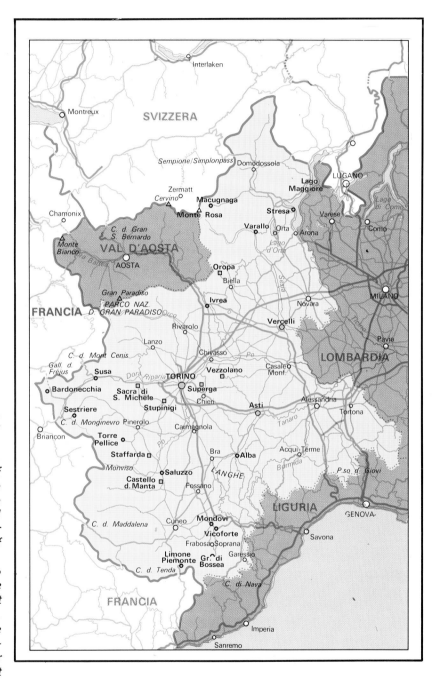

Weakened by the great effort of withstanding the Spaniards, the Savoys were no match for the French, who once more wrested control of the Savoy lands in 1631. After numerous attempts at regaining their autonomy, the Savoys, with the help of their Austrian allies, managed to defeat the French in 1706 and extend their territory to include Sicily which, however, was later exchanged with Sardinia. Piedmont was at the forefront in the struggle for Italian unity throughout the

whereas Romanesque architecture abounds: the Duomo of Ivrea (10th century), the Sanctuary of San Michele, and a host of other buildings in the lesser known centers. (This is mostly due to the great influence monastic culture exerted throughout the region.) There are also notable examples of Romanesque sculpture in Piedmontese churches, perhaps the foremost being works in the church of Sant'Andrea in Vercelli and the Sanctuary of San Michele. The Gothic style, on the other hand, manifested itself in overpowering architecture, leaving little space to ornamentation and decoration. Notable examples of Gothic in Piedmont include the church of San Domenico in Alba and the cathedrals of Saluzzo and Asti, but we must not forget the dozens of castles built in every corner of the region throughout the Gothic period. Gothic painting is probably best typified by the simple, refined style of Giacomo Jacquerio, a fine example being the frescoes he left in the Castle of Manta. Renaissance art never had much of an influence on Piedmontese artists. Baroque, on the other hand, was quick to catch on, and perhaps the most impressive Piedmontese art was produced in this period: dozens of castles, palaces, and churches were built and decorated in the elaborate style of the 17th and 18th centuries. In addition to the grandiose buildings commissioned by royalty, the Baroque masters produced smaller-scale projects — which is not to say they were small-scale at all — such as the elaborate open-air sanctuaries called Sacro Monte. The most prominent architects of the period were Richini, Guarino Guarini, and, perhaps the greatest of all, Filippo Juvara. The 18th century architectural tradition did not die with the century, but continued well into the 1800s when, for example, Antonelli designed his famous building, the so-called Mole (pronounced mo-lay) in Turin. One of the outstanding painters of the 19th century Piedmontese school was Pellizza da Volpedo, whose style resembles that of the French Impressionists, and who favored social themes.

Risorgimento period, also playing an active role in the long war of independence that the northern Italian regions were waging against Austria. The end result, thanks to the combined efforts of Vittorio Emanuele II, Camillo Cavour, and Giuseppe Garibaldi, was that the United Kingdom of Italy was born in 1860, with Turin as its capital. (It was capital until 1865.) Today it ranks as one of Italy's great industrial centers (e.g., Fiat in Turin and Olivetti in Ivrea).

ART - Roman remains are to be found in Susa, Turin, and Acqui, not to mention the excavated cities of Libarna and Industria. Early medieval monuments are rare (e.g., the Baptistry of Novara and the church of San Giovanni in Asti),

TURIN

Above: panoramic view of the city.
Left: portrait of Emanuele Filiberto of Savoy (1510-1573), by Giacomo Vichi (known as Argenta), from the collection of the Galleria Sabauda in Turin.

Originally a Celtic settlement, Turin became a Roman colony (and christened *Augusta Taurinorum*). Periodically overrun and plundered by the barbarians, it soon fell to the Byzantines, who were followed by the Longobards and Franks. Throughout the Middle Ages it was a major contender in the fierce feudal struggles, and then, in the 12th and 13th centuries, one of the most important of the city-states.

Afterward it was taken over by the Savoys who were its stable rulers from then on. In the 1400s Turin became capital of Piedmont. It never relinquished this position, despite endless vicissitudes, not always beneficial to the city, and the frequent incursions of the French. Turin's artistic heritage was greatly enriched in the 16th century thanks to two dukes, Emanuele Filiberto and Carlo Emanuele I, who also brought a notable level of economic well-being to their city. The period between the 16th and 18th centuries was important from an architectural and town-planning standpoint: Turin's appearance today dates from the work

of dozens of architects who, without eradicating the grid-like layout of the Roman city of *Augusta Taurinorum*, filled it with buildings of understated elegance. This aristocratic spirit, along with an intense cultural life (centered about the University of Turin founded in 1404 and the Royal Society of Science chartered in 1757), continued right into the 1800s when the city, one of the leaders in the Italian struggle for national unity, became capital of the newborn Kingdom of Italy under Vittorio Emanuele II of Savoy. Turin lost its position as capital of Italy in 1865, but soon after found a new one as its industrial capital.

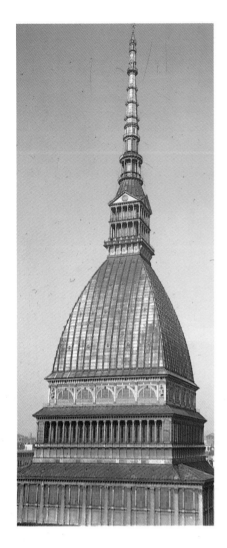

PALAZZO REALE - This 17th century palace was the residence of the House of Savoy up to the time of Vittorio Emanuele II. The interior is elaborately decorated (mostly in the Baroque style). The *Armory* belonging to the palace vaunts a superb collection of weapons of every conceivable type, armor, and related mementoes.

PALAZZO MADAMA - The original castle built in the 13th century on the site of an old Roman gate underwent several major modifications, the most radical of which were carried out in the 17th and 18th centuries. Later the palace — named after the *madame*, i.e. the royal ladies who had inhabited it — became the Senate of the Kingdom of Italy. The majestic facade was designed by Juvara in 1718.

CATHEDRAL - The Cathedral was erected in the late 1400s on the site of a cluster of three pre-existing churches. The only Renaissance building in Turin, it has been attributed to a Tuscan architect, Meo del Caprina. The three facade portals bear late 15th century reliefs. In a niche cut into the inside facade is the *Tomb of Giovanna d'Orlié* (c. 1439), while a 16th century altarpiece attributed to Spanzotti adorns the second righthand chapel. Most of the remaining works date from the 17th-18th centuries. The celebrated *Cappella della Sindone*, designed in the 17th century by Guarino Guarini as a fitting showplace for the *Holy Shroud*, is reached by way of the choir. The Shroud, bearing the imprint of the body of a man believed to be Jesus, has been in the Cathedral for centuries.

Above left: the so called «Mole Antonelliana», symbol of Turin. Above right: facade of Palazzo Madama. Facing page, above: detail of the Passion of Christ (dated c. 1470), one of the major paintings by the Flemish master Hans Memling, part of the collection of the Galleria Sabauda. Below: view from below of the spectacular dome designed by Guarini for the Cappella della Sindone in the Cathedral of Turin.

MUSEO EGIZIO - Turin's Egyptian Museum vaunts one of the world's finest collections of Egyptian art. It originated in the 18th century as the Savoy's private collection. The exhibits on the ground floor include great statues of the pharoahs such as *Ramses II* and *Tutankhamon*, sphinxes, and a 15th

Left: Basilica di Superga. Facing page, above: Palazzina di Caccia (Hunting Lodge), Stupinigi. Below: Castello del Valentino.

PALAZZO CARIGNANO

This building, sporting a majestic curved facade, ranks as one of the great examples of Turinese Baroque. Designed by Guarino Guarini in 1779, it served as the first Italian parliament building (from 1860 to 1865) and is now the *Museo del Risorgimento* with exhibits relating to 19th century Italian history.

MOLE ANTONELLIANA

This 167-meter-high building has come to be the symbol of Turin. Designed in 1863 by Alessandro Antonelli as a synagogue (although it is now only a monument), it is topped by a huge spire-crowned dome which may be reached by an elevator.

PARCO DEL VALENTINO

The park extends along the banks of the Po and is full of interesting sights. These include: the *Castle of Valentino*, a majestic Baroque building today the University's Department of Architecture; the so-called *Borgo Medievale*, a picturesque 19th century reconstruction of medieval Piedmont and the modern *Palazzo delle Esposizioni*.

STUPINIGI

This grandiose *Hunting Lodge* was designed by Filippo Juvara in 1730 for Vittorio Amedeo II of Savoy. Some of the major artists of the day were commissioned to work on the project which was not completed until 1772. Among the famous people who sojourned here were Napoleon Bonapart and Paolina Borghese.

century B.C. stone temple. Smaller objects are displayed on the upper floor, including sarcophagi, mummies, figurines, artifacts discovered during the exploration of the pyramids, a recontruction of a tomb, weapons, musical intruments, garments, and numerous papyri.

GALLERIA SABAUDA

The works in this collection were scattered about the various Savoy residences until the 19th century when Carlo Alberto had them all united into a single gallery. The highlights include: *Virgin and Child* by Fra Angelico, *Virgin and Child* by Mantegna, *Supper in the House of Simon* by Veronese, two *Views of Turin* by Bellotto, *St. Francis Receiving the Stigmata* by Jan van Eyck, *Scenes of the Passion* by Hans Memling, several works by van Dyck, and van der Weyden.

BASILICA DI SUPERGA

One of the masterpiece of its architect, Filippo Juvara, the church rises on a hilltop in a splendid natural setting. Building of the church, an X-shaped structure preceded by a Classical-style porch and set off by two charming belltowers, took fourteen years (1717-1731). The interior is plain but refined. In the underground chambers are the royal tombs of the Savoy family.

LAGO MAGGIORE

Views of the delightful Isole Borromee. Above: Isola Bella; below: Isola dei Pescatori.

Lago Maggiore is not Italy's biggest lake — it comes second after Lago di Garda. This fact does not stop people from all over the world from flocking here to enjoy its marvelous climate and remarkable landscapes. The charming little towns along its banks are popular resorts today, but their heyday was the *Belle Epoque* when their grand hotels overflowed with the *crème de la crème* of European society. The most renowned are *Arona* where St. Carlo Borromeo was born; *Stresa* famous for its refined elegance; *Pallanza*, with a magnificently landscaped estate, *Villa Taranto*; and, on the Lombard side, *Luino*, and *Laveno*. Especially noteworthy are the *Isole Borromee* opposite Stresa. The islands include: *Isola Bella* with its imposing *Palazzo Borromeo* (inside of which is a painting gallery) and stupendous Italian-style *garden* dating from the Baroque period, *Isola dei Pescatori*, with a picturesque village; and *Isola Madre*, which has an 18th century palace and a *Botanical Garden*.

LIGURIA

Liguria comprises a narrow tongue of land along the western Italian coast. It is mostly mountainous — here, in fact, the Alps end and the Apennines begin — with a tiny strip of coastal plain where most of the inhabited centers are located.

HISTORY - The first known settlements of Ligurians in the region, which extended even beyond the Apennines, date back to the late 7th century B.C. It was no easy task for the Romans to subjugate this tough people of pirates and sailors. Having finally succumbed to Rome in the 3rd century B.C., however, Liguria thrived as a prosperous center of trade and commerce, both on land and sea. At the end of the Imperial Age the region was sacked by the barbarians, thereafter conquered by the Byzantines, Longobards, and Franks, and throughout devasted by the Saracens in the course of their frequent incursions up the coast. Between the 10th and 12th centuries the territory was broken up into fiefdoms. Genoa emerged as the most important of these, due to her skillful handling of her major resource, maritime trade, and an aggressive expansionist policy with respect to the other coastal towns. By the late 14th century she controlled the whole Ligurian coast. In 1339 Simone Boccanegra crowned himself Lord of Genoa, which triggered a period of violence culminating in uprisings against the Sea Republic of Venice, the Aragonese, the Viscontis, and the French. In the 16th century the great admiral Andrea Doria, Lord of Genoa and ally of the Spanish king, Charles V, made a heroic stand against the French and the other Ligurian cities. Throughout the following centuries the region was compelled to defend itself from a new — and too close for comfort — enemy, the Savoys. Then, following an all too brief republican period at the end of the 18th century, Liguria was annexed

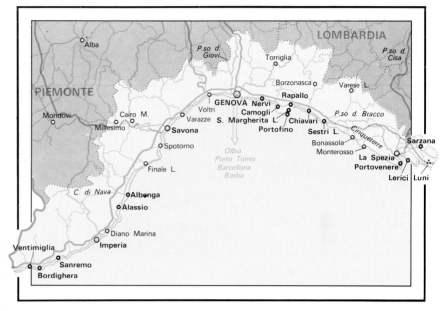

to Napoleon's great French empire. After Napoleon's fall and the Congress of Vienna (1815), it was annexed to another foreign state, this time the Kingdom of Savoy. During the Risorgimento, Ligurians were staunch supporters of unification, actively participating in the ventures of the Carbonari and the Giovane Italia Movement headed by Giuseppe Mazzini.

ART - The existing prehistoric remains, sculptural and architectural fragments at Luni, are connected with the Italic civilization of Central Italy. Roman ruins abound all over the region. Liguria's outstanding Early Christian monument is the Baptistery of Albenga with its remarkable mosaic decoration. Albenga also vaunts some fine examples of the Romanesque style (e.g., the Cathedral), as does Genoa. French, Tuscan, and Lombard influxes were felt throughout the Middle Ages. Prominent artists such as Giovanni Pisano and Giovanni di Balduccio, sculptors, and Manfredino d'Alberto and Taddeo di Bartolo, painters, were active in Liguria, sometimes over long peri-

ods. The feudal period was the time of a building boom in both the public and private sectors. Northern European Gothic influenced Ligurian architecture without eradicating the local styles then prevalent all over the region. The result was the erection of a host of splendid churches, towers, and palaces. Lombard and the Flemish schools had a great impact on Ligurian painting starting from the 15th century. Among the most important non-Ligurian artists in terms of influence were Foppa and Ludovico Brea (15th century). The 16th century was important from an architectural standpoint. The great princely palaces were built, mainly in Genoa, and decorated by the foremost decorators of the day such as Perin del Vaga, Montorsoli, Galeazzo Alessi, and Luca Cambiaso. The Baroque brought new ferments to the Ligurian art world; masters such as Peter Paul Rubens and Antonis van Dyck sojourned here. Moreover, the region was the birthplace of prominent artists such as Bernardino Strozzi, Orazio and Gregorio De Ferrari, and the extraordinary Alessandro Magnasco.

GENOA

From the start, Genoa's history has been closely linked to the sea. The basis for her position as a great Mediterranean sea power goes back to the Middle Ages, during which time she played an active role in the Crusades. In the 16th century Genoa thrived under the dogeship of Andrea Doria, yet the economic outlook was far from rosy since the world commercial center was shifting from the Mediterranean to the colonies of the North American continent discovered by Christopher Columbus. Successively, Genoa and the whole Ligurian region were conquered by the French Austrians, and Savoys. In the 19th century, Genoa contributed greatly to the *Risorgimento* cause. Genoese such as Mazzini, Mameli, and Bixio played important parts in the struggle. Genoa today is an active industrial city and the most important port in Italy.

PIAZZA DE FERRARI - This bustling square is situated in the heart of midtown Genoa in one of the city's finest neighborhoods. It was designed in the late 1800s when the whole downtown area was rebuilt.

SAN MATTEO - This magnificent 12th-13th century Romanesque-Gothic church was commissioned by the Doria family, who were also the owners of the houses bordering the lovely square.

CATHEDRAL - Founded long before the year 1000, the Cathedral, which is dedicated to St. Lawrence, underwent extensive rebuilding between the 11th and 12th centuries, and continued to be altered throughout the following ones. It ranks as Genoa's outstanding ecclesiastical building. Sculpted Gothic portals built in the 13th century stand out against the black and white striped marble facade. There are several noteworthy works in the interior. These include the *Cappella di San Giovanni Battista* (15th century) and the *Cappella Senarega*.

PORT - The port of Genoa, along with those of Marseille and Naples, ranks as the most important in the Mediterranean in terms of size as well as passenger and freight traffic. The port is the site of the *Lanterna*, an old lighthouse which from time immemorial has symbolized the city.

GALLERIA NAZIONALE - The museum building is the *Palazzo Spinola*. The 16th century palace with all its original furnishings, and artworks was bequeathed to the State in 1958 by the Spinola family. The museum is like a private gallery, reflecting the taste of the old aristocratic Genoese families.

VIA GARIBALDI - Around the mid-1600s the Genovese aristocrats decided to move en masse from the old city to a newer, more elegant residential area. This marked the birth of the *Strada Nuova* the present-day Via Garibaldi. The design and execution of the project were carried out by Galeazzo Alessi and Bernardino Cantoni. The finest buildings on Via Garibaldi are Palazzo Bianco, Palazzo Rosso, and Palazzo Municipale. The latter, designed by Rocco Lurago and built in

Facing page: panoramic view of the Port of Genoa. Above: facade of the church of San Matteo: Right: the 19th century Piazza de' Ferrari in downtown Genoa. Below: the controversial «Serpentone» («great snake») is one of the modern buildings in the newer section of the city.

1564, is Genoa's city hall. *Palazzo Bianco* (White Palace) was named for the color of the stone used to build it (1565). The classical-style palace, commissioned by Niccolò Grimaldi, is now a museum, the *Galleria di Palazzo Bianco*. Like Palazzo Bianco, *Palazzo Rosso* (Red Palace) was named for the color of the building stone. It was designed by Matteo Lagomaggiore in 1671 for the Brignole-Sale family who, in 1874, donated it to the City of Genoa. Today it, too, is a museum, the *Galleria di Palazzo Rosso*. The superb collection housed in Palazzo Rosso includes classical sculptures, *portraits* by Pisanello and Bordone, *Judith* by Paolo Veronese, *Ecce Homo* by Caravaggio, *portraits* by van Dyck, works by Titian and Tintoretto.

RIVIERA DI PONENTE

The Riviera di Ponente comprises the strip of land running north along the coast from Genoa to the French border. It is famous for its marvelous beaches, splendid bays, and delightful resort towns, not to mention locally-grown produce and flowers.

ALBENGA - The town, rising in the midst of an intensely cultivated plain of considerable size, is also a popular summer resort. Settled by the Ingauni, a Ligurian tribe, it did not achieve prominence until after the Roman conquest of 181 B.C. Among the most notable sights are the *Cathedral* (an Early Christian church); the *Baptistry* (5th century), and the *Museo Navale Romano*.

ALASSIO - This elegant resort is renowned for its superb beach and delight climate. Sights include a promenade along the shore, a yacht basin, and the *Muretto*, on the corner of Corso Dante and Via Cavour, which is a wall composed of tiles autographed by show business celebrities.

SANREMO - San Remo is a year-long resort. It boasts first-rate hotels, restaurants, and entertainment centers. It hosts important cultural and sports events, as well as the world famous *Festival della Canzone*, the annual competition among Italy's top pop stars. In addition, it ranks as one of the biggest flowers exporters in the world. The city became the watering place of European nobility in the 19th century luxurious hotels and elegant shopping districts were built to accommodate the high class tourism. The celebrated gambling *Casino* was erected in 1906. Old houses along narrow, winding streets make up the medieval district of *Pigna* covering the hillside.

Above: Alassio's pleasant beach.
Below: the popular Sanremo Casino.
Facing page: Portofino, with its charming pastel houses and port.

RIVIERA DI LEVANTE

The Riviera di Levante comprises the Ligurian coast between Genoa and the Gulf of La Spezia. Here the shoreline is dotted with beaches, bays, and promontories, with numerous inlets creating natural boat basins. The little fishing villages and resort towns along the way are set in luxuriant Mediterranean vegetation.

PORTOFINO - Famous world-over, Portofino vaunts a unique natural setting on the inlet of a wooded promontory separating the Gulf of Genoa from the Gulf of Tigullio. Tourists come year-round to bask in its superb climate and the beauty of its sea-mountain location. The *Porticciolo* and the pastel-hued houses surrounding it make a picturesque sight. *San Fruttuoso*, another stupendous inlet on the promontory, can be reached by motorboat. The tiny fishing village of San Fruttuoso is reflected in the clear waters of the bay. Nearby is the 8th century *Abbey of San Fruttuoso di Capodimonte*.

RAPALLO - This resort town with its charming villas, gardens, and grand hotels, was actually settled long before the Middle Ages when it was involved in bitter fighting first with the Genoese, then with the Venetians, and lastly with the Turks who looted and razed it several times over. The tradition of lace-making is still very much practiced. The beautifully-landscaped *Promenade* makes a pleasant walk. A narrow strip of land leads to the 16th century *Castle* rising on an islet.

SESTRI LEVANTE - This resort town vaunts a delightful setting on an isthmus joining a rocky promontory to the mainland, thus creating two facing bays, the *Baia delle Favole* and the *Baia del Silenzio*. A long scenic promenade leads to the promontory called *L'Isola* (The Island), on which there is a park.

CINQUETERRE - The name *Cinqueterre* (Five Lands) refers to the five tiny picturesque fishing villages nestling in five bays along the coast between Punta del Mesco and Punta del Montenero. The inhabited areas are closed off by mountains incredibly terraced and planted with grapevines. The main town is *Monterosso* which has a fine beach and several hotels. The church of *San Giovanni Battista* in Monterosso was built in the 13th-14th centuries, and contains a painting of the *Virgin* attributed to Mariotto Albertinelli. Inside the *Monastery of the Cappuccini Friars* is a *Crucifixion* by a follower of van Dyck. The charming *Via dell'Amore* runs along the coast joining Monterosso and Vernazza. *Vernazza* is set by a tiny bay. Its church, the *Parrocchiale*, was built in the 14th century. *Corniglia* is renowned for its superb wine. Its fine 14th century church vaunts a striking rose window. *Manarola*, with its charming cluster of pastel houses, is joined to *Riomaggiore*.

LOMBARDY

Lombardy can be divided into three main geological zones: mountains in the north, hills in the center, and plains in the south. South of the Alps proper, the Pre-Alps gradually flatten out, first into hills and then into the vast Padana plains. While the Po is the major Lombard river, several of its affluents, including the Adda, Oglio, Mincio, and Ticino, are also good-sized waterways. Lombardy is also dotted with lakes, the largest of which Lake Maggiore (east shore), Lake Lugano (south shore and west branch), and Lakes Como, Iseo, and Garda (west shore).

HISTORY - In the pre-Roman era, the territory north of the Po was inhabited by Celtic tribes. In the 3rd century B.C. when it was conquered by the Romans who annexed it to their Gallia Cisalpina, the major Lombard centers were Milan, Pavia, Brescia, Bergamo, and Mantua. In the 4th century, Milan, foremost city in a region that had come to play a key role in the events of the day, was made capital of the Empire of the West. Thereafter, however, hordes of barbarians (Huns and Ostrogoths) swept through the region. In the 7th-8th centuries, they were followed by the Longobards (after whom Lombardy - originally Longobardia — was named), who in turn were supplanted by Charlemagne's Franks. By the 9th century, Lombardy had disintegrated into a myriad of tiny fiefdoms. In the 12th century, some of these had become free communes, the most important of which were Milan, Brescia, Como, Pavia, and Mantua — as usual constantly bickering among themselves. They joined together, however, to defeat a common enemy from without, Frederick Barbarossa, who was beaten at Legnano in 1176 by the alliance of communes known as the Lombard League. The following years were hardly peaceful while the mighty families busily engaged in their bloody power struggles. The victors, the Visconti, ruled Lombardy unchallenged up through the Renaissance. After the fall of the Visconti Signoria, Lombardy became part of Charles V's Hapsburg Empire (later the Spanish Empire under Philip II), and then the Austrian Hapsburg Empire, until Napoleon conquered it and incorporated it into his Cisalpine Republic (1797). In the 1800s the Hapsburgs returned. Patriotic fervor against the Austrians was, however, intense. The uprising culminating in the famous Cinque Giornate di Milano (Five Days of Milan) in 1848 led to the ousting of the Austrian commander Radetzky. Garibaldi's patriots and the Piedmont army liberated the region once and for all. Today Lombardy ranks as Italy's foremost industrial region.

ART - The scanty Roman remains are mainly concentrated in the Milan and Brescia areas. There are outstanding examples of Early Christian and medieval metal-crafting in several Lombard centers, e.g., the Treasury of Monza, the Vuolvinius

Altar in Sant'Ambrogio, and the Brescia collections. Of great interest are the medieval frescoes of Santa Maria di Castelseprio. Lombard art, especially architecture, developed to a considerable extent in the Middle Ages. Among the finest buildings erected during this period are the basilicas of San Michele Maggiore in Pavia, and Sant'Ambrogio in Milan. Lombard painting, on the other hand, developed relatively late (around the 14th century) when Giovanni da Milano and Giovannino de' Grassi (a miniaturist) were active. Painters such as Bembo, the Zavattaris, and Foppa dominated the 1400s. In terms of architecture the 15th century was the period of

great undertakings, i.e., the Duomo of Milan (not finished, however, until five centuries later), the Duomo of Como, and the Charterhouse of Pavia. In addition, decoration of these huge buildings also required the services of an army of sculptors and artisans. The Renaissance produced a true flowering of Lombard art, thanks chiefly to the impressive output of architects of the ilk of Bramante in Milan and Leon Battista Alberti and Giulio Romano in Mantua, not to mention painters such as Bernardino Luini, Boltraffio, and Ambrogio De Predis (the three best-known followers of Leonardo), Lotto, Savoldo, and Romanino (from Brescia), and Moroni (from

Above: Milan's Piazza del Duomo as it appeared in the early 1800s in painting by Giovanni Migliara. Right: the same square in a recent aerial photo.

Bergamo). The Baroque period was equally exciting: the great Lombard villas were commissioned and Caravaggio, from the Lombard town of the same name, painted his revolutionary canvases. Artistic production did not let up in the 18th and 19th centuries, and continues intense and innovative to this day.

MILAN

Milan, the symbol of hard-working Italian industry, is a modern city of glass, metal, and poured concrete. (The tallest building, the Pirelli skyscraper, dominates the station area from its 127-meter height.) A seemingly endless residential belt girths the downtown area in which office buildings, deparment stores, and smart shops vie for the tight space. Yet the city is full of history and things to see, among them artistic treasures and historical monuments of great renown. The focal point of Milanese life is Piazza del Duomo, the square from which the complex web of streets making up the old historic center radiate star fashion. The history of Piazza del Duomo and the city itself goes back to Roman times. Even then Milan was the foremost of the Lombard centers—mainly due to its favorable position at the crossroads of the major trade routes between northern and central Italy passing through the Po Valley. In the 4th century it became capital of the Holy Roman Empire and, thanks to the great fervor of its celebrated bishop, St. Ambrose, an important center of Early Christian life. It continued to dominate the other Lombard cities throughout the Longobard and Frankish periods. Its power grew even more pronounced starting, in the 12th century when the Lombard League, with Milan at its head, defeated Frederick Barbarossa, thereafter reaching an apex from the 14th to 16th centuries when the Visconti and Sforza *Signorie* extended its territory and embarked on major building compaigns. Decline set in with the Spanish conquest (17th century), continued under the rule of the Hapsburgs (18th and 19th centuries), and lasted until the *Risorgimento* when the Milanese made it Italy's cultural and economic capital — a position it holds to this day. The economic vitality of the city is especially apparent in April when the *Fiera Campionaria*, Italy's most important trade fair and one of Europe's major expositions, dominates Milanese life.

DUOMO - It took 500 years to complete the Duomo, Milan's most celebrated monument, begun in 1387 by a crew of master stonecutters under the supervision of Simone da Orsenigo. Over the centuries, dozens of craftsmen shared in the building and decoration of the cathedral whose stylistic features, however, never strayed from the original International Gothic style as it was first conceived by its unknown (French? German?) architect. The facade, completed in the 1800s, has five Baroque portals enclosing modern doors. The building is topped by the famous *Madonnina*, a 4-meter-tall gilded copper statue of the Virgin, cast in 1774. The impressive interior has double aisles set off from the nave by composite columns with capitals and niches adorned with

Above: facade of the Milan Cathedral. Right: Galleria Vittorio Emanuele.

statues. Light is filtered through *stained glass windows*, the oldest of which date from the 15th century. The artistic highlights include: the 11th century *Tomb of Ariberto da*

Intimiano (right aisle), the *Tomb of Gian Giacomo de' Medici* carved by Leone Leoni in 1563 (right transept), and the *portal of the South Sacristy* whose fine Gothic sculpture was executed by Hans von Fernach in 1393. In the center of the choir is the *Sanctuary* with its 16th century altar. The wooden *choir stalls* were carved in the Baroque period. In the underlying *Crypt* are the mortal remains of St. Carlo Borromeo. In the left transept is a masterpiece of French Gothic art, the *Trivulzio Candelabra*, sculpted in the 13th century. Other noteworthy sights include the *portal of the North Sacristy* sculpted in the late 1200s and a well-stocked *Treasury*.

PIAZZA MERCANTI - This peaceful memento of medieval Milan is only a few yards from bustling Piazza del Duomo. Around the *piazzetta* are several buildings: Palazzo della Ragione (or *Palazzo Broletto Nuovo*) built in 1233 for Mayor Oldrado of Tresseno who is depicted on horseback in a relief on the exterior, the picturesque *Loggia degli Osii* commissioned in 1316 by Marco Visconti, the 17th Baroque palace century and the Gothic *Panigarola House*. In the center is a 16th century *well*.

GALLERIA VITTORIO EMANUELE - The remarkable Galleria, entered by way of the arcade on the north side of Piazza del Duomo, was designed in the late 1800s by Giuseppe Mengoni. At the crossing of the cross-shaped mall is a glass and metal dome. The Galleria is a favorite meeting-place for Milanese and out-of-towners alike.

LA SCALA THEATER - La Scala, the very symbol of Italian opera, has hosted a long list of memorable performances of and by such greats as Verdi, Puccini, and Toscanini. Designed in the neo-Classical style by Piermarini in 1777, it is noteworthy for its 18th century simplicity and elegance. Under the same roof is a *museum* with exhibits relating to theater and opera.

PINACOTECA AMBROSIANA - The original collection, begun by Cardinal Federico Borromeo, was put on exhibition in this building starting from the 17th century. Bombed during World War II, the museum had to be completely rebuilt and was only reopened in 1966. Works by Leonardo, Raphael, Caravaggio, and Titian among others, are displayed.

SFORZESCO CASTLE

SFORZESCO CASTLE - Work on this impressive complex of buildings girthed by massive walls was begun in the late 1300s by the Viscontis, and proceeded well into the 1400s under Francesco Sforza, then Lord of Milan. Supervisors were Giovanni da Milano and Filarete who designed the entrance tower (restored in the 19th century). Over the centuries the castle was embellished by a veritable army of craftsmen and artists. Today it is a museum. The collections, exhibited in the so-called *Duke's Court*, range from paintings and sculpture to musical instruments and furniture. The groundfloor *Sculpture Collection* features a masterpiece of Romanesque sculpture, the *Monument to Bernabò Visconti* carved by Bonino da Campione in 1357, a superb 13th century wooden *Crucifix*, Michelozzo's stunning Renaissance *Medici bank portal*, and the *Rondanini Pietà*, the incredibly moving sculpture Michelangelo never lived to complete. The ceiling decoration of the *Sala delle Asse* has been attributed to Leonardo da Vinci. The well-stocked *Armory* is also on the ground floor. Upstairs are two noteworthy collections: *Furniture* and the *Pinacoteca* hung with works by Andrea Mantegna, Giovanni Bellini, Bergognone, Boltraffio, Lotto, Moroni, Tintoretto, and many others.

SANT'AMBROGIO - Founded by St. Ambrose in 386, this celebrated church still has its transeptless, single-aisle plan — despite extensive remodeling carried out between the 9th and 11th centuries — making it the foremost example of Lombard Romanesque extant. The narthex and lefthand belltower date from the 12th century. In the choir of the impressive interior is a superb medieval *gold altar* crafted by Master Vuolvinius, above which is a *ciborium* adorned with 12th century

Left: Pietà Rondanini, the sculpture Michelangelo was working on when he died, now in the Castello Sforzesco Museum. Right: the facade of Sant'Ambrogio.

reliefs. The sanctuary of *San Vittore in Ciel d'Oro* is covered with 5th century mosaics.

BRERA PINACOTECA

Brera, one of Italy's outstanding painting galleries, was opened in 1809 in the building occupied by the Academy of Beaux Arts. A steady flow of acquisitions has enriched its collections over the years. The highlights, starting from the courtyard, include: *statue of Napoleon* by Canova, self-portraits dating from various periods, reconstruction of the *Oratory of Macchirolo* with frescoes by Giovanni da Milano, *Supper in the House of the Pharisee* by Paolo Veronese, *Miracle of St. Mark* by Tintoretto, *St. Mark Preaching in Alexandria* by Gentile and Giovanni Bellini, the superb *Visconti tarot cards* painted by Bonifacio Bembo, *Adoration of the Magi* by Stefano Zevio, paintings by Bergognone, Bernardino Luini (*Virgin of the Rose-Garden)* and Lanino *(*three of the foremost painters of the 15th-16th century Lombard school), several works by Carlo Crivelli, including the *Virgin of the Candle* and *Coronation of the Virgin*, the unforgettable *Dead Christ* by Mantegna, *Pietà* by Giovanni Bellini, the celebrated *Virgin Enthroned with Federico da Montefeltro Donor* by Piero della Francesca, *Marriage of the Virgin* by Raphael, and *Supper at Emmaus* by Caravaggio. There are also notable works by 19th-20th century masters including Hayez, Fattori, Boccioni, Duchamp, Man Ray and Carrà.

POLDI-PEZZOLI MUSEUM

The fine collection put together by Gian Giacomo Poldi-Pezzoli in the late 19th century was left to the City of Milan. Notably eclectic, it comprises paintings, clocks and watches, textiles, and arms and armor. The highlights include the *Armory*, one of the foremost in Italy, the *archeological collection*, *Persian carpets*,

Left: Marriage of the Virgin, an early work by Raphael, now hanging in the Pinacoteca di Brera. Right: Portrait of an Unknown Lady, by Antonio del Pollaiolo, in the Poldi Pezzoli Museum.

ceramics (Saletta degli Stucchi), and the *jewel collection*. The best known paintings include Cranach's *Portrait of Martin Luther*, Giovanni Bellini's *Crucifixion* and *Pietà*, Botticelli's *Deposition*, and Antonio del Pollaiolo's *Portrait of a Lady*.

SANTA MARIA DELLE GRAZIE
- The church begun by Solari in 1463 was remodeled in 1492 by Bramante whose drum-topped tribune is considered one of the masterpieces of Renaissance architecture. The striking cloister was also designed by Bramante. In the refectory belonging to the monastery adjoining the church is Leonardo's *Last Supper* painted by the master between 1495 and 1497. His revolutionary iconographic scheme proved more successful than his revolutionary fresco technique, which has not withstood the perils of time and weather.

Above: Leonardo's Last Supper in the church of Santa Maria delle Grazie. Left: detail of Christ's head.

COMO

Como, one of the most popular lake resorts in Italy, is situated on the tip of the western branch of Lake Como. The town's clearly marked grid layout testifies to its Roman origin. (It was, in fact, settled by the Romans in 89 B.C.) A long-standing enemy of Milan in the Middle Ages, it nevertheless succumbed to Francesco Sforza in the 14th century. Starting in the 16th century it became a leader in the textile sector, especially silk, a position it has retained to this day. Famous native sons include Pliny the Elder, his son, Pliny the Younger (1st century A.D.), and the scientist Alessandro Volta (18th-19th centuries). Among the sights: the 15th century *Duomo* the *Broletto* City Hall (1215), the nearby church of *San Fedele*, and the *Museo Civico* (on Via Vittorio Emanuele II). Outside the down-town section are the Romanesque basilica of *Sant'Abbondio* and the *Tempio Voltiano* (1927) at the end of the picturesque *Lungolario*. The starting point for delightful lake excursions is the nearby boatyard.

LAKE COMO - Also called *Lake Lario*, it is fed by the Adda River which descends from Valtellina and comes out at Lecco, i.e., the easternmost of Lake Como's three branches. The scenery along the shores and its environs is unforgettable. The region is popular with vacationers not only for its setting, but also for its mild climate. In addition to Como, there are several other charming towns located on the shores of Lake Como including *Cernobbio*, *Tremezzo*, *Cadenabbia* (famous for an estate, *Villa Carlotta*, built in 1747), *Menaggio*, *Grav-* edona (vaunting a lovely 12th century Romanesque church, *Santa Maria del Tiglio*), *Bellano*, *Varenna*, *Lecco* (today an active little city, once the home of Alessandro Manzoni, who set his novel «The Betrothed» here), and Bellagio (whose superb woodside setting and fine hotels made it an attractive vacation spot). Worthwhile sights include an 11th monastery, the *Abbey of Piona*, a treasure-house of 13th century artworks, and several villas in the Bellano area. Of the estates, the most famous are *Villa Melzi*, built in the 19th century, and *Villa Serbelloni*, remodeled in the 18th century and set in the midst of a huge park.

View of Como.

PAVIA

Pavia's Roman name was *Ticinum* since it is located on the Ticino River not far from where it flows into the Po. An important Ostrogoth center, it became even more important under the Longobards when, renamed Pavia, it was made capital of the Longobard kingdom. Its present appearance dates from the period of the Communes, throughout which it was one of the most powerful. In the 14th century it lost its autonomy, becoming one of the Visconti domains. The seat of a major university, it never, however, lost its standing as a great cultural center. Pavia's major thoroughfare, Strada Nuova, runs between the Covered Bridge and the Castle. Most of the sights of the city are to be found in this area which still retains the grid plan of a Roman city.

COVERED BRIDGE - The very symbol of Pavia, the Ponte Coperto is a reconstruction of the original medieval bridge bombed in 1944.

Above left: Pavia's Covered Bridge. Below left: Charterhouse of Pavia, a masterpiece of Lombard Renaissance art. Above: Visconti Castle.

DUOMO - Many prominent architects, among them Bramante, Leonardo, and Francesco di Giorgio Martini, worked on the cathedral, which was built between the 15th and 16th centuries. Rising on the site of two pre-existing buildings (whose remains are visible in the subterranean chamber), the Duomo features a complex Greek cross plan with a single aisle running all around. The whole is crowned by an octagonal dome designed by Bramante. The church is decorated mainly with 15th-16th century paintings and sculpture. In the *Treasury* are 14th-15th century manuscripts, vestments, reliquaries, and other finely-crafted objects.

VISCONTI CASTLE - This impressive square structure was commissioned by Galeazzo Visconti and his son Gian Galeazzo and erected in the late 14th century. Two of the towers and one side were destroyed in the 1500s. The castle is occupied by the *Musei Civici*, i.e., two museums, in turn divided into several sections. Of major interest are the *Archeology Section* (local Roman remains such as bronzes, inscriptions, glassware, ceramics, etc.) and the *Sculpture Section* (Pavian-Longobard inscriptions, reliefs, and architectural fragments, and Romanesque mosaics). Other exhibits include jewelry and engravings.

SAN PIETRO IN CIEL D'ORO - Originally a Longobard basilica, San Pietro was rebuilt as a Romanesque church in the 12th century. Its facade, somewhat resembling San Michele's, is adorned with colored ceramics. Its sole portal is sculpted with reliefs.

CHARTERHOUSE OF PAVIA - (10 km). This masterpiece of 15th century Lombard architecture was begun by Gian Galeazzo Visconti as a family tomb. The project was continued by Francesco Sforza, although it was not completed until the 16th century. A chronological list of the architects who had a hand in the great undertaking comprises: Bernardo da Venezia, Giacomo da Campione, Giovanni and Guiniforte Solari, Amadeo, and Lombardino. The superb *facade* of the church is adorned with colored marbles, sculpture, and reliefs. Inside are several works by Bergognone, an altarpiece by Pietro Perugino, *tomb statues of Ludovico the Moor and Beatrice d'Este* by Cristoforo Solari, and *Gian Galeazzo Visconti's tomb* by Gian Cristoforo Romano. Outside are two charming cloisters, *Chiostro Piccolo* and *Chiostro Grande*. Formerly a Certosine monastery, the Charterhouse now belongs to the Cistercian order.

MANTUA

One of the great Latin poets Virgil was born in Roman Mantua (to be exact in nearby Pietole) in 70 B.C. Of scarce importance up the Middle Ages, in the 12th-13th century it became a free commune and joined the Lombard League. Around the end of the 13th century it lost its autonomy, succumbing to the Bonacolsi family who were succeeded in 1328 by the mighty Gonzagas. Mantua blossomed under the rule of the Gonzaga dukes whose court was also a drawing card for great artists from all over Italy.

PALAZZO DEL TE - A masterpiece of Renaissance architecture, the Gonzaga's country estate was designed by Giulio Romano who completed the project in 1535. The sumptuous interior was entirely decorated by Giulio Romano.

SANT'ANDREA - The church dated 1470, ranks as one of Alberti's masterpieces. The dome was added by Juvara in the 18th century. The striking facade was inspired by Classical triumphal arches. The artists whose works adorn the vast interior include Correggio, Giulio Romano, and Lorenzo Costa.

PIAZZA DELLE ERBE - On the square, the heart of old Mantua, are several important buildings: the 11th century *Rotonda di San Lorenzo*, a round building characterized by typical Romanesque simplicity and solidity, the *Clock Tower* (dated 1473), the *Palazzo della Ragione*, a 13th century building with a portico added in the 15th century, and the *Broletto* (or *Palazzo del Podestà*), Mantua's 13th century city hall. A *statue of Virgil* (also 13th century) adorns the Broletto's main facade facing out on Piazza Broletto.

PALAZZO DUCALE - The Gonzaga's incredible palace is a complex of buildings, all built in different periods. The most important are: the *Appartamento della Guastalla*, the *Appartamento degli*

Above left: rear view of the Gothic Palazzo della Ragione. Below-left: Palazzo Ducale. Above: Mantegna's frescoes decorating the Camera degli Sposi in the Palazzo Ducale. Right: Castello San Giorgio.

Arazzi, (named after its *tapestries*, designed by Raphael), the *Sala dello Zodiaco* (with frescoes dated around 1580 attributed to Lorenzo Costa), the *Sala del Labirinto* ᵢ *Appartamento Ducale* (with a ceᵢ ing painting of a maze), the *Appartamento dei Nani* (an unusual suite of tiny rooms). In another building, the 14th century *Castello di San Giorgio*, is the celebrated *Camera degli Sposi* frescoed by Mantegna (1472-1474). Scenes pertaining to the life of Ludovico Gonzaga and his wife Barbara of Brandeburg are shown in a trompe l'oeil setting consisting of a pavillion where putti and ladies cavort with an incredible illusionistic effect.

47

LAKE GARDA

Garda, Italy's biggest lake (370 km²), is shared by three regions, i.e, Lombardy on the west, Veneto on the east, and Trentino on the northern tip. It is fed from the north by the Sarca River which exits in the south as the Mincio. Its scenery varies from mountainous and jagged in the north to gently hilly in the south. Throughout the lake region the climate is pleasant and mild. Farming is a major economic activity. Important crops comprise citrus fruit, olives, and grapes, while several of the local wines are highly prized. Among the lake towns the foremost is *Sirmione*, located along a narrow strip of land extending into the lake which was a popular vaca-tion spot with the Romans who filled it with luxurious villas. Its impor-tance did not wane in the Long-obard period and continued way into the 13th century when Mastino della Scala built a great fortress, the *Rocca Scaligera*, from which he could control the entire lake region. Today the *Rocca* is a *museum*. On the far side of the peninsula are the *Grottoes of Catullus*, a vast arche-ological zone consisting of the ruins of a fine *Roman estate*. *Gardone Riviera* - This elegant resort vaunts fine hotels and facilities. Nearby is the *Vittoriale*, Gabriele D'An-nunzio's extravagant villa with its original furnishings and mementoes of the adventurous life of the writer

Rocca Scaligera in Sirmione.

(who died here in 1938). *Riva del Garda* - This elegant town, under Austrian rule until World War II, has long been a famous resort. Major sights include the *Rocca*, inside of which is a *museum*. In addition to exhibits pertaining to local costumes and customs, there are collections of prehistoric and Roman pieces, and medieval sculpture. The 17th cen-tury church of the *Immacolata* con-tains works by Palma the Younger. *Malcesine* - Another scenic lake town, *Malcesine*, vaunts a charming port and medieval castle.

TRENTINO-ALTO ADIGE

Trentino-Alto Adige occupies the northernmost region of Italy, extending from Lake Garda to the Alps. Its hyphenated name reflects a longstanding ethnic-linguistic division: the southern part Trentino (capital: Trento) is Italian speaking, whereas the northern part, Alto Adige or Sudtirol (capital: Bolzano), is roughly two-thirds German speaking, with Italian and Ladino minorities. Geologically the region is homogeneous; typically alpine, it is characterized by a succession of great mountains (the tallest of which Mt. Ortles rises 3905 meters) and deep-plunging valleys. Major ranges comprise the Ortles-Cevedale, Adamello-Presanella, Brenta, and of course Dolomites.

HISTORY - Settled in prehistoric times, the region was colonized by the Romans around the 1st century B.C. It was not long before Trento, the connecting point between the Padana plain and the territories beyond the Alps (by way of the Resia and Brennero passes), became its most important center. Annexed by the Holy Roman Empire in the 9th century, the region was thereafter ruled by a long series of bishop-princes headquartered at Trento and Bressanone whose authority was delegated by the central imperial powers; in the 13th century the counts of Tirolo joined their ranks. In 1363 the region was ceded to Rudolph IV of Hapsburg (whose family would go on to dominate European politics for the next six centuries). Nevertheless, the Trentino and Alto Adige valleys continued to be the scene of frequent bloodshed as their inhabitants were constantly forced to defend themselves from the repeated attempts of the Venetians, Lanzichenecchi, and French to invade their territories, not to mention their own frequent autonomistic and antifeudal uprisings-often "put down" by plague epidemics and natural disasters.

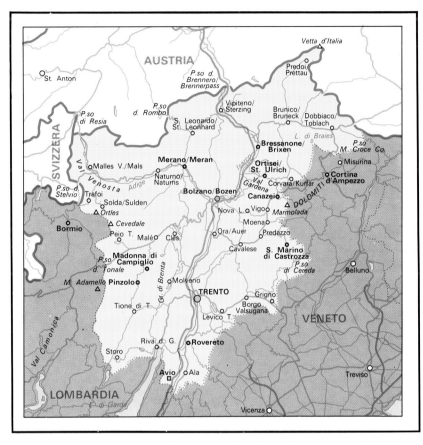

After a flickering period of peace and prosperity under the enlightened rule of Empress Marie Theresa (1740-1780), the region was annexed to Tirol (capital: Innsbruck) becoming victim of a new absolutist policy in the 19th century. Consequently, the Risorgimento movement grew stronger and bolder in Italian-speaking Trentino, but when the patriots passed to action, Austrian repression was swift and harsh with the end result that the region could only adhere to united Italy following World War I. In 1972 it was granted a special charter under which it retains full regional autonomy.

ART - Although nothing has come down to us from the Roman period, several noteworthy medieval monuments have survived (e.g., the churches of Naturno and Malles in Val Venosta, the Collegiata of San Candido in Val Pusteria, and the cathedrals of Trento and Bressanone). The most characteristic architecture of the medieval period is not ecclesiastical, however, but civic, i.e., the castles built — oft times in the most inaccessible and picturesque locations — to defend the underlying valleys. Although the Renaissance came late to the region, it found a staunch supporter in a Trento bishop, Bernardo Clesio, who commissioned the building of several churches as well as the Castle of Buonconsiglio. The artistic production of the Baroque period (17th century) focused mainly around the Alto Adige churches, whose stylistic keynote is a combination of German and Trentino-Lombard motifs.

TRENTO

This natural-shelter valley girthed by a protective mountain wall was settled by the prehistoric epoch. Later a wealthy Roman center dotted with sumptuous buildings and palaces, it was destroyed by the Goths and Longobards while its inhabitants frantically rushed to safety on the Verruca Peak, today known as Doss Trento. Its recovery in the 7th-8th centuries was mainly due to the fact that anyone headed toward the Brennero Pass was obliged to cross it. In fact, the Holy Roman emperors who granted temporal power to the bishops-princes, did so in order to acquire allies at this strategic crossroads between northern and southern Europe. Thereafter relegated to a minor position on the outskirts of the Hapsburg Empire, the city lost both economic and political importance. It was liberated by the Italian army in 1918.

PIAZZA DEL DUOMO - In the middle of this remarkable square is an impressive fountain, the *Fontana del Nettuno*, a Baroque-style work sculpted by Francesco Antonio Giongo in 1768. On the Via Belenzani corner are the *Case Rella*, medieval houses with picturesque facades frescoed by Marcello Fogolino around the mid-1500s. The *Duomo*, like its 5th century predecessor dedicated to St. Vigilius, was built between the 12th and 13th centuries. It was designed by a Ticenese architect, Adamo d'Arogno, who gave it its distinctive Lombard Romanesque style.

CASTLE OF BUONCONSIGLIO - The buildings making up the castle were for many centuries the sumptuous residence of the bishop-princes who ruled the city. The oldest section is the crenelated *Castelvecchio* over which rises the circular *Torre Grande* built in the 1200s.

Above: Piazza del Duomo with the Neptune Fountain and the 16th century Rella houses. Below: Trento's Duomo.

BOLZANO

The largest city and capital of Alto Adige is bilingual; its inhabitants speak both German and Italian. Spread over the valley situated where the Talvera and Isarco rivers flow together, it was settled in pre-Roman times. Throughout the Middle Ages it was a bone of contention between the Longobards and Baiuvaris in an incessant struggle whose outcome was the Germanization of the local population. Thereafter it was ruled by the princes of Trento who were followed by the Austrian Hapsburgs, becoming Italian along with the whole Alto Adige (or South Tirol) region at the end of World War I. Business-oriented Bolzano is a major industrial center and, thanks to a favorable climate and the closeness of the Dolomites, a leading resort.

DUOMO - The church was built in the 12th century and remodeled in the 14th century as a Gothic building; the lower part of the *belltower* dates from the 12th century, while the upper part dates from the early 1500s. The facade features a fine 14th century *rose window*, Gothic portals, and a restored porch. Another fine portal, the *Porticina del Vino* (literally, Wine Door), dated 1387, is visible in the apse area. The *Cappella delle Grazie* was added in the 15th century. The highlights of the interior comprise an early 16th century *pulpit* with reliefs by Hans Lutz, several 14th century *frescoes*, and the Baroque *main altar* sculpted by a Veronese master, Giovanni Battista Ranghieri (1710).

PIAZZA DELLE ERBE - This is the city's open-air fruit and vegetable market and the starting point for its main thoroughfare, *Via dei Portici*. On the corner is a bronze fountain, the *Fontana del Nettuno*, an 18th century Baroque work.

Rear view of Bolzano's Duomo with its unusual patterned roof and elegant Baroque belltower.

DOLOMITES

The Dolomites belong to the Eastern Alps. Extending over a vast territory stretching from Valsugana to Val Pusteria and from the Adige to Piave valleys, they touch on three provinces (Trento, Bolzano, and Belluno) belonging to the Trentino-Alto Adige and Veneto regions. The Dolomites differ from the rest of the Alps: they are characterized by enormous valleys of wood-or meadowlands set off by steeply vertical masses of isolated mountain ranges. The mountains are mainly composed of a rock called *dolomite* (named after Déodat de Dolomieu, an 18th century French geologist) formed millions of years ago as undersea coral deposits. Erosion and weathering modeled the rock, creating strange formations resembling everything from towers to spires, while the «chips» that gradually accumulated became the characteristic Dolomite gravel beds. The region started drawing large numbers of tourists at the turn of the century, rapidly becoming one of the major year-round vacationlands in Italy. The Dolomites are superbly organized to fulfill every tourist whim they vaunt excellent hotels and restaurants, as well as ski and climbing facilities. The major sights are: *Val Gardena*. A typical Dolomite valley of wide open meadowlands and soaring mountain peaks, Val Gardena offers incomparable scenery, as well as excellent tourist facilities for both summer and winter vacations. Skiers may choose from over 100 kilometers of trails. *Ortisei*,

52

Left: Mt. Latemar rising beyond Lake Carezza. Above: Sassolungo viewed from Passo Sella.

the main center in the valley and a renowned ski resort. There are some interesting exhibits pertaining to valley Ladino culture in the local museum, the *Museo della Val Gardena*. From Ortisei you can hike up to *Alpe di Siusi*, an enormous scenic plateau at an average of 2000 m above sea level. The valley is flanked by two scenic mountain ranges, the Sassolungo and the Sella. *Sassolungo*, not of overbearing size, is divided into eight sections, all of which characterized by

exceptionally vertical walls, whereas *Sella* is a great compact mass of dolomite rock. *Lake Carezza* in a superb setting of fir trees with the pointed peaks of *Mt. Latemar* (2842 m) reflected in its waters. (Latemar is the only Dolomite peak composed entirely of greycolored stone.) The *Val di Fassa*, a pleasant valley of meadows and prairie lands. The main Val di Fassa towns are *Moena, Vigo di Fassa, Pozza di Fassa*, and *Canazei*. Traversing the valley, the road heads to the *Catinaccio Range* (tallest peak: 3002 m), among the most striking of the Dolomite mountains. In the middle of the Catinaccio rise the spectacular peaks called

Torri del Vaiolet. Among the sheerest of the Dolomite mountains, they have oft times been the scene of daring climbs and exploits. *Canazei*, a major ski resort and vacation center. Its popularity is to a great extent due to its breathtaking setting in the midst of spectacular mountains such as Sella, Sassolungo, and Marmolada. The *Passo Pordoi*, at 2239 meters, is the highest pass of the Dolomites. From the pass, you can take a cable car to the top of *Mt. Sass Pordoi* (2950 m) of the Sella Range where the view is well worth the effort. The descent follows the Cordevole River opposite the south side of the Sella mountains.

MADONNA DI CAMPIGLIO

The present-day town rises on the site of an old mountain shelter. Its setting in the center of a charming wooded valley lying between the Brenta and Presanella ranges is utterly superb. It is renowned all over Europe as one of the most stylish and best-equipped of the alpine winter resorts. Most of the populated area is composed of hotels and modern dwellings, chiefly villas. As a result, there are few historic sights, apart from a fine 15th century International Style altarpiece displayed inside the modern church of *Santa Maria*. There are approximately 70 km of ski trails in the area, as well as ski lifts of every kind and size,

including one connecting the stations of *Folgarida* and *Marilleva*. The most popular descents are Mt. Spinale, Pradalago, Nambino, and Tre 3. (The latter is where one of the major European ski championships are held.) Ski-trekking is practiced in the vicinity of the village of *Campo Carlo Magno*, the Austrian Emperor Franz Joseph's favorite winter playground. Another favorite sport is ice-skating (on the frozen-over local lake). One of the most inspiring of the alpine mountain ranges, the *Brenta* can be reached either by one of the several footpaths ascending from the charming Vallesinella and Val Brenta valleys

Brenta Range viewed from Lake Pradalago.

or by taking the conveniently-located cabin car lift from Madonna di Campiglio to the Grostè Pass (2443 m). Unlike their granite neighbors, the Brenta mountains are made of calcareous rock that constant erosion has altered and molded into hundreds of different shapes and sizes. Consequently, they very much resemble the Dolomites (from which they are separated by the Adige Valley) — and, in fact, they are known as the *Brenta Dolomites*. Numerous trails and footpaths make them ideal for nature hikes.

VENETO

Like many other Italian regions, the Veneto comprises different geological zones. Three principal divisions are distinguishable: a vast area of plain along the coast between the Po delta and the mouth of the Tagliamento River (broken up by the Euganei Hills and Berici mountain range); a pre-Alpine strip between the Asiago and Belluno plateaus; and an extensive mountainous zone which includes a good-sized chunk of the Dolomites.

HISTORY – The Veneti controlled the whole region until the advent of the Romans who gradually colonized it starting in the 2nd-1st century B.C. The Roman period was particularly positive for all the Veneto cities. They prospered on trade thanks to an efficient network of roads, land reclamation, ports, and other public works, all of which carried out by the Romans. During the 4th and 5th centuries, Aquileia became the main religious center of the local church. At the same time, however, the region was forced to defend herself from constant attacks of the barbarians whose arrival meant death and destruction. By the 10th century the Veneto had disintegrated into a host of little fiefdoms. In the cities, however, following a brief period of church domination, a commune movement was born, gradually gained momentum, and finally reached its apex in the 12th century when the communes of Verona, Padua, Treviso, and Vicenza joined together to form the so-called Veronese League. At the same time, albeit in a completely different way, Venice was beginning to make great strides economically and politically. First wholly under the control of the emperor of the Orient, then gradually attaining more and more independence, Venice ultimately became a republic ruled by a doge rather than a commune. In the 14th century, the Veneto underwent the same politi-

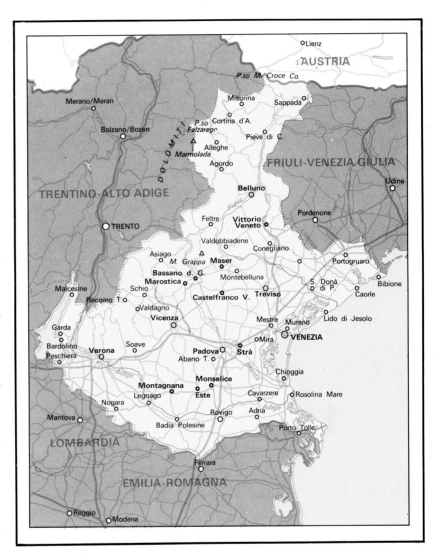

cal process that was taking place in many other regions of Italy: the communes gave way to the Signorie or lords, e.g., the Carraresi in Padua, the Scaligeri in Verona, and the Caminesi in Treviso. Once they had firmly taken control, the great Signorie set about extending their territories. The ensuing wars brought about the intervention of the Venetians — until that time completely removed from matters involving the mainland — who felt it better to nip in the bud any possible threat arising from powerful en-

emies at their borders. The Venetians soon managed to conquer both the Veneto and Friuli (1420), relinquishing their control only in the late 18th century. The 15th through 18th centuries were intense for the Venetians: they grew richer and richer on trade and commerce, defeated the Turks in battle, constantly renewed their attempts at territorial expansion at the expense of their neighbors, and staunchly defended their mainland possessions from outside threats. In the 18th century, however, trade began

Above: early 16th century Venice in a detail of a painting by Carpaccio (Healing of a Man Possessed by the Devil, Venice, Accademia). Right: View of Piazza San Marco from the Isle of San Giorgio.

to level off. In 1797 the great Sea Republic of the *Serenissima fell* to Napoleon's army, and her territories were annexed to Austria with the French emperor's consent. Attempts to oust the foreign powers were common occurrences in the course of the 19th century. Finally, in 1866, the region, once more free and independent, adhered to the Kingdom of Italy.

ART - The most important Roman remains in the Veneto are in Verona (i.e., the Arena). During the Middle Ages, the clear-cut division of the territory into mainland and coastal cities had a great impact on its art: whereas the former were in-creasingly exposed to Longobard and then Emilia-Romagna influxes, the latter (e.g., Venice and Torcello) came under the sphere of influence of the Orient, which meant the predominance of the Ravennate-Byzantine style. During the 12th-14th centuries, the prevailing style in Padua, Verona, and Vicenza was Romanesque and then Gothic, while Venice was in the throes of creating her own very personal fusion of Byzantine, Romanesque, and Gothic (best revealed in the Basilica of San Marco and the Palazzo Ducale). During this period, Italy's foremost painters (Giotto, Altichiero, Giusto de' Menabuoi, Pisanello, and Tommaso da Modena) were active in the inland centers. In the 15th century the Renaissance came to the Veneto. Tuscan masters such as Paolo Uccello, Donatello, Filippo Lippi, Andrea del Castagno, and the great Sicilian, Antonello da Messina, worked in the region, influencing exponents of the local schools, such as Mantegna in Padua. Venetian art, especially architecture, remained under the sway of the Gothic until the end of the 15th century. The period that followed, however, turned out to be one of the most exciting in European art, as the Bellinis, Carpaccio, and Giorgione broke with the Byzantine tradition and created a new style, the forerunner of the great Venetian colorism of the 16th century. During the glorious 1500s, in fact, Titian, Tintoretto, and Veronese, each in his own inimitable way, dominated Italian painting. These masters created the Venetian school, where effect is conveyed primarily through color, as opposed to the Central Italian school (e.g., Leonardo, Raphael) where line and drawing predominate. In architecture, Palladio was the unchallanged master, designing incomparably beautiful villas and churches in every corner of the region. The Veneto, however, produced great artists right into the 18th century. Among the best-known are the painters Piazzetta, the Longhis, the Tiepolos, Guardi, and Canaletto, and the great neo-Classical sculptor, Antonio Canova, whose apprenticeship was spent in Venice.

VENICE

Venice is universally acclaimed one of the world's most beautiful cities. It is certainly one of the most unusual. Actually, however, the buildings which appear so delicately suspended above the water are strictly earthbound, i.e., they are built on hundreds of islets and firmly reinforced by huge pylons sunk into the ground. The canals (*rii*) which separate the islands are the equivalent of our everyday roadways — with the Grand Canal as Main Street. The area it stands on was a fishermen's village in the Roman era. Not until the Middle Ages, however, did it became a clearly defined political and social entity, when it came under the Byzantine sphere of influence, as opposed to the mainland cities which were dominated by the Longobards. In the 9th century, when most of Italy was under Frankish control, Venice embarked on a new form of government, i.e., a duchy headed by a duke (*Doge*, in Venetian dialect) and backed by the local nobility. Having severed all ties with the Empire of the East, she enjoyed a centuries-long era of prosperity and glory: the *Serenissima* stood out as a leader in sea trade (especially with the Orient) and in culture. Her artistic development was totally unique. Her mixed Eastern-Western background made her a meeting place for two different cultural heritages. She never went through a feudal period, nor did she exist as a city-state. Rather, the Venetian form of government was that of an aristocratic republic — in itself unique for its times — the doge elected and aided by counsellors. The great wealth amassed thanks to the business acumen of the Venetian traders (among them Marco Polo in the 13th century), was a prime factor in sparking a great building boom. Venice reached the height of political and economic power during the 15th and 16th centuries. She managed to greatly expand her territories on the mainland and was successful in defeating the Turks in battle. At the same time, Venetian art was thoroughly revolutionizing Italian painting: the Bellinis, Carpaccio, Giorgione, Titian, Tintoretto, and Veronese were active during these years. Then, in the 17th and 18th centuries, as Venice found herself crushed by the new European powers, decline, both economic and political, began to set in. In 1797 she was annexed to Austria and did not regain her independence until 1866 when she adhered to the Kingdom of Italy.

Preceding pages: Piazza San Marco.
Above: facade of San Marco.

PIAZZA SAN MARCO

PIAZZA SAN MARCO - Originally, San Marco was a grass-covered open space traversed by a canal and bounded on either of its short sides by a church. Subsequent transformation and embellishments made in into one of the most beautiful squares in the world. Today it is bounded by buildings on all four sides. On the east in the Basilica and on the west, the *Ala Napoleonica* (early 19th century). The long buildings on the north and south are the *Procuratie*, which served as the living and working quarters of the famous *Procuratori* (magistrates). The *Procuratie Vecchie* (Old Court) on the north side was built between the late 1400s-early 1500s. The *Procuratie Nuove* (New Court) on the south was begun by Scamozzi in the late 1500s, although the great project was completed by Longhena in 1640. Two other important features complete the square: its attractive geometric paving, which dates from the 18th century, and two towers: the *Bell-tower* and the *Clock Tower*. The *Museo Correr* occupies the upper floor of the Procuratie Nuove.

BASILICA OF ST. MARK'S

BASILICA OF ST. MARK'S - In 828 the mortal remains of St. Mark the Evangelist were brought to Venice from Alexandria, Egypt. On this occasion it was decided to built a church worthy of containing such a precious relic, and one befitting a burgeoning city anxious to show off its wealth and grandeur. Most of the buildings of the grandiose basilica took place between the 11th and 15th centuries. The result is a harmonious blend of Byzantine gilding, Gothic gables, Romanesque round arches, and Islamic domes. Five great *portals*, separated by Romanesque columns and reliefs, dominate the two-story facade. Although the portal domes are all adorned with *mosaics*, only the first one on the left, dated 1270, which shows how the Basilica looked in

the 13th century, is original. The others were executed in the Baroque period. Four of the five arches of the upper level also bear mosaic decoration (18th century). Their elaborate carved frames were sculpted by the Dalle Masegne family during the 14th and 15th centuries. On the terrace separating the two levels are the famous gilded copper *Horses* (recently replaced by copies as the originals were undergoing extensive restoration). The four horses, brought to Venice from Constantinople by Doge Enrico Dandolo in 1204, were sculpted in Greece, probably around the 4th century B.C. On the corner of the Basilica (Doges' Palace side) is another celebrated sculpture group,

the so-called *Tetrarchs*. This fascinating porphyry carving has been classified as a 4th century B.C. Syrian work. From the largest portal (the one in the middle), you enter the Basilica's atrium whose ceiling is completely covered with *mosaic* decoration. The finest are undoubtedly the *scenes from Genesis* (13th-14th centuries). The interior in in the shape of a Greek cross, with single aisles in each arm of the cross, and *matronei* runningn the length of the upper level. *Mosaics* cover the walls and the floor (subject: the *lives of Christ and St. Mark*). The Byzantine style mosaics were executed between the 12th-13th centuries by Venetian craftsmen, while those of the inside facade were designed by

Interior of the Basilica of San Marco.

Tintoretto and others. Even older mosaics (predating the year 1000) are to be found between the apse windows. The great *Christ* in the apse, however, dates from the 16th century. A carved screen separates the nave from the choir. The fourteen statues adorning it were sculpted in the 14th century by the Dalle Masegnes. On either side are pulpits: the 14th century *double pulpit* and so-called «Reliquary Pulpit.» The relics of St. Mark are preserved inside the richly-deco-

61

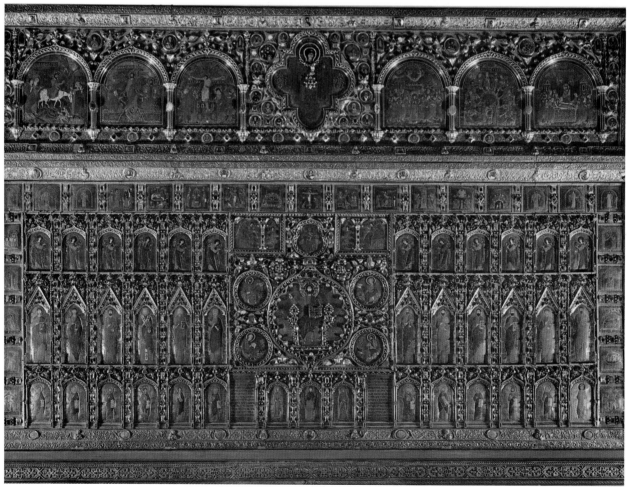

rated *main altar*. Behind the altar is one of the masterpieces of medieval art, the *Pala d'Oro* (Golden Altar). Made of gold, gemstones, and enamels, it was crafted between the 10th and 14th centuries. The enamel in the center depicts *Christ* with the *Evangelists*, while the *Virgin, Apostles*, and *Prophets* are portrayed in the others. On the right wall of the left transept is a famous Byzantine icon known as the *Madonna Nicopeia* (Virgin Victorious). Dated around the 10th century, it was brought to Venice from Constantinople by the returning Crusaders in 1204.

PIAZZETTA - Until the 16th century the Piazzetta, i.e., the square between the San Marco Quay and Piazza San Marco, was a marketplace for foodstuffs and the scene of public executions. On top of the two columns standing in the middle are statues of *St. Todaro* (or Theodore, one of the first patron saints of Venice) and a *Lion of St. Mark*. To your left (back to the water) is the *Libreria Marciana*, or Libreria Sansoviniana, designed in the mid-16th century by Jacopo Sansovino for the rare book collection bequeathed to the city by a 15th century Greek Humanist scholar, Cardinal Bessarione. Today the building houses a library, the *Biblioteca Nazionale Marciana*, and Venice's *Archeological Museum* (Greek and Roman sculpture). Opposite the Libreria is the Doges' Palace.

DOGES' PALACE - The stunning combination of delicate Gothic tracery, pointed arches, and pat-

San Marco. Above left: Noah's Ark, detail of one of the 13th century vestibule mosaics. Below left: Pala d'Oro. Right: details of some of the mosaics inside the Basilica: Christ's Entry into Jerusalem, from the right transept (above) and Christ Enthroned, from the ceiling of the main apse (below).

terned stonework makes the building appear light and airy, almost as if it were weightless. The palace was built in the 9th century as the doges' residence, and then altered several times by famous architects such as the Dalle Masegnes, Rizzo, and da Ponte. The majestic *balcony* on the lagoon side was sculpted by the Dalle Masegnes in 1404, wheares the one facing int the Piazzetta, executed by followers of Sansovino, dates from 1536. The elaborate portal you pass beneath to enter the building, the *Porta della Carta*, was carved by members of the Bon family in 1442. In the *courtyard* are two 16th century *bronze wells*. On the left is the so-called *Foscari Arcade*. The monumental staircase of the adjoining *Cortiletto dei Senatori*, the *Scala dei Giganti* (Giants' Stairs), was designed by Rizzo in the 1500s. A series of decorated halls — most of them the work of the great 16th century Venetian masters — starts on the second floor. We shall list only the highlights. In the *Sale della Pinacoteca*, once the doges' private apartments: *Lion of St. Mark*, by Carpaccio, *Pietà*, by Giovanni Bellini, and works by Jerome Bosch; in the *Sala delle Quattro Porte*: frescoes by Tintoretto and a Titian painting depicting *Doge Antonio Grimani kneeling before Faith*; in the *Sala del Collegio*: a superb ceiling adorned with paintings by Veronese; in the *Sala del Senato*: paintings by Tintoretto (on the ceiling, *Venice, Queen of the Seas*); in the *Sala del Consiglio dei Dieci*: paintings by Veronese; in the *Sala d'Armi*: arms and armor; in the enormous *Sala del Maggior Consiglio*: *Paradise*, by Tintoretto, one of the biggest canvases ever painted (7 × 22 meters). Lastly, crossing over the Bridge of Sighs, you can descend into the *Piombi*, the gloomy palace dungeons where, among other personalities, Casanova was imprisoned (and from which he escaped).

PONTE DEI SOSPIRI - The Bridge of Sighs, which connects the Doges' Palace and the dungeons is one of the most renowned sights in Venice. Built by Antonio Contin in the 17th century, it is a remarkably graceful Baroque structure. Inside, there are two levels of corridors whose only light comes from windows covered by stone tracery. The sighs in the bridge's name are probably a reference to the unhappy sighs of the prisoners being led to the dank dungeons and not, as some say, sighs of lovers.

GRAND CANAL - Venice's major waterway, the Grand Canal bisects the whole city. Running from the railway station to San Marco (approximately 1 1/2 kilometers as the crow flies), it is shaped like an upside down «S». Its vital statistics are: almost 4 kilometers long, maximum depth 5 meters, and average breadth 50 meters. Heavily trafficked by *vaporetti*, gondolas, and

Doges' Palace. Left: facades viewed from the docks. Above: Sala del Maggior Consiglio with Tintoretto's painting of Paradise visible on the far wall. Right: detail of the allegorical painting representing the Triumph of Venice, one of the scenes adorning the ceiling of the same hall.

craft of every size and shape, the canal is a unique sight, its banks lined with an incredible parade of medieval palaces and churches. Where it starts (by the railroad station) is a Baroque building with a fine 17th century facade, the church of the *Scalzi*. The bridge crossing the canal here, *Ponte degli Scalzi*, was built in 1934. A bit farther, on the left side, where the *Cannaregio Canal* intersects the Grand Canal, is *Palazzo Labia*. On the right is *Fondaco dei Turchi*. Originally a Turkish storehouse, the building underwent extensive restoration in the 19th century. After the church of *San Stae*, is *Palazzo Pesaro*, a majestic building with a rusticated stone fa-

cade. Designed in the 17th century by Baldassarre Longhena, today it houses two important museums, the *Galleria d'Arte Moderna* and the *Oriental Museum*. A bit beyond on the left side is the renowned *Ca d'Oro*, with a stunning facade of Gothic marble tracery. It was designed by Bartolomeo Bon and Matteo de' Raverti in the 15th century. Inside is the *Galleria Franchetti* featuring works by Bellini, Titian, Carpaccio, and Guardi. Beyond the Rialto, on the left bank, are two Venetian-Byzantine style palaces, *Palazzo Loredan* (the Venice City Hall) and *Palazzo Farsetti*. A bit farther on the same side is *Palazzo Corner Spinelli* designed by Codussi in the 16th century. Just beyond the bend in the canal appears is the striking facade of *Ca' Foscari*, an elegant 15th Gothic design consisting of three superimposed loggias. Just beyond, at the tip of the bend, is *Palazzo Rezzonico (Museum of 18th Century Venice)*. Opposite is an 18th century palace, *Palazzo Grassi*. Leaving the bend, you pass beneath the *Accademia Bridge*, a wooden structure built in 1930. The *Accademia Museum* is on your right. Beyond, on the left, is *Ca' Grande*, built by Sansovino in 1537. The last monument on the right bank is the church of *Santa Maria della Salute*. On the left is San Marco. From the canal you can see the *Giardinetti Park*, the *Libreria Marciana*, the *Piazzetta*, and the *Doges' Palace*.

RIALTO BRIDGE - This is the oldest, loveliest, and best known of the three bridges spanning the Grand Canal. Originally of wood (as you can see in a famous painting by Carpaccio in the Accademia), it had a special mechanism that allowed the middle section to be moved for the passage of oversize craft. In the 16th century (following its destruction in a terrible fire), a competition was announced for its rebuilding. Among those who unsuccessfully submitted designs were name artists such as Michelangelo, Palladio, and Sansovino; the winner was a native of Venice, Antonio da Ponte, who terminated the project in 1592. The Rialto spans the Grand Canal at its

Left: Bridge of Sighs, the famous covered bridge leading from the Doges' Palace to the gloomy dungeons known as Piombi. Above: Rialto Bridge. Right: Ca d'Oro, one of the most beautiful of the many beautiful palaces and mansions along the Grand Canal.

narrowest point (28 meters), stands 7.5 meters at its center, and is reinforced by 6,000 pylons sunk into the ground at either end. Lined with shops, it is one of the most popular spots in Venice.

SS. GIOVANNI E PAOLO - This

huge church was begun in 1246 as part of a monastery. The facade with its portal by Bartolomeo Bon was left unfinished in the mid-1400s. The area in and around the apse is especially noteworthy. The fact that there is no belltower is quite unusual. Several historical Venetian figures are buried in the church. The most important are: *Admiral Marcantonio Bragadin* (right aisle, 16th century tomb) and *Doge Pietro Mocenigo* (inner facade, 15th century tomb by Pietro Lombardo).

Among the other notable works adorning the building are: the *St. Vincenzo Ferreri Altarpiece*, by Giovanni Bellini (second righthand altar); *St. Antonino Begging*, by Lorenzo Lotto (right transept); and a splendid chapel, the *Cappella del Rosario*, with paintings by Veronese and a canvas attributed to Moretto. The statue in the square is Andrea del Verrocchio's masterpiece of 1496, the *Monument to Bartolomeo Colleoni* (*Condottiero* of the Republic of Venice).

SANTA MARIA DELLA SALUTE

- The Senate of the *Repubblica di Venezia* deliberated building of the church in 1630 in thanksgiving for the end of a plague epidemic. Longhena, who was awarded the commission, brilliantly overcame numerous practical problems relating to land slippage by reinforcing the dome drum with the esthetically-pleasing curlicews that make the building so distinctive and unusual. The church has an octagonal plan, two domes, and faces out on the Grand Canal. The interior consists of a great hall encircled by columns. The side altars are adorned with paintings by Titian, Morlaiter, and Luca Giordano. The magnificent *main altar* standing in the choir was designed by Longhena himself, and decorated with statues of saints carved by various sculptors. Alongside it is a fine 16th century bronze *candlestick*, while behind it is a 15th century *Virgin and Child*. The most important works, however, are in the *Sacrestia Grande* (Large Sacristy): *St. Mark Enthroned*, a youthful work by Titian; a 12th century Byzantine mosaic depicting the *Virgin and Child*; *Wedding at Cana*, by Tintoretto; *Sacrifice of Isaac, David and Goliath*, and *Cain and Abel*, by Titian.

Above: church of Santi Giovanni e Paolo. Right: Santa Maria della Salute viewed from the Grand Canal.

SAN GIORGIO MAGGIORE -

The church, situated on the Isle of San Giorgio across the lagoon from San Marco, is a 10th century building remodeled by Palladio in the second half of the 16th century. Adjoining the elegant church, with its striking white marble facade and soaring belltower, is a brick complex, once a monastery and now an important cultural organization.

LIDO

- An elongated island in the Venetian lagoon, the Lido is a popular summer resort. Bordered by a great stretch of sandy beach, it vaunts excellent tourist facilities, including fine hotels, a casino, and restaurant. The Venice Film Festival is held here every year.

SANTA MARIA GLORIOSA DEI FRARI

The most Gothic of the Venetian churches was built between 1330 and 1340 on the site of a preexisting building, but not consecrated until 1492. The project was carried out by Franciscan monks (frari). Like SS. Giovanni e Paolo, many illustrious Venetians are buried inside. Two of Titian's most famous paintings are hanging here: the *Assumption of the Virgin*, dated 1518, and the *Ca' Pesaro Altarpiece*, dated 1526. Other notable works include an altarpiece portraying *St. Ambrose and other saints*, by Alvise Vivarini and Marco Basaiti; and a triptych depicting the *Virgin Enthroned* by Giovanni Bellini in the Sacristy. Among the tomb monuments, two belong to great artists: *Titian's*, in the nave, built in the 19th century over the spot where the master was supposedly buried and *Canova's*, in the left aisle, designed by the sculptor himself.

SAN ROCCO

The original church designed by Bartolomeo Bon in the 15th century was rebuilt in the 18th century by Scalfarotto. The interior is adorned with marvelous paintings by Tintoretto: *scenes from the life of St. Roch*.

SCUOLA GRANDE DI SAN ROCCO

Several architects worked on the *Scuola* commissioned by the Confraternity of St. Roch following the plague epidemic of 1515. There are eight Tintoretto canvases painted between 1583 and 1587 in the downstairs hall, a huge room partioned into three sections by columns. Upstairs is the impressive *Salone Maggiore*, completely covered with Tintoretto paintings executed between 1576 and 1581. The scenes on the walls are taken from the *New Testament*, while those on the ceiling are *Old Testament* subjects. In the Sala dell'Albergo are a dramatic *Crucifixion* and three paintings of the *Passion of Christ*.

Left: Titian's Assumption of the Virgin in the church of Santa Maria Gloriosa dei Frari. Right: 18th century facade of the church of San Rocco.

ACCADEMIA GALLERY

ACCADEMIA GALLERY - The *Accademia di Pittori e Scultori* was founded in 1750. Piazzetta, its first director, was succeeded by Tiepolo in 1756. In the late 1700s it was moved to its present location on the Grand Canal inside a former monastery, the Convento della Carità. Many prominent artists, including Canova, trained here, although gradually the Accademia became more of a museum than an art school. The plural «*Gallerie,*» as the museum is called in Italian, is used because originally there were two separate collections, one of plaster casts and one of paintings. Today, it ranks as one of the world's great art museums. The first exhibition hall is primarily devoted to the 14th century Venetian school. Major works include: *Coronation of the Virgin*, by Paolo Veneziano; *Mystic Marriage of St. Catherine* and *Annunciation Altarpiece*, by Lorenzo Veneziano; *Madonna della Misericordia* and *Coronation of the Virgin*, by Jacobello del Fiore. Room II: *Sacra Conversazione* and *Virgin of the Orange Tree* by Cima da Conegliano; the *Calling of the Sons of Zebedeus* by Marco Basaiti. Room III: *Sacra Conversazione*, attributed to Sebastiano del Piombo. Room IV: *St. George*, by Mantegna and *St. Jerome and donor*, by Piero della Francesca. Room V: *Pietà*, *Madonna degli Alberelli*, and *Allegories*, all by Giovanni Bellini, and Giorgione's masterpiece, the unsettling *Tempest*. Room VI: works by Tintoretto and Titian. Room VII: *Portrait of a·Gentleman*, by Lotto. Room VIII: works by Palma the

Lamentation, by Giovanni Bellini, in which the Virgin is atypically depicted as an old woman; the background is a cityscape of buildings from two towns, Vicenza and Ravenna.

Elder. Room X: *Banquet in the House of Levi*, a huge canvas by Paolo Veronese, and the *Miracles of St. Mark* cycle, by Tintoretto. Rooms XI through XV are devoted to Tintoretto, Veronese, 16th century Venetian school, Tiepolo, and 18th century landscapists. Room XVI: four mythological scenes by Tiepolo. Room XVII: landscapes by Guardi, Bellotto, and Canaletto, pastels by Carriera, and genre scenes by Pietro Longhi including the *Fortune-Teller*, the *Dancing Lesson*, and the *Pharmacist*. Room XVIII: sculpture by Canova. Room

XX: the renowned series of 15th century Bellinis and Carpaccios depicting the *Miracles of the Reliquary*, and especially: *Healing of a Possessed Man*, by Carpaccio, and *Procession in Piazza San Marco*, by Gentile Bellini. Room XXI: Carpaccio's remarkable cycle of the *Story of St. Ursula*, the most famous of which are *St. Ursula's Dream* and

The Tempest, by Giorgione. To this day, nobody has been able to interpret the subject of the this remarkable painting.

the *English Ambassadors at the Court of Brittany*. The following hall is devoted to the 15th century, while the last room contains outstanding works by Titian (*Presentation of the Virgin*) and Giovanni Bellini.

MURANO – Around the 10th-11th centuries it became one of the major lagoon centers. The tradition of *glassblowing*, still the basis of the city's great renown, dates back to that period, although it received its greatest boost in the 13th century. Much of the city appears as it did in the 15th-16th centuries when its villas and gardens were favorite vacation spots with the Venetian aristocrats. The *Glass Museum* is on the Canale di San Donato. Its exhibits

Left: Tintoretto's Miracle of the Slave. Below: view of the Grand Canal and the Isle of San Giorgio in a striking 17th century rendition by Francesco Guardi.

comprise glass from different periods, among which the celebrated 16th century *Barovier Goblet*. Next to the museum is *SS. Maria e Donato*, a Ravennate-style church with a 12th century apse covered with geometric patterns, and a square *belltower*. The highlights of the striking interior include the floor *mosaics* and frescoes. One of the musts in Murano is a walk along the charming *Angeli* and *Vetrai canals*.

TORCELLO - This tranquil little island, today partially uninhabited, was once a mighty urban center and Venice's major rival. It was founded in 452 by refugees from the mainland city of Altino and by the 7th century had become an important bishopric. Torcello's decline was a result of two factors: overpowering competition from Venice and malaria, which in a way was just as overpowering. The island, is unrivalled for atmosphere. One devoté was Ernest Hemingway who spent long periods living and working on Torcello. The Ravennate-style *Cathedral* was built between the 8th and 11th centuries, whereas its square *belltower* dates from the 9th century. Inside the church, the choir is separated from the nave and aisles by a carved *screen* with remarkable 15th century icons and a wooden *Crucifix*. The mosaic adorning the inside facade (*Last Judgment*, 12th century) and apse zone (*Virgin and Child*, 13th century) are among the great masterpieces of Byzantine art. Next to the Cathedral is a 10th-11th century polygonal building, the church of *Santa Fosca*. Its Greek-cross interior is quite striking. Outside, opposite Santa Fosca, is the so-called *Caregon* (chair, in the local dialect), which was once called «Attila's Throne,» although it was probably just a bishop's chair. The two other buildings facing into the square, *Palazzo dell'Archivio* and *Palazzo del Consiglio*, were built in the 14th century. Today they are a museum, the *Museo dell'Estuario*.

Above: church of Santa Fosca on the Isle of Torcello. Below: apse of the church of Santi Maria e Donato.

VERONA

View of Piazza delle Erbe with Torre del Gardel and Palazzo Maffei in the background.

Many extraordinary remains of Verona's past have been preserved throughout the centuries. The city achieved prosperity by the Roman period thanks to a strategic position at the crossroads of the major communications networks. There was a drawback though: such a central position also left it open to outside attacks, which were indeed frequent. In the 12th century the Free Commune of Verona joined the Lombard League in a concerted effort to oust Barbarossa. In the 13th, it was ruled by the *Signoria*, first under Ezzelino II da Romano and then under the Scaligeri, who brought political and economic well-being to the city, and, in addition, summoned important artists and architects to work under their patronage. Art flourished throughout the 16th century, mainly under the impetus of Paolo Caliari, known as "*Il Veronese*," one of the foremost Venetian painters of the times. Modern-day Verona is a great center of Italian agriculture. Of course, we must not forget opera, i.e., the performances in the Arena, known and appreciated world over.

PIAZZA ERBE - This bustling marketplace is bordered by picturesque old buildings. In the center are: the *Market Column*, the *Stocks*, the *Column of St. Mark's*, and the *Fountain of Madonna Verona*.

PIAZZA DEI SIGNORI - Some remarkable buildings look out on the square. *Palazzo della Ragione*, topped by an old belltower, Torre

76

dei Lamberti, was built in the late 12th century in a Romanesque style. *Palazzo dei Giudici* is a 17th century reconstruction of a pre-existing building. The elegant *Loggia di Fra' Giocondo* attributed to a Veronese monk, comprises an elaborate eight-arch portico.

CASTELVECCHIO - Begun in 1354 by Cangrande II as a defense fortress, Castelvecchio still makes an impressive sight with its majestic towers and ramparts outlined against the skyline. After serving as a prison and then an army barracks,

it became a museum, the *Museo Civico*. We shall mention only the highlights of each room. Room I: Romanesque sculpture, Longobard metal objects, and medieval bronzes. Rooms III and IV: 14th century works, including a fine *Crucifixion*. Room VI (in the *Torre Maggiore*): two 14th century Veronese *bells*. Rooms VIII and IX (the first of the Scaligero Royal Palace): 13th and 14th century paintings. Room XI: *Madonna della Quaglia* (Virgin of the Quail) by Pisanello, *Virgin of the Rosegarden* by Stefano da Verona, and paintings by Jacopo

Ponte Scaligero, the 14th century bridge crossing the Adige River from Castelvecchio.

Bellini. Room XIV and XV: 15th century Venetian school, e.g., two *Virgins* by Giovanni Bellini and *Sts. Catherine and Veneranda* by Carpaccio. Room XIX: two fine paintings by Mantegna and the *Virgin of the Passion* by Crivelli. The remarkable 14th century *statue of Cangrande I* (originally atop his tomb) is displayed between Rooms XX and XXI.

PIAZZA BRA - The square the natives call "*La Bra*" (a shortened form of *braida*, a Germanic-root word for open space) was once the local livestock marketplace. The area around the Arena was paved in the 18th century, and since then, dubbed "*Il Listón*", it has always been a favorite with the *Veronesi* as a place to stroll and shop. Beyond the Arena is Verona's *City Hall* (1838), *Palazzo della Gran Guardia* (17th century), and the arcades known as *Portoni della Bra* (1389).

ARENA - This huge amphitheater was built by the Romans in the 1st century A.D. Throughout the Mid-

dle Ages, however, it ceased to be a showplace and sadly became a handy stone quarry. Only recently has it been restored and returned to its original function, this time as an open-air opera house. The surviving structures include a wing of the outer walls in the three Classical orders (Doric, Ionic, Corinthinian), the inner walls, the stage, and the impressive 30-meter-tall cavea seating 22,000.

The double-tier exterior of the Arena entirely built of local white stone. The Arena of Verona is the third largest Roman amphitheater extant, preceded only by the Colosseum in Rome and the Capua Amphitheater.

SAN ZENO

SAN ZENO - The renowned Romanesque basilica of San Zeno was founded in the 5th century and rebuilt during the 11th and 12th centuries. The rose window on the linear facade (called Wheel of Fortune) dates from the 13th century. The outstanding artistic feature of the church facade, however, is its *portal*, comprising a porch resting on columns bordered by two rows of reliefs depicting *scenes from the Old and New Testaments*. This masterpiece of Romanesque art was executed by Niccolò and helpers. In the lunette is a sculpture of *San Zeno*. Vigorous *Old and New Testament scenes* plus *scenes from the life of San Zeno* by various 12th century masters are embossed on the *bronze panels* of the door. There are many fine works inside the church. The highlights are: *Crucifixion* by Lorenzo Veneziano (inner facade); 12th century *baptismal font* (beginning of the right aisle); fragments of 14th-15th century frescoes (right aisle); *Altarpiece by Mantegna*, one of the masterpieces of 15th century Italian painting (main altar); painted statue of *San Zeno laughing*, provincial school (small left apse); 15th century *Crucifixion* (apse dome), and the *crypt*. From the left aisle you enter the charming Romanesque *Cloister* (1123).

ARCHE SCALIGERE - The Arche are 14th century tombs belonging to the *Signori* of Verona. They are located by the *Arca di Cangrande I* (1329) atop the portal of the church of *Santa Maria Antica*. (The statue of Cangrande is a copy; the original is in the Castelvecchio Museum.) The later tombs, the *Arca di Mastino II* (1345) and the *Arca di Cansignorio* (by Bonino da Campione, 1375), have the same elaborate structure and decorative style.

San Zeno. Above left: framing the Basilica are the crenelated Torre di San Zeno Maggiore and the church's 13th century belltower. Below: bronze panels from the Basilica's great portal representing the Beheading of St. John the Baptist (left) and the Expulsion of Adam and Eve from Paradise (right). Right: the central panel of Mantegna's triptych.

JULIET'S HOUSE - A thoroughly romantic atmosphere is conveyed in the charming court of this 13th century dwelling with its pointed-arch portal and, of course, balcony. The story of two Veronese youths, Juliet Capuleti and Romeo Montecchi, who fell in love despite the fact that their families were bitter enemies became known world over through Shakespeare's play written at the end of the 16th century. (Shakespeare himself, however, never actually visited Verona.) Although no documentary evidence exists, this house is believed to have really belonged to the Capuleti family.

SANT'ANASTASIA - Work on the church was begun in the 1200s (by Dominican monks) on the site of a much earlier building erected by Theodoric, and continued well into the 15th century. The huge double portal of the unfinished facade has a splendidly carved 14th century entablature. The Gothic-style interior has single aisles topped by a fine cross-vaulted ceiling. One of the two holy water fonts resting on 16th century *caryatids* at the beginning of the nave (left) has been ascribed to Veronese's father. By the right aisle is the *Fregoso Altar*, built by Sanmicheli (16th century). A fresco by

Above: House of Juliet. Right: detail of Pisanello's fresco of St. George and the Princess in the church of Sant'Anastasia.

Altichiero (c. 1395) depicting the *Cavalli Family being presented to the Virgin* adorns the Cappella Cavalli. In a nearby chapel is Pisanello's celebrated fresco of *St. George and the Princess*, revealing the master's love of elegant line and courtly treatment of his subjects.

82

PADUA

By the 1st century B.C. Roman *Pataviam* was one of the region's principal centers. Its importance plunged with the fall of the Roman Empire, only to rise again with the birth and development of the communes in the 11th and 12th centuries. In the 13th century, under the *Signoria* of Ezzelino da Romano, Padua's glorious university was founded. However, Padua reached her apex of splendor in the 14th-15th centuries under the *Signoria* of the Carraresi family. During this period, great artists — for example, Giotto, Dante, and Petrarch — were active in the city, a local school of painters, foremost of which Guariento, began to make their mark, and dozens of splendid buildings were designed and erected. In the 15th century, despite the fact that politically it was subject to Venetian domination, Padua retained her standing as an artistic leader.

Artists such as Donatello and Mantegna were active in the 1400s, and they were followed by Titian, Sansovino, and a host of others, not to mention the great architect Palladio who was born here in 1508. Padua, to a large extent stimulated by the intense intellectual life of a great university, never relinquished her leadership in cultural-artistic affairs of the Veneto region.

BASILICA DI SANT'ANTONIO - Work on this great religious complex, built to house the relics of Padua's beloved St. Anthony (who was actually born in Lisbon, Portugal, although he died here in 1231), began in 1232 and lasted well into the 14th century. Its composite style reveals Romanesque-Gothic motifs (facade and apse) and Oriental influxes (belltowers and domes). The facade is divided into two registers. The single-aisle interior has *ma-*

tronei galleries and hemispherical domes. The *Cappella di San Felice* (or San Jacopo) taking up the whole righthand transept is covered with 14th century frescoes illustrating the *life of St. Jacob*, a *Crucifixion*, and other scenes, by Altichiero. The apse is encircled by an ambulatory and radiating chapels. The middle chapel, the *Treasury*, is a masterpiece of Baroque architecture. Inside the cabinets are precious relics. In the left transept is the *Arca del Santo*, designed by Riccio in the early 16th century. The altar was built by Tiziano Aspetti in the late 16th century. On the back is an urn containing a *silver casket* with the mortal remains of St. Anthony. The main altar is decorated with *bronze reliefs by Donatello* and his school, executed in the years 1443-1450. In front of the church is the *Gattamelata Monument*, an equestrian statue by Donatello.

84

Left: Palazzo del Capitanio, a late 16th century building. The clock in the Arco dell'Orologio (whose ground floor is a passageway connecting Piazza dei Signori and Piazza Capitaniato) was installed in 1344 and thus ranks as Italy's first public timepiece. Above: Basilica of Sant'Antonio.

EREMITANI - The church was named after the Monastery belonging to the Eremitani Friars. Built in the late 1200s in the Romanesque-Gothic style, it underwent extensive restoration after being heavily bombed in World War II. On the right side of the facade is a fine 15th century portal with reliefs depicting the *Months,* by Niccolò Baroncelli. Medieval and Renaissance tombs line the great aisleless interior. Of especial note are the *tombs of Ubertino da Carrara* and *Jacopo da Carrara* (14th century), and the *Mausoleum of Marco Mantoa*

Benavides by Ammannati (1546). In the choir are remains of Guariento frescoes depicting *scenes from the life of St. Augustine.* At the far right end of the church side is the *Cappella Ovetari.* Once covered with celebrated *frescoes by Mantegna,* the Vivarinis, and Giovanni d'Alemagna, it was unfortunately ruined by bombs in 1944. The subjects of the surviving paintings are the *Martyrdom of St. Christopher,* the *Martyrdom of St. Jacob,* and the *Assumption of the Virgin* that Mantegna painted in the mid-1400s.

SCROVEGNI CHAPEL - The chapel was commissioned by Enrico Scrovegni in 1305 as expiation for the sins of his father who had made a fortune as a moneylender. Its interior is frescoed with *scenes of the lives of Christ and the Virgin by Giotto,* one of the most important works in Western art. When Giotto

came to Padua shortly after having completed the great fresco cycle at Assisi, he was at the height of his artistic maturity. These frescoes reveal, not only superb technical mastery, but also emotional levels rarely reached before — or after — in the history of painting. The scenes are arranged in three registers above a fake marble border interspersed with personifications of the *Virtues* and *Vices.* The cycle begins at the figure of *God the Father* in the lunette opposite the entrance and continues all around from right to left and top to bottom with *scenes from the lives of Joachim and Anna,* the *Virgin* (*Annunciation, Nativity, Flight into Egypt*), and *Christ,* culminating in the stunning renditions of the *Last Supper, Kiss of Judas, Crucifixion, Deposition,* and *Resurrection.* On the entrance wall is a grandiose *Last Judgment.* The *Virgin* on the altar is by Giovanni Pisano.

85

VICENZA

Vicenza was never a particularly powerful or important city, nor was it governed by art patron-lords, since for most of its history it was dominated by others. Nevertheless, it is one of the Italian cities boasting the largest number of art monuments. Historically, the most exciting years were the prosperous 1500s when Andrea Palladio, of Vicenza, was embellishing the whole Veneto region-with his masterpieces of architectural design.

BASILICA - Palladio's masterpiece and the outstanding architectural monument in Vicenza, the Basilica was built in the mid-1500s around an earlier building, the 15th century Gothic-style *Palazzo della Ragione* which at the time was badly in need of repair. Palladio submitted his plans in 1549 and supervised construction until his death in 1580. The building consists of two superimposed loggias, the lower Doric and the upper Ionic. Above the upper loggia is the enormous *Hall* (22 × 52 meters) covered by a barrel roof and lit by pointed windows.

TEATRO OLIMPICO - It was designed by Palladio who died a few months after construction was begun, and finished in 1584 by Scamozzi. Originally built for performances of the Accademia Olimpica, it is still being used as a theater today. The incredible building is ranked as one of the world's most beautiful theaters. Inspired by Classical models, it has permanent stage sets, adorned with ninety-five statues, built by Scamozzi.

LA ROTONDA - This stupendous round building was designed and erected by Palladio and Scamozzi (1550-1606). It became a prototype for dozens of villas and other kinds of buildings all over Europe.

Left: Giotto's fresco of the Last Judgment in the Scrovegni Chapel, Padua. Above: Palladio's Basilica. Below: Palladio's Rotonda.

CORTINA D'AMPEZZO

Cortina, set in a picturesque valley entirely girthed by majestic Dolomite peaks, is one of the most exclusive resorts in the world. Today renowned for its fine hotels, restaurants, and shops, as well as top notch skiing and winter sports facilities, it originated as a tiny mountain village in 1830. One of the nicest excursions you can make from Cortina is a long hike (approximately 20 km) or ride, to *Lake Misurina*, an enchanting scenic lake, and beyond to the *Tre Cime di Lavaredo*. The Lavaredo mountains come to tower-like peaks (three major and several minor ones), all of which smooth and vertical on the north side, whereas their steepness decreases descending toward the Misurina Valley.

Above: Cortina d'Ampezzo with the mountains of Pomagagnon and Cristallo in the background. Left: the triple peaks of Lavaredo viewed from Lake Misurina.

FRIULI-VENEZIA GIULIA

Friuli-Venezia Giulia is the east-ernmost region of Italy. It has such a variety of landscapes that a 19th century writer was moved to de-scribe it as a «pint-sized compen-dium of the universe.» Prominent geological features are the snow-capped Carnia mountains (tallest peak: Mt. Coglians, 2781 m), the Adriatic lagoons, the gently-rolling Morenici Hills, and the arid Carso Plateau which, especially in the Tri-este area, is dotted with grottoes and dolinas.

HISTORY AND ART HISTORY -

In the prehistoric era, this whole area was inhabited by tribes whose existence is documented by bones and artifacts found in the grottoes around Trieste. The highlands were settled in the 10th century by the so-called Castellieri. In the 5th century, the Celts overran the region, driving the local population closer and closer to the coastal zones. Aware-ness that the Celtic threat was in-creasing led the Romans to found the city of Aquileia in the 2nd century B.C. as a bulwark in the defense of Northern Italy. Other colonies followed in the wake of Aquileia until finally the whole terri-tory was engulfed in the X Regio of Rome. Today there are notable Ro-man remains, especially in the Tri-este area. In 452 A.D. Attila and his Huns overran Aquileia whose sub-sequent decline lasted eight hun-dred year. The major center in the 6th century was Cividale, capital of a powerful Longobard duchy. (A splendid 8th century temple has come down to us from the Long-obard period.) Grado and Istria, on the other hand, remained under Byzantine rule for long centuries, while Carso was being settled by Slavic tribes. In the 8th century the Franks swept through the whole region, splintering it into a myriad of little fiefdoms. These united under the common necessity of defending their lands from the Slavic pirates —

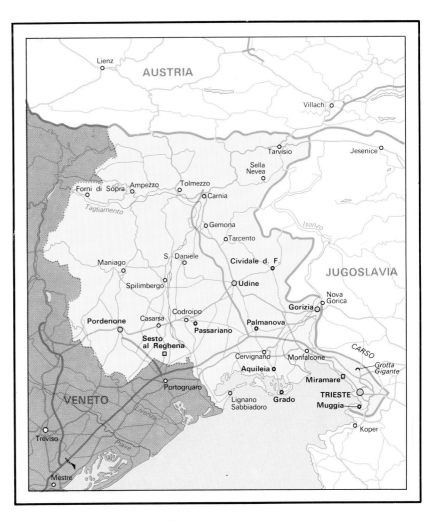

which led many towns and cities to ask for the protection of their neigh-bors, the Venetians. The most im-portant examples of 12th-13th cen-tury Romanesque architecture are to be found in Trieste, Udine, and Aquileia. The political importance of the patriarch began to gain momen-tum in the 11th century when the Patriarch of Aquileia was successful in uniting all the Friulian cities in a common front against the Ungari threat on the East. The church was thus able to dominate the region up until the 14th-15th centuries, despite the growth of the communes and the increasing power of the Republic of Venice which, however, man-

aged to take control when Friuli, ravaged and thus weakened by in-ternal disputes, failed to receive the backing of the German emperor. Local Renaissance and Baroque art continued to be influenced by the Venetian school. The foremost 16th century master, Pordenone, studied under Titian, while Tiepolo's influ-ence lasted well into the 18th cen-tury. By the 18th century Trieste had gained notable importance as a business center and ranked as major Adriatic port. In 1866 Friuli became part of the Kingdom of Italy, where-as Venezia Giulia remained under Austrian rule until the end of World War I.

TRIESTE

Settled in pre-Roman times, Trieste (then known as *Tergeste*) became a prosperous Roman colony. Thereafter, it was a Byzantine and Frankish possession before becoming a Free Commune. It succumbed to the Venetians in the 13th century and the Austrians in the 14th. Its importance was secondary until the 18th century, when Emperor Charles VI declared it a free port and made it the main Mediterranean trading station of the Austrian empire. From then on it was a cosmopolitan center of trade and commerce. Throughout the 19th century anti-Austrian sentiment ran high; in the 1918 the city was annexed to the Kingdom of Italy. Three literary giants were active in Trieste during the early 1900s: James Joyce, Italo Svevo, and Umberto Saba.

ROMAN THEATER - When the theater was built between the 1st and 2nd centuries A.D., it was right on the water — in fact, the water actually reached the stage during high tides. The theater was excavated in 1938 along with the ten statues that originally adorned the proscenium (now in the Museo di Storia ed Arte). Excavations have brought to light the semicircular cavea with four rows of seats and a rectangular stage.

CATHEDRAL OF SAN GIUSTO - The foremost monument in Trieste rises on top of the Hill of San Giusto, the site of the Roman Capital (remains of which are partially incorporated in the church and belltower). The cathedral was built in the 14th century by uniting two pre-existing ecclesiastical structures. In one of the original buildings are the relics of St. Justus, the patron of Trieste. A 14th century rose window adorns the plain facade. The center portal is framed by two sections of a Roman stele. In a niche above the belltower entrance portal is a 14th century statue of *St. Justus*. The double-aisle interior (resulting from the unification of the two churches) contains some noteworthy works of art: the Romanesque *Baptistry* entered by way of the left aisle, the *Cappella del Tesoro* (a bit farther down on the same side as the Baptistry) with a Baroque gate, a 13th century *Crucifix*, and a painting of *St. Justus* on silk (also 13th century). The apse mosaic off the middle aisle on the left portrays the *Virgin and Child with Archangels Michael and Gabriel* (12th century). The mosaic in the apse off the first righthand aisle shows *Christ between Sts. Justus and Servolus* (13th century). Against the wall are Byzantine columns dating from the 6th century. The painted sculpture of the *Pietà* in the first chapel of the far right aisle was crafted in Alto Adige in the 16th century.

MUSEO DI STORIA ED ARTE - This collection along with that of the adjoining *Orto Lapidario* was founded in the mid-1800s. Highlights include Roman artifacts, paintings, and masterpieces of the minor arts.

Left: panoramic view of the city. Above: Cathedral of San Giusto on a hillside. Right: Castello di Miramare, located approximately four miles from Trieste.

MIRAMARE CASTLE - Designed in the late 19th century by Carlo Junker, the castle was built for Hapsburg Archduke Maximilian and his wife Charlotte. Its impressive setting is a 55-acre park (one of the biggest in Northern Italy) overlooking the water. Brother of Emperor Franz Joseph, Maximilian was crowned emperor of Mexico in 1864. Three years later, however, he was captured and shot to death by the republican army. His wife eventually went crazy. In summer months, their tragic story is recreated in a *son et lumiére* show held daily on the castle grounds. The castle, a remarkable example of 19th century eclecticism, is decorated in an elegant and original style.

UDINE

Udine, today the major Friuli city, was just one of the many castle towns dotting the region in the Middle Ages. In 1238, it became seat of the patriarch and, in the early 1400s, major contender in the struggle between Gorizia and Treviso, before falling to Venice under whose control it remained from the 15th to 18th centuries.

PIAZZA DELLA LIBERTÀ - The square is surrounded by aristocratic buildings of various periods. These include the *Arco Bollani* designed by Palladio in 1556, the *Porticato di San Giovanni*, built in the 16th century the clock tower, and *Palazzo del Comune* a fine example of the Venetian Gothic architecture (1456).

CASTLE - The elegant castle was designed by Giovanni Fontana in the 16th century. The staircase before the main entrance is instead by Giovanni da Udine. There are two museums inside the castle, the *Museo Civico* and the *Galleria d'Arte Antica e Moderna*. The highlights of the colletion include: Greek and Roman works, a *Crucifix* by Canova; *St. Francis in Ecstasy* by Caravaggio, *Christ* by Carpaccio, and *Consilium in Arena* by Tiepolo.

DUOMO - Built between the 13th and 14th centuries and rebuilt in the Baroque period, the Duomo vaunts its original portal. Inside there are paintings by Tiepolo, Pordenone and Vitale da Bologna.

ORATORIO DELLA PURITÀ - This 18th century Oratory is adorned with exceptional *frescoes* by Giovan Battista Tiepolo (*Assumption of the Virgin* on the ceiling and *Immaculate Conception* on the altar) and his son Gian Domenico.

Above: Piazza della Libertà with the San Giovanni Arcade and the Clocktower. Below: Duomo.

EMILIA-ROMAGNA

Emilia is the northwestern and Romagna the southeastern part of the single political entity designated Emilia-Romagna. It is shaped rather like a triangle, with the Apennines making up the south side, the Po the north side, and the Adriatic coast the east side. This three-part division is reflected in its geological makeup: in the northwest a vast valley formed by the Po and its affluents, along the coast an extensive stretch of sandy beach, and, running diagonally, a natural inland border created by the great range of Ligurian/Tusco-Emilian mountains.

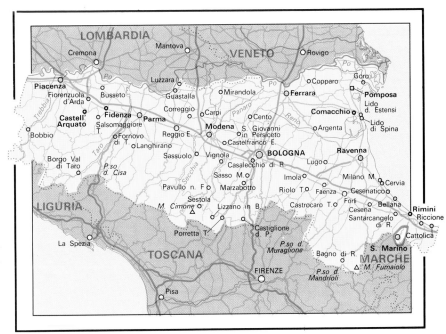

HISTORY - We have ample proof (flints, remains of dwellings, etc.) of the prehistoric settlements that once dotted the region. There are also considerable traces of later civilizations such as that of the Villanovians (10-6th centuries B.C.), in turn supplanted by the Etruscans, Celts, and, in the 2nd century, by the Romans. Ravenna's period of glory began in the 5th century when it became capital of the Holy Roman Empire of the West. It continued under Odoacre the barbarian king who toppled the empire in 476), the Ostrogoth Theodoric (who rose to the throne in 593), and the Byzantine exarchates (who were the prime force opposing the Longobard dominion in the western part of the region). Thereafter, decline set in until the political-cultural reawakening of the communal period. From the 9th through 11th centuries, Emilia-Romagna was ruled by a succession of bishops. In the early 1100s, the newborn communes were able to stop Frederick II of Swabia on his way to conquer them. The great duchies (d'Este in Ferrara, Da Polenta in Ravenna, and Malatesta in Rimini) were the keynote of the 14th and 15th centuries. At the outset of the 16th century, the conquests of Cesare Borgia (son of Pope Alexander VI) laid the way for the church's domination which ex-

tended everywhere except Parma and Piacenza (controlled by the Farnese) and Modena and Reggio (controlled by the d'Este). Occupation (the French starting at end of the 18th century followed by the Austrians shortly afterward) and bitter fighting (insurrections in Bologna and Parma) preceded annexation to the newborn Kingdom of Italy in 1860.

ART - In the 5th-6th centuries, there was a great outpouring of Byzantine art in Ravenna where new churches were built and embellished with exquisite mosaics. Later, in the 11th and 12th centuries, the great Romanesque churches of Modena, Ferrara, Parma, and Piacenza were built, and master sculptors such as Wiligelmus, Benedetto Antelami, and Niccolò were commissioned to provide their sculptural decoration. Bologna's rise as a cultural-artistic center dates from the 12th-13th centuries. During this period the Gothic churches of the new Tuscan style of sculpture, brought by Nicola Pisano, was gain-

ing ground. At the same time, masters such as Vitale da Bologna, Simone dei Crocifissi, and Tommaso da Modena, influenced by the innovations coming from the north (France) and south (Florence) were developing a local painting school, while in Rimini painters looked mainly to Giotto and his school. The outstanding artistic center during the Renaissance period was Ferrara which produced architects such as Biagio Rossetti and painters such as Cosmè Tura, Francesco del Cossa, and Ercole de' Roberti in the 1400s and Dosso Dossi in the following century. Other major art centers were Bologna, Forlì, and Parma. Shortly afterward, in the mid-1500s, Bologna became the region's leading artistic center due to the presence of a sculptor, Giambologna, and a school of painters, the Carracci, Guido Reni, and Guercino. Its artistic tradition has never died out: modern masters from or active in the region include Carrà, Morandi, and De Chirico, whose «metaphysical art» was greatly influenced by his long years of activity in Ferrara.

BOLOGNA

Bologna has been renowned as a cultural center since Roman times. Decline set in with the fall of the Empire and lasted until the rise of the communes in the 11th-12th centuries. By this time the University of Bologna was already a cultural magnet attracting students from all over the world. During these fruitful years, when the city was being embellished with churches and palaces, the Bolognese were also successful in repelling the advance of the Swabian emperor Frederick II. Independence was followed by a long period of papal domination which, despite a revolt every once in a while from the inside and an attempt at conquest from the outside, lasted from 1361 to 1796, the year Napoleon's army entered Bologna. It currently ranks as one of Italy's most economically productive centers.

PIAZZA MAGGIORE - Impressive medieval buildings are situated around Bologna's most important square. Among these is *Palazzo del Podestà*, in the 13th century the headquarters of the Commune, although its present appearance dates from a 14th century remodeling, and the *Palazzo dei Banchi*, originally bankers' offices, which was designed by Vignola in the 16th century. The adjoining square, *Piazza del Nettuno*, was named after the impressive fountain *(Fontana del Nettuno)* by Giambologna adorning it. Joined on one side to Palazzo del Podestà is *Palazzo di Re Enzo* (1246), where the son of Frederick II, Enzo, was imprisoned.

SAN PETRONIO - Designed by Antonio di Vincenzo 1390, this immense church went through three building campaigns (15th, 16th, and 17th centuries) to reach completion. On the *central portal* are Jacopo della Quercia's renowned reliefs of biblical scenes (c. 1425). The side chapels of the single-aisle Gothic *interior* are closed off by choir screens and adorned with 15th century stained glass windows. Fine frescoes adorn several: *New Testament scenes* and *scenes from the life of St. Petronius* by Giovanni da Modena (first and fourth left), and *Virgin and Saints* by Lorenzo Costa

Neptune Fountain, by Giambologna, with crenelated Palazzo di Re Enzo in the background.

(seventh). At the far left is the Cathedral Museum. On the nave floor is a fascinating 17th century *sundial*. Vignola's *tribune* adorns the main altar. The highlights of the right aisle are a *statue of St. Anthony* attributed to Sansovino (ninth chapel), inlaid *choir stalls* (eighth chapel), *St. Jerome Altarpiece* by Lorenzo Costa (sixth chapel), and a *Pietà* by Amico Aspertini (fifth chapel). Here, in 1530, Charles V of Spain was crowned emperor by Clement VIII.

SAN FRANCESCO - This fine Gothic church was built around the mid 1200s. Several features testify to French influence, e.g., the radiating chapels and rampant arch of the apse. In front of these are three tombs, the so-called *Arche dei Glossatori*, (i.e., annotators of juridical works, 13th century). Inside is a late

Above: Arcaded Palazzo del Podestà on Piazza Maggiore. Right: San Petronio.

14th century marble altar by the Dalle Masegne workshop. Other noteworthy sights are the *cloisters* and two *belltowers*.

TORRI PENDENTI - Like Pisa's celebrated leaning towers, they have come to symbolize the city. The taller of the two, *Torre degli Asinelli*, affords a marvelous panorama from its 97.6 meter summit. Named after the Asinelli family, it was probably commissioned by the Commune in the 12th century for use as a watch tower. The lower one (48.16 meters), *Torre Garisenda,* has a much greater inclination.

It was built around the end of the 11th century, probably by the Garisendi family after which it was named, and cut down in the 14th century to prevent collapse.

PINACOTECA NAZIONALE - The collection originated in the early 1800s. It features outstanding works by 14th-18th century Emilian School painters, as well as other Central Italian masters. Pre-Renaissance section: Vitale da Bologna (*St. George and the Dragon*), Giotto and his workshop, (*Virgin and Saints*), Simone dei Crocifissi, and Jacopino da Bologna. Renaissance

Above: apse of the church of San Francesco with the 13th century tombs known as «Arche dei Glossatori». Right: Ecstasy of St. Cecilia, by Raphael, in the Pinacoteca Nazionale.

section: the Vivarinis, Cima, Costa, Raphael (*Ecstasy of St. Cecilia*), Parmigianino (*Madonna di Santa Margherita*), and Francia; Baroque section: the Carraccis (note the *Annunciation* by Annibale), Guido Reni (*Beggars' Pietà*, *Victory of Samson*, and *Portrait of the Artist's Mother*), Domenichino, and Guercino.

MODENA

Modena was settled by the Romans in the 2nd century B.C. During the prosperous communal period, great building projects were undertaken and a university, rivaling Bologna's as a prominent intellectual center, was founded. Rivalry with Bologna was not confined to cultural matters, however: in 1249 the armies of the two cities met on the battlefield, and Modena was soundly beaten. Shortly afterward in 1288 the defeated city passed into the hands of the d'Este family until the arrival of Napoleon's army in 1796. Modern-day Modena is active in both industry and agriculture. (Ferrari cars, for instance, are manufactured in nearby Maranello.)

DUOMO - This superb Romanesque church designed by Lanfranco in the 11th century was built in the 11th and 12th centuries over a pre-existing building inside of which important relics, the mortal remains of St. Geminianus, were preserved. Consecrated still unfinished in 1106 in the presence of Countess Matilde di Canossa, it was not completed until the 13th century. Its most remarkable feature are the facade reliefs recounting the *story of Genesis* carved in the 12th century by Wiligelmus. The *rose window* was designed by a Northern Italian master, Anselmo da Campione. Inside the belltower known as *«La Ghirlandina»* is a wooden *bucket* that was stolen by the Modenese from the Bolognese in 1325 and immortalized in a 16th century heroic-comic poem, *«La Secchia Rapita»* (The Pilfered Bucket). The single-aisle *interior* has several *capitals* carved in Wiligelmus' workshop, the pillar

Left: facade of the Duomo. Right: the tower known as «La Ghirlandina».

pulpit carved by Arrigo da Campione dated 1322, the *Pontile*, or apse partition adorned with fine 12th century Northern Italian reliefs, and the *pulpit* which was also executed by a Northern Italian master.

PALAZZO DEI MUSEI - The building was erected in 1753 as the royal arsenal and before being turned into a museum complex in 1883, it served as the local poorhouse. Today it comprises the *Galleria* and *Museo Estense* (which features a notable collection of 14th-17th century works), the *Museo Civico, Galleria Campori, Museo Lapidario* (inscriptions), and *Biblioteca Estense* (the d'Este library).

FERRARA

Ferrara was settled around the 7th-8th century by the banks of the Po River and along its outlying canals. By the end of the 15th century the city had attained such a notable level of prosperity that Duke Ercole I d'Este could turn his mind to improving and modernizing its appearance. This renovation plan which enhanced without destroying the existing urban structure made Ferrara "the first modern city in Europe," as the great historian Jakob Burkhardt described it.

CATHEDRAL - This majestic Romanesque church was built between the 12th and 14th centuries. The *facade* is adorned with elegant loggias and carved portals whose reliefs date from the 12th-13th centuries. The *belltower* was designed by Leon Battista Alberti.

D'ESTE CASTLE - The project comprising the turreted brick castle surrounded by a moat was started in 1385 and completed in the 16th century. The most interesting sights include a notable 15th century courtyard and the *Salone dei Giochi*.

PALAZZO DEI DIAMANTI - Biagio Rossetti's great Renaissance masterpiece was commissioned by Sigismondo d'Este and begun in 1492. It was named after the over 12,000 diamond-faceted stones covering its facades. Two art museums, the *Pinacoteca Nazionale*, and the *Museo Boldini* are inside.

PALAZZO DI SCHIFANOIA - Rossetti remodeled a late 14th century building, turning it into this delightful palace, between 1466 and 1493. The interior is superbly appointed. One of the most important Renaissance fresco cycles decorates the *Salone dei Mesi* on the second floor. It was painted by leading Ferrarese masters (Cossa and de' Roberti) in the mid 15th century.

Above: Castello Estense. Below: facade of the Cathedral.

RAVENNA

Roman Ravenna was a strategic border town and as such was given a suitable port structure, i.e., the nearby Port of Classe. The city's period of glory, however, did not begin until the 5th century when the Byzantine emperor Honorius set up his court in the city and embarked on a great building campaign. Ravenna's power and prestige increased under Honorius's successors: Odoacre and Theodoric (Roman-barbarians) and Justinian and his wife Theodora (Byzantine). The artistic output of this remarkable period is a unique blend of Byzantine and Classical elements, the so-called Ravennate style, which reached its highpoint in the art of

the mosaic. The 7th century, however, marked the beginning of a long decline which lasted till the period of the communes and the advent of the Da Polenta family, during which time recovery was swift. In the 15th century Ravenna became a Venetian possession and from the 16th to 19th centuries it was one of the papal states.

SAN VITALE - This eight-sided brick building topped by a dome was built in the mid 5th century on the spot where Vitale, a 1st century Christian, was supposedly martyred. The superb interior is adorned with mosaics (dated c. 520-550), ranked among the great

San Vitale. Above: interior. On the following page, two of the Basilica best known mosaics: the Emperor Justinian and his entourage (above) and the Empress Theodora and her entourage (below).

masterpieces of Western art. Their subjects are: *Abraham's Hospitality* and the *Sacrifice of Isaac* between *Jeremiah* and *episodes from the life of Moses* (left lunette) and the *Sacrifice of Abel and Melchisedec* framed by additional *scenes from the life of Moses* (right lunette). The mosaics along the walls of the main chapel are also remarkable for their purely decorative motifs. The scenes depict *Justinian and his entourage of digni-*

MAXIMIANVS

taries, priests, and soldiers (left) and
*Theodora and her entourage of ma-
trons and ministers* (right). In the
semidome is the traditional figure of
Christ.

**MAUSOLEUM OF GALLA PLA-
CIDIA** - The tiny 5th century brick
building bears the name of the empress believed to have commissioned it for her tomb. The interior
is wholly covered with superb early
5th century mosaics.

SANT'APOLLINARE NUOVO -
Theodoric commissioned the church
in the early 6th century as a place of
worship for the Aryan sect. (Shortly
after, however, it became a Catholic
church.) A simple building, it is
preceded by a classical porch and
flanked by a striking 9th century

Sant'Apollinare Nuovo. Above: nave. Right: detail of the nave mosaics depicting a procession of saints and prophets and the facade of Theodoric's palace.

belltower. The interior of the stupendous basilica features a single-aisle plan. Among the notable sights are the Byzantine *capitals* of the nave columns and a 6th century *marble pulpit* (nave). The outstanding feature of the church, however, is its three-register mosaic decoration partially commissioned by Theodoric in the 6th century. In the upper right and left registers are *New Testament scenes*, while figures of *prophets* and *saints* alternate between the windows. In the lower lefthand register are a scene of the *Port of Classe* and a *procession of 22 Virgins and the Magi* culminating at the *Virgin enthroned*, while in the lower righthand register are a view of *Theodoric's palace in Ravenna,* a *procession of 26 male martyr saints,* and *Christ enthroned.*

103

SAN FRANCESCO - The original late-5th century building was restructured in the 10th century. Inside note the altar composed of a 5th century sarcophagus, the *urn of St. Liborius* and 16th century sculptures by Tullio Lombardo.

DANTE'S TOMB - Italy's greatest poet, Dante Alighieri, having been exiled from his native city of Florence, was awarded refuge in Ravenna. Dante died in 1321 and was buried in the church of San Francesco; thereafter, his mortal remains were placed in the special temple-shrine designed by Camillo Morigia in 1780.

MAUSOLEUM OF THEODORIC - Theodoric commissioned this massive building in 520 as his own tomb. The two-story building is topped by a huge stone dome that cracked as it was being put in place.

SANT'APOLLINARE IN CLASSE - Attractively situated on the outskirts of the city, this striking 6th century church is one of the few extant remains of Classe, the old port of Ravenna. Alongside is a monumental *belltower* dating from the 10th century. The single-aisle interior lined with Roman columns vaults several notable works, including the remarkable mosaic decoration of the apse-choir zone: *God the Father* flanked by *Evangelist symbols, sheep* (= Apostles), *palm trees* (= Passion of Christ), and *angels*, create a frame for the great semi-dome scene of the heavenly garden dominated by an immense cross. On either side of the cross are *Moses and Elijah and sheep* (= Apostles) below which stands an oversize figure of *St. Apollinare* with a flock of twelve sheep (= the Church).

Above: Dante Alighieri's tomb housed in a chapel alongside the church of San Francesco (pictured below). Above right: exterior of the church of Sant'Apollinare in Classe in front of which is a copy of a Roman statue of the Emperor Augustus. Below right: view down the nave, wholly covered with 6th century mosaics.

RIMINI

Rimini is the «capital» of the Romagnola Riviera, an immense stretch of white sand beaches and resort facilities that covers several townships, the most important being Cervia, Cesenatico, Bellaria, Rimini, Riccione, and Cattolica. Although signs of its future development were already apparent a century ago, the real boom began in the postwar period with the arrival of mass tourism whose needs were swiftly met by the creation of resort facilities such as hotels, restaurants, bars, entertainment centers, bathing and sports facilities, and the like. This incredible success is due to a number of factors, including quality accommodations and cuisine at low prices, easy accessibility from any-

where in Europe, as well as the natural resources of the coast (wide sandy beaches, extensive stretches of shallow water, and great stretches of pine woods). A highway and the railroad tracks separate the beach zone proper from the old city centers. The downtown section of Rimini is a good example of a resort that has preserved much of its historic past intact. It was settled in Roman times when, known as *Ariminus*, it stood at the intersection of two of the great Roman roads, the Via Emilia and the Via Flaminia. In the 14th century, the Malatesta family rose to power. The most famous of them, Sigismondo Malatesta, dominated 15th century Rimini life.

ARCH OF AUGUSTUS - This superb triumphal arch, the oldest extant, was erected to commemorate a victory of Augustus' in 27 B.C. right where the Via Emilia intersects the Via Flaminia. The battlements are a medieval addition. Nearby are remains of a Roman *amphitheater*.

TEMPIO MALATESTIANO - This unique building has a complicated history. Originally it was built by Franciscan monks during the mid 1200s, but two centuries later Sigismondo Malatesta decided to have it totally remodeled. The commission was split in half: the inside was designed by a Gothic architect, Matteo de' Pasti, while plans for the exterior were drawn up by Leon

Battista Alberti, one of the great theorists of Early Renaissance architecture. Work on the project was suspended in 1460 and, despite the fact that the Franciscans later resumed the task, the building was never fully completed (e.g., the facing). The emblems and symbols belonging to the Malatesta family attest to Sigismondo's profound desire to achieve personal glorification through a great work of art. Despite its unfinished state, the *facade* is extremely elegant, a totally new rendering of Classical motifs such as rounded arches, tympanums, and fluted Corinthian columns. Along the right side of the building are seven arch-niches containing 16th-17th century *sarcophagi*. The striking *interior* designed by Matteo de' Pasti is a treasure house of Early Renaissance art. A notable fresco by Piero della Francesca depicting *Sigismondo Malatesta and St. Sigismund* adorns the *Cappella delle*

Left: Rimini's Lungomare. Right: Leon Battista Alberti's facade of the Tempio Malatestiano. Below: interior.

Reliquie. The fine carved *tomb of Sigismondo's wife, Isotta degli Atti* (second right chapel), has been attributed to Matteo de' Pasti. In the same chapel is a *Crucifix* by Giotto. Agostino di Duccio also contributed to the decoration of the church: there are some fine *reliefs* in the pillars of the third chapel on the left side and in the chapel known as the *Cappella dell'Arca degli Antenati e dei Discendenti*.

Above: Crucifix painted by Giotto inside the Tempio Malatestiano.
Above right: panoramic view of San Marino girthed by medieval walls.
Below right: the so-called Montale, one of the several watchtowers along the walls.

SAN MARINO

According to tradition, this pint-sized state picturesquely situated on the slopes of Mt. Titano was founded by a Dalmatian stonecutter, Marino, who settled here with a group of fellow Christians to flee the persecutions of the emperor Diocletian. Thereafter, the tiny village expanded in both size and importance. In the Middle Ages it became a free commune whose republican laws have been in effect, practically unchanged, ever since. Despite repeated attempts from outsiders (neighboring cities and later the papal state) to conquer it, San Marino, thanks to the proud spirit of its populace and the inaccessibility of its territory, has managed to preserve its independence over the centuries. It participated in the Italian Risorgimento, not only on the battlefield, but also by giving political asylum to the freedom fighters,

among whom Garibaldi, when the need arose. The 61-kilometer-square republic is governed by two *Capitani* elected by a board of twelve (*Il Consiglio dei Dodici*) every six months. It has an army and a national guard and issues its own stamps, as every stamp collector well knows. Tourism is one of its major economic resources.

PIAZZA DELLA LIBERTÀ - The foremost square in San Marino, Piazza Libertà, overlooks a spectacular view of the Republic's western territory and the region of Montefeltro. Around it are a 19th century reconstruction of a medieval building, the *Palazzo delle Poste*, the *Arcipretura Vecchia*, the *Palazzo Pubblico*, which is also a 19th century reconstruction, and the *Statue of Liberty* of 1896.

SAN FRANCESCO - First built in the 14th century, the church was partially restructured in the Baroque period: the porch dominating the simple medieval facade was erected in 1631. Inside is a fine 14th century wooden *crucifix*. In the adjoining loggia on the left side of the church is a *Pinacoteca* with some fine paintings including an *Adoration of the Magi* by a 15th century Marche master, *John the Baptist* by Lanfranco, *St. Francis* by Guercino, and a *Virgin and Child* attributed to Raphael.

LE ROCCHE - The earliest of the three castles, known as *La Guaita*, was built in the 11th century and later rebuilt. It is surrounded by impressive crenelated walls. The second, known as *La Cesta*, is taller. Erected in the 13th century and then rebuilt several times, it is now a museum of arms and armor, the *Museo delle Armi Antiche*. The third, *Il Montale*, rises isolated in the countryside. A dungeon is still visible inside the 13th century structure.

Above: Palazzo Pubblico and the «Statue of Liberty» in Piazza della Libertà. Below: Porta San Francesco, the most important of the city gates.

TUSCANY

The Tuscan region is mostly hilly and mountainous. Valleys of considerable size (Lunigiana, Garfagnana, Mugello, and Casentino) are sandwiched between the Apennines. The rare plains are either of the coastal type (e.g., Versilia and Maremma) or alluvional (e.g., the Arno Valley). The coastline alternates long stretches of beach (Versilia, Cecina) with promontories and cliffs (Piombino, Argentario).

HISTORY - Tuscan history begins around (1000 B.C.) when the land lying between the Arno and Tevere Valleys was settled by the Etruscans, whose origin (Eastern?) and language (pre-Indo-European) are still unknown. Around the 7th-6th centuries B.C., the territory under Etruscan control extended as far as the Po Valley plains and Corsica. In the 5th century, after being soundly beaten by the Greeks and Carthaginians, the Etruscans were compelled to give up their newly-acquired dominions and retreat within their original borders. Then in the 4th century, subjugated by Rome, they disappeared forever. In the Early Middle Ages, Tuscany became a Longobard duchy. During the 12th century, Pisa, facilitated by the Crusades, established intensive trade relations with the Orient, and Florence and Siena embarked on equally intense industrial (textiles) and financial (banking) activities. This led to internecine squabbles which eventually resulted (12th century) in the supremacy of Guelph Florence (backed by the Pope and the Anjous) over the pro-Ghibelline centers such as Siena. Tuscany prospered up until the mid 1200s when a succession of setbacks (famine, plague, and financial crises) wrought havoc on the Florentine and Sienese economies. In 1436 Florence's ostensibly democratic government fell to the Medicis who would rule the city for the next three centuries. Cosimo the Elder and

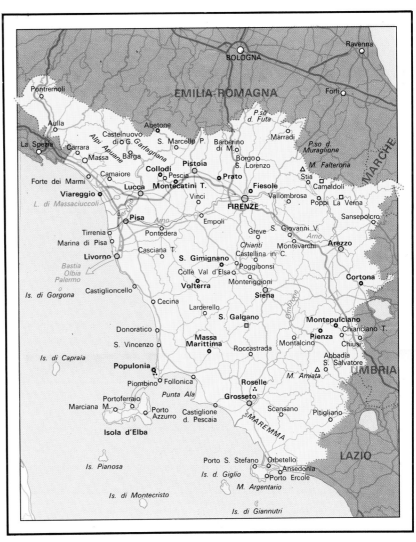

Lorenzo the Magnificent made the city into the cultural and economic capital of Italy, and the greatest world power of its day. In the 16th century, the Medici Signoria gave way to the Medici grandduchy. Under Grandduke Cosimo I, Siena was subdued, the academies and university were founded, and all the Tuscan cities except for the Republic of Lucca came under Medici rule. Cosimo's successors, however, were unable to follow in his footsteps and the Tuscan state fell from power, both economically and politically. The last Medici grand-

duke Gian Gastone died in the middle of the 18th century without leaving any heirs. Thereafter, the Lorraine dynasty gained political control of the region and, especially under the enlightened rule of the great reformer Pietro Leopoldo, brought renewed prosperity and peace. At the turn of the 19th century, Tuscany became part of the French empire, with Lucca as the duchy ruled by Napoleon's sister, Elsa Bonaparte. An active participant in the Risorgimento struggle, the region adhered to the Kingdom of Italy in 1860.

ART - Most of the manifestations of Etruscan art that have survived in Tuscany (tombs and tomb fittings) come from the great Etruscan cities (i.e., Volterra, Chiusi, Fiesole, and Populonia) which reached their greatest splendor between the 7th and 5th centuries B.C. On the other hand, few Roman remains, aside from the Luni and Arezzo amphitheaters, the Fiesole theater, and some villas, have survived. Artistic activity flourished once more in the Romanesque period (11th-12th centuries) when the great basilicas and tiny country churches (pievi) were built and then adorned outside (portal sculpture) and inside (frescoes and sculpture). The styles born in Pisa and Florence influenced art and architecture throughout their respective spheres of influence. In the 13th century, a new style born from the mixture of Northern European Gothic with local Romanesque produced numerous architectural masterpieces including Florence's Pal-azzo Vecchio, Siena's Palazzo Pubblico, and Pisa's Camposanto. The foremost artists of the period were Arnolfo di Cambio, architect, Giovanni Pisano, sculptor, and Giotto di Bondone, painter. Their contemporary was Dante Alighieri, who wrote the Divine Comedy at the turn of the 13th century. The only painting school able to challenge Florence's supremacy in the 13th-14th centuries was Siena's represented by Simone Martini and the Lorenzetti brothers. In the 15th century, the so-called Early Renaissance period, a host of works of the most remarkable originality were produced in Florence: Brunelleschi designed the dome of the Cathedral and Palazzo Pitti, Leon Battista Alberti devised a new set of architectural precepts, Ghiberti cast the great doors of the Florentine Baptistry, Donatello produced remarkable sculptures of saints and heroes. In painting, Masaccio, Paolo Uccello, and Fra Angelico (among others) further developed Giotto's innovative use of perspective and space. The Renaissance artists strived to reach a harmonious naturalistic style based on perspective, foreshortening, and scientific treatment of light and shade. Originating in Florence, this great cultural debate not only spread throughout Tuscany and Italy, but soon affected the art and culture of the whole world, especially in the 15th and 16th centuries when artists of the ilk of the Lippis, Botticelli, Leonardo and Michelangelo were active in the great Medici courts. The late 16th century was dominated by the intellectual Mannerists, the most famous of which were Agnolo Bronzino, Pontormo, Rosso Fiorentino, and Giorgio Vasari. Although Tuscany's artistic output declined in the 17th-18th centuries, the region once more became an artistic center in the 19th century with the birth of the «Macchiaiolo» movement somewhat akin to French Impressionism.

112

FLORENCE

Florence, dubbed "cradle of the Renaissance," "Athens of Italy," and just plain Firenze in Italian, was for over a thousand years a quiet town in the Tuscan countryside. Settled by the Etruscans, a Roman encampment, and then a domain of the Holy Roman Empire, its political and economic rise only began around the 11th-12th centuries when, despite warring between the Guelph and Ghibelline factions and recurrent revolts of the populace, prosperity from trade laid the way for its future leadership position. In fact, by the 12th century, when it was a city-state and the first guilds (the famous *Corporazioni delle Arti*) were already functioning, the Florentine *fiorino* had become one of

Above left: Benozzo Gozzoli's Cavalcata, frescoed in the chapel of Palazzo Medici-Riccardi in Florence. Above: panoramic view of the city.

the strongest currencies in all of Europe. In the 13th century, the city's prosperity increased even more. This was the century dominated by Dante Alighieri, whose *Divina Commedia* written in the language spoken by the Florentines and not erudite Latin, laid the basis for modern Italian. In painting Giotto and in architecture Arnolfo di Cambio made their remarkable contributions. In the 14th century, a time of combined economic hardship and plague (the Black Death of 1348 chronicled by Boccaccio in *Decameron*), Northern Gothic, known in painting as the International Style, was the strongest influence on the major Florentine artists, most of whom followers of Giotto. In 1434 with the fall of the Communal form of government, Cosimo de' Medici, known as the Elder, seized power, thereby giving rise to what would be three centuries of Medici rule. By the second half of the century, the Renaissance (literally,

rebirth) was well underway, as Cosimo's grandson, Lorenzo the Magnificent, presided over a remarkable court imbued with Classical-inspired Humanist culture. Under the patronage of the great Renaissance prince, the arts flourished as few times before (and after) in the history of mankind, producing names such as Lorenzo himself, Poliziano, and Pulci in literature, Botticelli, the Lippis, Ghirlandaio, and Paolo Uccello, in painting, Brunelleschi, Michelozzo, and Alberti in architecture, and Donatello, Verrocchio, and the della Robbias in sculpture. Lorenzo was also a clever politician, managing to attain a correct balance of power among the major contenders of his day, but his successors failed to live up to his greatness, with the result that the Medicis were driven from the city in the late 1400s and the citizenry proclaimed the Republic of Florence. Savonarola, Machiavelli, Michelangelo, and Leonardo were among the promi-

nent figures who witnessed and participated in the events of those days. Shortly afterward, however, the Medici triumphantly returned. Cosimo I, the first Medici grandduke, skillfully consolidated Florence's dominions in Tuscan territory, without relinquishing the great tradition of art patronage started by his predecessors. He was succeeded by Francesco I, also a notable art patron, one of whose projects was founding of the Uffizi collection. The Medici and their successors, the Lorraine granddukes, continued to promote artistic endeavors of every sort, commissioning great villas and monumental palaces for themselves, although the political importance of Florence had in the mean-

time greatly declined. The outstanding events of the 19th century were the *Risorgimento* struggle and Florence's brief period as the capital of the newly-established Kingdom of Italy (1865-1871).

BAPTISTRY - Probably built around the 5th century, the Baptistry is a striking eight-sided green and white marble building. The sculpted *doors* on three sides are celebrated works: on the south, *scenes from the life of St. John the Baptist* by Andrea Pisano (1330), on the north, *scenes from the New Testament* by Ghiberti (1401), and, on the east, one of the great masterpieces of Early Renaissance art, the *Gates of Paradise* (as Michelangelo reputedly

Baptistry. Above: exterior. Right: closeup of the Gate of Paradise. The ten panels recount the Old Testament stories of Adam and Eve, Cain and Abel, Abraham, the Deluge, Jacob and Esau, Joseph, Moses and the Tablets of the Law, Joshua, Saul and David, Solomon and the Queen of Sheba.

described them), sculpted with *Old Testament stories* by Ghiberti (1425-1452). The *mosaics* adorning the interior (some of which attributed to Cimabue) date from the 1200s.

GIOTTO'S BELLTOWER - Giotto started work on the stunning green and white belltower in 1334, al-

114

Left: Baptistry dome mosaics. Above: aerial view of Florence's religious complex.

though the project was completed after his death in by Andrea Pisano and Francesco Talenti. Some of the *reliefs* on the base of the building (copies, the originals are in the Museo del Duomo) while sculpted by Andrea Pisano are believed to have been designed by Giotto himself. The view from the 85-meter-tall tower is well worth the climb.

CATHEDRAL - When the old church of *Santa Reparata* (c. 4th-5th century) could no longer contain Florence's growing Christian community, Arnolfo di Cambio was commissioned to design a cathedral to be built right over it (1289). After his death in 1302, it was continued by artists of great renown such as Giotto, Andrea Pisano, and Brunelleschi. The facade, having been

Duomo. Left: 19th century facade. Both Brunelleschi's dome and Giotto's belltower are visible. Above: interior.

erected in the 19th century, does not belong to the original project. Brunelleschi worked on the remarkable dome from the 1420s to 1434. Of note are the cathedral's lateral portals: the early 15th century

Porta della Mandorla (north side) and the 14th century *Porta dei Canonici* (south side). The feeling of stark majesty pervading the *interior* is enhanced by the oversize pillars and impressive *stained glass windows* (14th-15th century). On the left wall are two celebrated frescoes commemorating 15th century military figures: *John Hawkwood* painted by Paolo Uccello in 1436

alongside the chiaroscuro *Niccolò da Tolentino* painted by Andrea del Castagno in 1456. On the same side some feet beyond is a panel depicting *Dante and his Divine Comedy* by Domenico di Michelino (1465). A *Crucifix* by Benedetto da Maiano dated 1497 adorns the main altar. The dome is covered by the world's largest fresco, an impressive Last Judgment by Vasari, Zuccari, and

helpers. A flight of stairs in the right aisle leads down to the *Crypt of Santa Reparata* which not only contains remains of the original Florentine cathedral (architecture, fragments, carved tombs, and frescoes), but also the recently-discovered tomb of the great Brunelleschi.

MUSEO DELL'OPERA DEL DUOMO - The museum houses works originally part of the nearby religious complex. Its best-known treasure is Michelangelo's dramatic *Pietà*. Left unfinished, the group was sculpted around 1550 for the master's own tomb. Other highlights include sculpture by Arnolfo, Donatello, and Nanni di Banco (from the original Cathedral facade), the two Cathedral *Cantorie* (one sculpted by Luca della Robbia in 1438 and one by Donatello in 1455), Donatello's wooden *Mary Magdalene* carved in 1455 for the Baptistry, Andrea Pisano's reliefs for the Belltower as well as reliquaries, vestments, and a 15th century *altar frontal* crafted by celebrated artists among whon Verrocchio, Pollaiolo, and Michelozzo.

ORSANMICHELE - The original building that Arnolfo erected in 1290 on the site of the church of San Michele in Orto as a covered trade center for the local wheat dealers was rebuilt in the 14th century after being totally destroyed by fire. The new structure with its great arches and tracery windows is typically Gothic in style. In the niches around the outside are 14th-15th century statues of the *Patron Saints of the Guilds* that commissioned them from the great artists of the day, e.g., Donatello, Nanni di Banco, Ghiberti, and Verrocchio. Inside the striking church interior, adorned with frescoes, sculpture, and stained glass windows, is Andrea's celebrated *Tabernacle of the Madonna delle Grazie* (1359) framing a painting of the *Virgin* by Bernardo Daddi.

Michelangelo's Pietà, in the Museo dell'Opera del Duomo. The hooded figure of Nicodemus is a self-portrait of the artist.

PIAZZA DELLA SIGNORIA -
From the early 1400s to this day, the square has been the scene of the major Florentine political events. A plaque, for example, marks the spot where the reformer monk Savonarola was burned at the stake in 1498. The south side of the square is dominated by the three great arches of the *Loggia della Signoria* (which is also known by two other names: *Loggia dei Lanzi* because the Medicis' Swiss guards, the *Lanzichenecchi*, used to station under it in the 16th century and *Loggia dell'Orcagna* because it was once erroneously attributed to Orcagna.) Designed in the 1380s by Benci di Cione and Simone Talenti for public

ceremonies, it became an open air sculpture museum as great works such as Benvenuto Cellini's *Perseus* (1554) and Giambologna's *Rape of the Sabine Women* (1583) were set up inside it. The *Neptune Fountain* in front of Palazzo Vecchio is composed of an immense statue representing *Neptune* sculpted by Ammannati and statues of *seagods* and *seahorses* by Giambologna. Giambologna also sculpted the nearby *equestrian statue of Cosimo I dei Medici* (1594). Across the way is the *Alberto della Ragione Collection of Italian Modern Art.*

PALAZZO VECCHIO - Arnolfo
designed the building in 1299 and its

Aerial view. Several important monuments are recognizable: the Uffizi (right middleground), Piazza della Signoria with Palazzo Vecchio (center middleground), Orsanmichele (left middleground), the Bargello and the Badia (background).

tower in 1310, although modifications were made in the 14th-15th centuries and in the 16th by Vasari and Buontalenti. The distinctive crenelated building with its rusticated stone facing and asymmetrical tower was a symbol of the Free Commune of Florence whose headquarters it was during the Middle Ages, even

121

when it thereafter belonged to those who toppled the Commune, the Medicis. From 1865 to 1872 the Italian Chamber of Deputies, it is now Florence's city hall. The emblems below the crenelation represent the Tuscan cities, while atop the 16th century portal is the symbol of Christ the king. The statues in front are (left to right): the *Marzocco lion* by Donatello (copy), *David* by Michelangelo (copy), and *Hercules and Cacus* by Bandinelli. The main *courtyard* designed by Michelozzo (15th century) was frescoed and stuccoed by Vasari (16th century). The *putto* adorning the *fountain* is a copy of Verrocchio's 1476 original. The immense *Salone dei Cinquecento* (Hall of the 500), designed by Cronaca in 1495, was decorated by Vasari around the mid-1500s. On the south end is Michelangelo's statue of *Victory* (1534). Off the hall is the *Studiolo* of Francesco I. Designed by Vasari and the Humanist scholar Borghini in 1572 for Francesco's collections, it was decorated by the foremost Mannerist artists of the 16th century. On the same floor, are the *Quartiere del Mezzanino* by Michelozzo now a small art museum, the *Loeser Collection*, featuring 14th-16th century Tuscan painting and sculpture) and the *Sala dei Duecento* (Hall of the 200) designed by the da Maianos. On the third floor are the Medici apartments: the *Quartiere di Eleonora di Toledo* (Cosimo I's wife) designed by Vasari, with a notable *chapel* decorated by Bronzino; the *Quartiere degli Elementi*, again by Vasari; the striking *Sala dei Gigli* with a carved portal by Benedetto da Maiano, frescoes (including one by Ghirlandaio dated 1485), and a coffered ceiling by Giuliano da Maiano. The *Cancelleria* was Machiavelli's office in the 15th century.

Left: Palazzo Vecchio, now Florence's town hall. Right: Benvenuto Cellini's bronze Perseus holding up the freshly severed head of Medusa, sculpted in 1554.

Above left: two of the celebrated halls of Palazzo Vecchio. Above: Sala dei Gigli (Lily Room), named after the lily pattern decoration of its walls. It also bears notable frescoes by Ghirlandaio.

Below left: Salone dei 500 (Hall of the 500), the most impressive of the palaces audience halls, is adorned with frescoes painted by Vasari and his school (ceiling, walls), tapestries, and sculpture, outstanding of which is Michelangelo's allegorical statue of Victory in a niche on the south side. Above: the Uffizi during the annual May Flower Festival viewed from Palazzo Vecchio with a 19th century copy of Michelangelo's David visible in the foreground.

GALLERIA DEGLI UFFIZI - The building was commissioned in the 1560s by Cosimo I as offices (*uffizi*) from which to administer the affairs of state of his domain, the Grand-duchy of Tuscany. Vasari, the architect picked by Cosimo, came up with a striking design consisting of two porticoed wings joined by a great archway on the river side. A few years later he completed a second project, this one in record time: the Corridoio Vasariano which runs from the Uffizi, crosses the river, and ends a half a kilometer away at Palazzo Pitti. The building was turned into an art gallery by Bernardo Buontalenti in 1582 who received the commission from Cosimo's successor Francesco I. Buontalenti not only reorganized the rooms, but also added some new elements, e.g., the striking Tribuna. The collection, enriched over the years by Francesco's successors, became property of the state in 1743 when the last of the Medicis, Anna Maria Ludovica, left it to the City of Florence. As space does not allow listing of all the masterpieces in the museum, only the most famous will be mentioned: Three altarpieces representing the *Virgin Enthroned* (*Maestà*) by Cimabue, Giotto, and Duccio; *Annunciation*, by Simone Martini; *Adoration of the Magi*, by

125

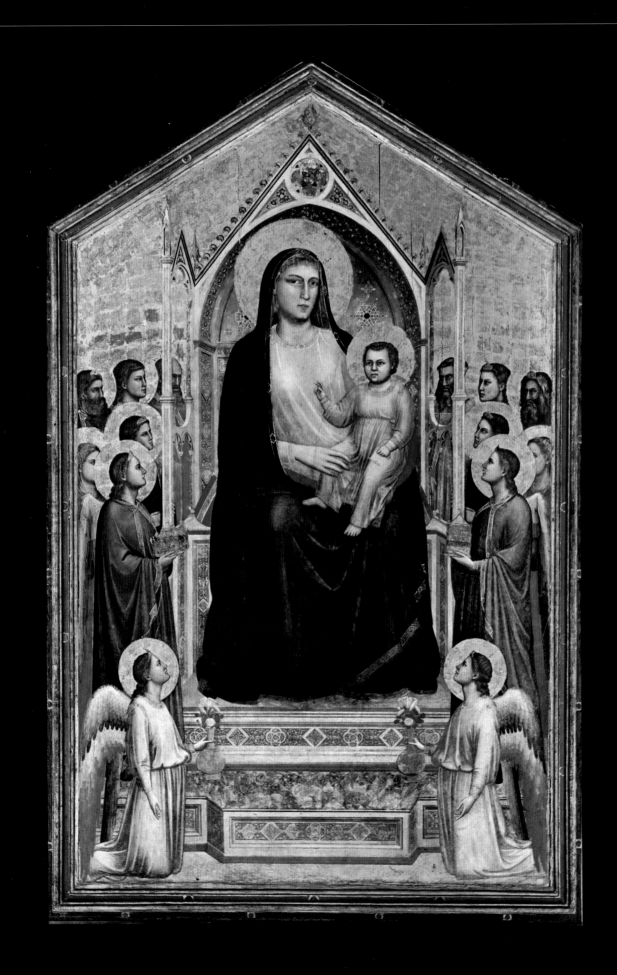

Left: Giotto's Maestà (or Virgin Enthroned), painted c. 1310 for the high altar of the Ognissanti Church in Florence.

Above: Annunciation, painted by Leonardo da Vinci when he was still an apprentice in Verrocchio's studio.

Below: Battle of San Romano, one of three panels of the same series that Paolo Uccello painted around 1456.

Above: Birth of Venus, by Botticelli, dated 1486. Below left: Michelangelo's Doni Tondo. Above left, facing page: Portrait of Duke Federico da Montefeltro painted by Piero della Francesca in Urbino c. 1465. Above right, facing page: Portrait of Pope Leo X with Cardinals Giulio de' Medici and Luigi de' Rossi, one of Raphael's last works (1519). Below: Buontalenti's Tribuna. Following pages: Botticelli's Spring.

Gentile da Fabriano; *Portraits of Battista Sforza and Federico da Montefeltro*, by Piero della Francesca; *Virgin and St. Anne*, by Masaccio and Masolino; *Battle of San Romano*, by Paolo Uccello; *Virgin and Child*, by Filippo Lippi; *Birth of Venus*, *Spring*, *Calumny*, and *Madonna della Melagrana*, by Botticelli; *Portinari Altarpiece*, by Hugo van der Goes; *Annunciation* and *Adoration of the Magi*, by Leonardo; *Doni Tondo*, by Michelangelo; *Virgin of the Goldfinch* and *Portrait of Leo X*, by Raphael; *Venus of Urbino*, by Titian; and

Bacchus, by Caravaggio. Other renowned painters represented include Pontormo, Giorgione, and Canaletto and, among the non-Italians, Rubens, Van Dyck, Dürer, and Goya. Lastly, the *Corridoio Vasariano* is hung with self-portraits of Italian and foreign masters starting from the 13th-14th century to our day.

PONTE VECCHIO - From Antiquity there was always a bridge crossing the Arno at this point, to connect Florence's most populated area with the Via Cassia. Every time one was destroyed by floods, another was built in its place. (This one dates from the 14th century). The jewelry shops lining the bridge replaced the butcher shops banished by Ferdinando I in the late 1500s. The windows along the top belong to the Corridoio Vasariano.

SANTO SPIRITO - An Early Renaissance building designed by Brunelleschi in 1444, it was finished by Manetti in 1487. The belltower (1517) was designed by Baccio d'Agnolo. The *interior* is a notable example of Brunelleschi's masterful use of space: an effect of harmony and balance is a achieved through the regular succession of spaces marked by the columns sweeping the eye to the focal point of the building, the dome-crowned crossing. Among the masters whose works are hanging in the church are Filippino Lippi, Sansovino, and Rossellino.

PALAZZO PITTI - This remarkable palace was designed by Brunelleschi around the mid-1400s for a rival of the Medicis, Luca Pitti. The original building was much smaller (running the length of only the seven central windows). It was remodeled and

Above: Ponte Vecchio. The upper story windows belong to the Corridoio Vasariano, the covered passageway that connects Palazzo Vecchio to Palazzo Pitti via the Uffizi and Ponte Vecchio. Above right: facade of Palazzo Pitti. Below right: Sala Verde (Green Room), in the Monumental Apartments.

enlarged in the 16th century as a showplace worthy of its new owners. Another Medici project, landscaping of the immense palace grounds, was carried out by Tribolo. Extensive modifications were also made in the 17th and 18th centuries. Today the palace is a museum, or rather complex of museums, the most important of which are the *Palatine Gallery, Monumental Apartments, Gallery of Modern Art*, and *Silver Museum*. Among the masterpieces of art displayed in magnificent halls frescoed by Ciro

Ferri and Pietro da Cortona in the 17th century, we shall mention only a sampling of the Palatine Gallery treasures: *La Bella* and *Man with a Glove*, by Titian; *Return from the Hayfields, Four Philosophers*, and the *Consequences of War*, by Rubens; *Virgin and Child*, by Filippo Lippi; and *Mary Magdalene*, by Perugino. The collection features several famous Raphaels including Virgins (*Madonna del Granduca, Madonna della Seggiola, Madonna dell'Impannata*) and portraits (*Tommaso Inghirami, Agnolo and Maddalena Doni, La Velata* or *Veiled Lady*, and *La Gravida* or *Pregnant Lady*). There are notable portraits by van Dyck, Velazquez, Botticelli and Sustermans.

Palazzo Pitti, Palatine Gallery. Above: Raphael's Madonna della Seggiola (Virgin of the Chair), painted c. 1515. Facing page, clockwise from upper right: The Four Philosophers, a group portrait by Rubens; Titian's Man with a Glove; Van Dyck's Portrait of Cardinl Bentivoglio; and Raphael's La Velata (Lady with a Veil).

Above: «The Tribute Money,» one of Masaccio's frescoes in the Brancacci Chapel of the Santa Maria del Carmine Church, dated c. 1420.
Below: Leon Battista Alberti's facade for the Santa Maria Novella Church.
Above right: interior of the church of San Lorenzo.

SANTA MARIA DEL CARMINE –

Founded in the 13th century, it underwent extensive remodeling. Its present appearance dates from the 18th century. The church's claim to fame is the *Brancacci Chapel*, in the right transept, frescoed by Masaccio. Masaccio's master, Masolino, commissioned by a wealthy merchant, Felice Brancacci, began work on the chapel in 1425, but the project was soon taken over by his pupil whose treatment of figures in believable space made the frescoes among the most important to have come out of the Early Renaissance. The scenes by Masaccio are the *Expulsion from Paradise*, *The Tribute Money*, *St. Peter Healing a Lame Man*, and *St. Peter Raising*

Tabitha from the Dead (in conjunction with Masolino). The cycle was finished by Filippino Lippi.

SANTA MARIA NOVELLA - Built by Dominican monks in the mid-1200s, the church has a remarkable facade begun in the 14th century and completed by Alberti in the 15th (upper section and portal). The geometric patterns recall the Tuscan-style Romanesque of the 11th-12th centuries (e.g., San Miniato, Baptistry, etc.). The entranceway to the remarkable *cloisters* is to the left of the facade. The first, the *Chiostro Verde* (c. 1350), is adorned with 15th century frescoes. Next you enter the *Refectory* which Paolo Uccello frescoed around 1430. The most famous scenes are those of the *Flood* and *Sacrifice of Noah*. From the other side of the Chiostro Verde you enter the *Chiostro Grande*, then the *Chiostrino dei Morti*, and finally the *Cappellone degli Spagnoli*. The Cappellone, built in 1350 and taken over by Eleonora da Toledo's Spanish entourage for their

religious services in the 16th century, was superbly frescoed by Andrea di Bonaiuto (c. 1355) with scenes relating to the *history of the Dominican order* and the *life of St. Thomas of Aquinus*. Inside the immense Gothic church are numerous masterpieces of Renaissance art: Masaccio's *Trinity* frescoed around 1427, a *Crucifix* by Giotto, frescoes by Nardo di Cione and an Orcagna altarpiece (*Cappella Strozzi*), a celebrated Brunelleschi *Crucifix* (first chapel to the left of the choir), stupendous *scenes from the lives of the Virgin and St. John the Baptist* frescoed by Filippino Lippi in the late 15th century.

PALAZZO MEDICI-RICCARDI - A superb example of 15th century Florentine civic architecture, the palace was designed by Michelozzo in the mid-1400s for Cosimo the Elder and later embellished under Lorenzo the Magnificent-Purchased by the Riccardi family in the 17th century, it underwent remodeling and enlargement. The first floor of

the exterior is faced in rough stone, the second in rusticated stone and the top one in planed blocks. Two of the ground floor windows (the corner ones) are traditionally ascribed to Michelangelo. From the courtyard radiate the *Museo Mediceo* (temporary exhibitions) on the left, an attractive *garden* in the center, and the *Cappella* (stairs to the right). Built by Michelozzo, the chapel was frescoed in 1460 by Benozzo Gozzoli with a scene ostensibly showing the Wise Men on their way to Bethlehem (actually portraits of the Medicis). Upstairs is the Galleria, an impressive hall frescoed by Luca Giordano in 1683.

SAN LORENZO - The Medicis commissioned Brunelleschi to remodel the original building. The facade, despite plans drawn up by Michelangelo, was never completed. The superb Brunelleschi interior is adorned with notable works, among them two bronze *pulpits* by Donatello (1460s), Rosso Fiorentino's striking *Marriage of the Virgin*

a *tabernacle* by Desiderio da Settignano, and an *Annunciation* by Filippo Lippi. The *Tomb of Giovanni and Piero dei Medici* by Verrocchio (1472) is in the *Old Sacristy*, designed by Brunelleschi and decorated by Donatello.

MEDICI CHAPELS - There are two tomb complexes: the *Cappella dei Principi*, the granddukes' grandiose burial hall lavishly faced with colored marbles and semiprecious stones, and the *New Sacristy* designed by Michelangelo in 1524.

Some of his most celebrated sculpture adorns the tombs (*Day* and *Night* above Giuliano di Nemours, *Dawn* and *Dusk* above Lorenzo di Urbino, and the *Virgin and Child* above Giuliano and Lorenzo the Magnificent).

Sacrestia Nuova, with architecture and sculpture by Michelangelo. The tomb of Giuliano, Duke of Nemours, adorned with reclining figures personifying Night and Day is on the left, that of Lorenzo, Duke of Urbino, with personifications of Dusk and Dawn, is on the right.

PALAZZO STROZZI - Perhaps the most famous example of Renaissance civic architecture, the distinctive palace was commissioned by the Strozzi family and designed by Benedetto da Maiano in 1489. Its great *cornice* and lovely inner *court-yard* were designed by a contemporary of Benedetto's, Cronaca.

SANTISSIMA ANNUNZIATA - Built by Michelozzo between 1444 and 1481 on the site of a pre-existing 13th century oratory, the church

Above: Chimera, an Etruscan bronze dating from the 5th century B.C. in the Museo Archeologico. Below: Palazzo Strozzi, a fine example of 15th century civic architecture. Right: Annunciation, by Fra Angelico, in the San Marco Museum.

was completed by Alberti who designed the dome (lined up with the Cathedral's by means of Via dei Servi's straight-edge configuration). The outer portico dates from the 1600s. The most striking building facing out on the square is the *Spedale degli Innocenti*, by Brunelleschi (1419).

ARCHEOLOGICAL MUSEUM – The museum building is a 17th century palace, *Palazzo della Crocetta*, set in an attractive garden. The collections (established in the late 1800s) comprise Egyptian, Greco-Roman, and Etruscan art. In the ground floor halls are several

noteworthy ceramics including the celebrated *François Vase*, a 6th century B.C. Greek black figure vase unearthed by a Frenchman, François, in an Etruscan tomb in Chiusi, as well as Attic and mock Etruscan vases, and Etruscan funerary urns (outstanding of which is the so-called *Mater Matuta*). The highlights of the upstairs *Egyptian Collection* are a red basalt *pharoah's bust* (18th century B.C.), and two painted *statues of servant girls engaged in household tasks*. The second section, the *Etrusco-Greco-Roman Antiquarium*, features masterpieces of Etruscan art (the Chimera) and Greek sculpture (the Haranger and the Idolino).

SAN MARCO MUSEUM

SAN MARCO MUSEUM - The museum building, the Monastery of San Marco, was built by Michelozzo in 1452. Among the famous men who lived here were Fra Angelico, Savonarola, and Fra Bartolomeo.

The main courtyard, the *Chiostro di Sant'Antonino*, was frescoed by Fra Angelico, as was the *Chapter Room* opposite the entrance (Crucifixion). In the so-called *Ospizio del Pellegrino* (Pilgrims' Lodgings) is a collection of superb Fra Angelico panel paintings, including the celebrated *Linaioli Altarpiece* (1433), the *Bosco ai Frati Altarpiece*, the *St. Mark Altarpiece*, the remarkable *Last Judgment*, and smaller panels with *scenes from the life of Christ*. The most striking painting in the room, however, is the *Deposition*, acclaimed Fra Angelico's masterpiece (c. 1435). Upstairs are the monks' spare cells rendered precious by the marvelous *New Testament scenes* that Fra Angelico and his helpers, frescoed on the walls between 1439 and 1445.

ACCADEMIA (ACADEMY GALLERY)

ACCADEMIA (ACADEMY GALLERY) - Established in 1784, the museum features 13th-16th century Florentine school paintings and some of Michelangelo's most famous sculptures. The main exhibition halls, the *Salone* and *Tribuna* designed by Emilio De Fabris in the late 1800s, host Michelangelo's sculpture. Along the Salone are the four *Slaves*, roughed out masterpieces of enormous vigor, meant for Pope Julius' (never finished) tomb in Rome (c. 1518), *St. Matthew* (c. 1505), the only one of the planned group of apostles ever carved for the Cathedral of Florence, and the *Palestrina Pietà*, a dramatic example of the master's late style. In the Tribuna stands the *David*, an early work of exceptional effect, that needs no introduction. It was commissioned by the Republic of Florence as the symbol of Florentine freedom and set right in front of Palazzo Vecchio, the city's civic center (where it stood until replacement by a copy became necessary for preservation in the 1800s). The rest

of the museum focuses on Florentine painting, from the pre-Renaissance through Mannerist periods.

BARGELLO - The forbidding castle was built in 1225 as headquarters for the *Capitano del Popolo*, a kind of governor. Thereafter, police headquarters (starting from the 16th century), it also served as a dungeon and the scene of public executions. The bell in its crenelated tower is only rung on occasions of extraordinary importance (e.g., end of World War II and the flood of 1966). A museum since 1859, it vaunts one of the world's foremost collections of Tuscan sculpture. The *Museo Nazionale* starts in a *courtyard* filled with 16th century sculpture and emblems of various *podestà* (mayors) who governed the city. In the Salone del Cinquecento are famous 16th century masterpieces: Michelangelo's *Tondo Pitti, bust of Brutus, Drunken Bacchus,* and *Apollo David,* as well as sculpture by Cellini, Sansovino, Ammannati, and Giambologna. Upstairs is another collection of sculpture masterpieces, including Donatello's *St. George* (1416) and his two celebrated *Davids* (one in marble and a bronze one wearing a hat), as well as the reliefs of the *Sacrifice of Isaac* submitted by Ghiberti and Brunelleschi for the north door of the Baptistry (1402). (Ghiberti's delicate rendering won out over Brunelleschi's more dramatic version.) The *Cappella del Podestà* was frescoed by a follower of Giotto. In the *Paradise scene* on the the end wall is a celebrated *portrait of Dante.* On the third floor is a unique collection of della Robbia *glazed terracottas* (chiefly religious subjects on sky blue grounds), 15th and 16th century creations by Giovanni, Andrea, and Luca della Robbia.

Left: Michelangelo's David in the Accademia, one of the most celebrated sculptures of all times. Facing page, clockwise from upper right: Michelangelo's Pitti Tondo; Verrocchio's bronze David; Donatello's David; Donatello's Putto; and Luca della Robbia's Madonna del Roseto.

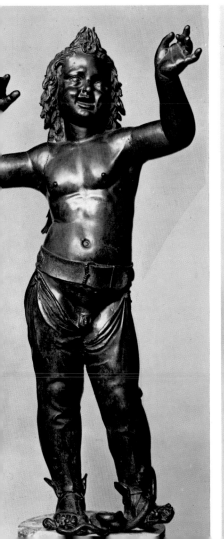

SANTA CROCE - This magnificent Franciscan Gothic church was begun around the mid-1200s (according to tradition by Arnolfo di Cambio), although it was not consecrated until 1443. Italy's Westminster Abbey, it vaunts Giotto's remarkable frescoes, as well as the tombs of famous Italians. The facade is a 19th century imitation of Gothic. In keeping with the Franciscan tradition, the interior is simple and stately. The nave walls, once covered with Giotto frescoes, are lined with tombs and monuments including Vasari's *Tomb of Michelangelo*, Canova's *Monument to Alfieri*, a *monument to Machiavelli*, as well as the *tombs of the composer Rossini, the poet Ugo Foscolo* (right aisle), *Galileo, and Ghiberti* (left aisle). The church is a veritable compendium of 15th century sculpture: Benedetto da Maiano' *Pulpit*, Donatello's *Cavalcante Annunciation*, Rossellino's *Tomb of Leonardo Bruni* (right aisle) and Desiderio da Settignano's *Tomb of Carlo Marsuppini* (left aisle). Most of the chapels in the righthand transept and side were frescoed in the 14th century (*Cappella Castellani* and *Cappella Baroncelli* by Gaddy, *Cappella Rinuccini* by Giovanni da Milano). Giotto's famous frescoes adorn two chapels of the east end, *Cappella Peruzzi* and *Cappella Bardi* (1317, *scenes from the life of St. Francis*). In the central *Cappella Maggiore* frescoed by Agnolo Gaddi is a wooden *crucifix* (unknown master). The last chapel on the left, the *Cappella Bardi di Vernio*, was frescoed by Maso di Banco (14th century). Nearby is a *crucifix* by Donatello. In the pleasant *cloister* (entrance to the right of the church) is the *Tomb of Florence Nightingale*. At the far end is Brunelleschi's *Pazzi Chapel*, one of the masterpieces of Early Renaissance architecture.

Above: 19th century facade of Santa Croce. Below: Brunelleschi's Pazzi Chapel. Above right: interior of Santa Croce. Below left: Donatello's Cavalcante Annunciation. Below right: detail showing the Ascension of St. John, by Giotto, in the Peruzzi Chapel.

PIAZZALE MICHELANGELO -
With the whole city spread out below your feet, you see, from left to right; the Cascine Park, the dome and immense mass of the Cathedral surrounded by the towers and bell-towers of medieval Florence, Santa Croce, with the Arno in the foreground and the Florentine hills in the background. In the center of the square is a copy of the *David* commemorating Michelangelo.

SAN MINIATO AL MONTE -
This superb Romanesque church was built between the 11th and 12th centuries. Inside, at the end of the nave is the *Cappella del Crocifisso*, designed by Michelozzo in 1448 and embellished with della Robbia terracottas. Above is the choir, surrounded by marble partitions sustaining a pulpit and adorned with an immense 13th century mosaic. On the left side is the *Cappella del Cardinale di Portogallo*, a Renaissance chapel with the *cardinal's tomb* by Rossellino.

LUCCA

Lucca originated as a Roman settlement at the intersection of three consular roads. In the Middle Ages it prospered on textile manufacture and trade. This period was the time of great building activity. During the Renaissance period, when banking became one of the city's chief activities, great palaces and mansions were built in and around it. The city's impressive girth of walls date from a later period (16th-17th centuries). In 1799, after having withstood centuries of attempts by the Tuscans to add Lucca's territory to the grandducal domains, Lucca succumbed to the French. Thereafter, it was a principality governed by Elisa Baciocchi, Napoleon's sister, before becoming part of the Kingdom of Italy.

Preceding page: Piazzale Michelangelo (above) and San Miniato (below). Below: the Arena of the ancient Amphitheater in Lucca, today Piazza del Mercato.

DUOMO - The original 11th-13th century Romanesque building dedicated to St. Martin was rebuilt in the Gothic style during the 14th-15th centuries. Its facade is adorned with impressive Romanesque sculpture. The *facade* dates from the first building campaign. The portal sculpture is superb, especially the *Nativity* and *Deposition* of the left portal, both attributed to Nicola Pisano. The *interior* is a treasure-house of artworks: a 13th century sculpture depicting *St. Martin and the Beggar*; a painting by Tintoretto (*Last Supper*); and Jacopo della Quercia's renowned *Tomb of Ilaria del Carretto*. Along the left aisle is the *Tempietto del Volto Santo*, crafted by Matteo Civitali in 1498, which contains a 11th-12th century Byzantine *Crucifix*.

SAN MICHELE IN FORO - The *facade* of this striking 12th-14th century church, is topped by an immense statue of *St. Michael*. The *Virgin and Child* on the right corner is by Civitali. Inside the church are various works, including a *Virgin and Child* by Andrea della Robbia, and a Filippino Lippi altarpiece.

MUSEO NAZIONALE DI VILLA GUINIGI - The museum building, the recently-restored 15th century brick *Villa Guinigi*, sports a distinctive porticoed facade. Roman, medieval, and 18th century sculpture adorn the grounds. Ground floor: Roman archeology and sculpture of the following periods: Early Christian, Romanesque, Gothic (e.g., a fine Pisan-Lucchese style partition with *Samson and the lion* carved in the 13th century and an *Annunciation* by a follower of Nino Pisano), as well as Renaissance (e.g., *Ecce Homo* by Civitali). Upstairs: *portrait of Alessandro dei Medici* by Pontormo, and 14th-15th century Lucchese school paintings.

PISA

Pisa, an important port from Roman times, ranked as one of the great Mediterranean sea republics throughout the Middle Ages. In the 11th century, it wrested control of Sardinia, the start of a political and artistic influence not to be relinquished for centuries. Some of the great wealth the city accumulated between the 11th and 13th centuries was lavished on gigantic building projects such as the Campo dei Miracoli religious complex, including their sculptural decoration commissioned from masters such as Nino Pisano (12th century) and Giovanni Pisano (13th century). In 1284, however, Pisa suffered a terrible

defeat at the hands of the Genoese in the sea battle of Meloria. The results were political and economic decline and inevitably (from 1406 on) complete dependence on Florence. Under the Medici grand-dukes, however, recovery was swift (at least economically, due to enlarging of the port, and, culturally, after the University of Pisa was opened).

CAMPO DEI MIRACOLI - The buildings on this grassy square (actually Pisa's Piazza del Duomo) constitute one of the foremost complexes of medieval religious architecture. Despite the fact that the buildings

date from different periods (11th to 14th century), the impression they convey is of utter stylistic harmony.

CATHEDRAL - Although ground was broken in 1064, construction continued well into the 13th century. The tomb of its first architect, Buscheto, is visible at the first arch on the left side of the facade. One of the foremost examples of Pisan Romanesque, the building has all the

Above: aerial view of the Campo dei Miracoli. Right: facade of the Cathedral.

typical features of this style: blind arch motifs, inlay patterns, and ornamental sculpture. The facade *doors* date from the 16th century when they were put in to replace Bonanno's originals of 1186 that had been destroyed in a fire. All that is left of Bonanno's work is the *Porta*

Above: nave and choir of the Cathedral with Giovanni Pisano's Pulpit in the foreground. Right: Leaning Tower of Pisa.

di San Ranieri, the door to the right transept. Dated 1180, it is composed of twenty bronze panels sculpted in a simple, vigorous style. Inside are several noteworthy sights, among them Giovanni Pisano's remarkable carved *pulpit* with *New Testament scenes* in the nave (c. 1310). At the crossing hangs a lighting fixture, the so-called *Galileo's Lamp*, which supposedly sparked the great Pisan scientist's insight into the movement of the pendulum. Other highlights are: Tino di Camaino's *Tomb of Arrigo VII* (right transept), the great apse mosaic depicting *Christ between the Virgin and St. John the Baptist* (the figure of *St. John* has been attributed to Cimabue), and the sensitive *St. Agnes* by Andrea del Sarto (righthand column in the choir). In the *Treasury* (enter from the Sacristy) are some noteworthy objects, especially reliquaries, and Giovanni Pisano's celebrated *statue of the Virgin* carved out of ivory (late 1200s).

LEANING TOWER - Construction of the belltower, the symbol of Pisa throughout the world, was begun in 1173, possibly under the supervision of Bonanno, and completed two centuries later. It stands 60 meters tall and is inclined 5 meters off perpendicular. Its characteristic inclination is not a recent phenomenom, having begun almost as soon as work on the project got underway (probably due to land slippage, a common phenomenon in Pisan territory). However, the fact that it shows no sign of diminishing has prompted the city to sponsor studies aimed at stabilizing the situation. So far, despite the efforts of engineers and architects all over the world, no solution has been found.

BAPTISTRY - The original project drawn up by Diotisalvi around the middle of the 12th century was altered in the course of the next one hundred years by such master architects as Nicola and Giovanni Pisano. The circular building faced in striped marble is divided into three horizontal registers decorated by arch and gable motifs. A partitioned tile roof surmounts the building. Inside is a masterpiece of medieval sculpture,

Nicola Pisano's carved *pulpit*. The reliefs adorning the six sides executed in a monumental, very Classical style represent *scenes from the life of Christ*. The baptismal font is a 13th century masterpiece by Guido Como.

CAMPOSANTO

The wall along the north side of the Campo dei Miracoli belongs to the cemetery (*Camposanto* in Italian). The great *tabernacle* adorning the main portal is by a follower of Giovanni Pisano. The building was begun in 1277 around a famous relic, i.e., earth from the Calvary brought from the Holy Land by the Pisan navy in the 1200s. Destroyed by bombs in 1944, it was restored and its sinopias put on display in a special museum (south side of the square). The interior, which looks like any quiet Gothic cloister, is nevertheless a treasurehouse of art masterpieces. Under the portico are Roman and Early Christian works (including the renowned *Phaedra Sarcophagus* dating from the 2nd century A.D.),

inscriptions, plus medieval sculpture and frescoes (many of which in poor condition) painted by masters such as Benozzo Gozzoli, Taddeo Gaddi, and Piero di Puccio. In the next room are the celebrated frescoes depicting the *Triumph of Death*, the *Last Judgment*, *Hell*, and *scenes of life in an Anacorete monastery*. Art historians are split over the attribution: Trani or Orcagna. The *altar of St. Ranieri* in the nearby *Cappella Ammannati* is adorned with reliefs by Tino di Camaino.

SANTA MARIA DELLA SPINA

This tiny jewel of Gothic architecture (dated 1323) was named after a relic donated by a Pisan merchant. The relic, a thorn (*spina*) from Christ's crown is preserved in a 16th century tabernacle which, along with sculpture by Tommaso Pisano, adorns the interior. The building, moved here from its original location right on the water to protect it from floods, is embellished with sculptural decoration executed by followers of Giovanni Pisano.

Left: Baptistry exterior. Above: Nicola Pisano's Pulpit. Facing page: porticoed corridor of the Camposanto (cemetery) and detail of Traini's Triumph of Death fresco in the Camposanto.

SAN PAOLO A RIPA D'ARNO

Founded in the 9th century, the church was rebuilt in the Romanesque style and subsequently remodeled over the centuries. Its typical Pisan Romanesque facade features blind arches and arcading. The interior has a single-aisle plan. The capitals atop the granite columns lining the nave are original. The most interesting features are: a tomb (*Tomba di Burgundio*), made from a Roman sarcophagus (right aisle), a 14th century *Virgin and Child* by Turino Vanni, and a 14th century stained glass window with a *scene of Christ and the Apostles* (aspe). Detached from the main building is the *Cappella di Sant'Agata*, a 12th century brick structure with an unusual pyramid-shaped cusp roof.

Above: Piazza dei Cavalieri. Below: the Romanesque facade of San Paolo a Ripa d'Arno.

PIAZZA DEI CAVALIERI - Gothic buildings surrounded this square, the site of the forum of Roman Pisa, until it was rebuilt by Cosimo I dei Medici in the 16th century. One of the famous sights is the *Torre dei Gualandi*, now incorporated into a 16th century palace, *Palazzo dell'Orologio*, where Count Ugolino was left to starve to death (as recounted by Dante in the *Divine Comedy*). Vasari was commissioned by Cosimo to build *Palazzo dei Cavalieri*, which sports a distinctive facade of graffiti patterns. Originally the headquarters of the Order of the Knights of St. Stephan, it is now the Scuola Normale Superiore, Italy's finest university. Vasari also designed the church of *Santo Stefano* adorned with war trophies belonging to the order, Tuscan Mannerist paintings, and a *reliquary-bust* by Donatello.

Museo di San Matteo. Above: Sala di Giovanni Pisano. Below: detail of Masaccio's St. Paul.

MUSEO NAZIONALE DI SAN MATTEO

The collection, begun in the 18th century, is displayed in a lovely old Benedictine monastery. The exhibits in the first four rooms date mainly from the Roman and medieval periods. Celebrated sculptures by Giovanni Pisano (*Dancers, Female Saint with a Reliquary*, and the *Madonna di Arrigo*) are displayed in Rooms V and VI. A perfect blend of Gothic and Classical elements, they date from the 13th century. Other highlights include: *St. Dominick* by Traini (Room VI), two *crucifixes* by Giunta Pisano (Rooms VI and XX), *Virgin and Child* by Simone Martini, *Madonna del Latte* by Nino Pisano (Room XXI), and Masaccio's *St. Paul* (Room XXIV). In addition, there are tapestries (Room XXIII) as well as works by Antonio del Ghirlandaio and others.

155

AREZZO

Arezzo was a major Etruscan and, in the following period, Roman center. The great rival of Florence and Siena, it reached the height of power in the early 1300s under the *Signoria* of Guido Tarlati, (by the end of the century, however, it had become a dominion of Florence). The homeland of a number of famous men (Petrarch, Piero della Francesca, Michelangelo, and Vasari among them), Arezzo today is an active city with a picturesque medieval downtown section.

PIAZZA GRANDE - The irregularshaped square is borderd by buildings dating from different periods. The most important are the porticoed *Palazzo delle Logge* by Vasari, *Palazzo della Fraternita dei Laici*, which is half Gothic (lower section) and half Renaissance (up-

per section), the 17th century *Court Building*, and the Romanesque apse of the Pieve.

PIEVE DI SANTA MARIA - Built between 1140 and the early 1300s, the church ranks as one of the outstanding examples of Tuscan Romanesque architecture extant. Its rectangular facade is adorned with Pisan style arcading and superb 13th century sculpture (*central portal*). Alongside is an unusual belltower pierced by forty Gothic windows. The single-aisle interior has the raised choir-lowered crypt plan typical of Tuscan Romanesque. Some great works are displayed inside: a superb *altarpiece* by Pietro Lorenzetti over the main altar, a *Crucifix* by Margaritone d'Arezzo, a 14th century silver *reliquary*, and a 14th century *baptismal font*.

Above: Piazza Grande, Arezzo. Right: view of Siena, with Piazza del Campo in the center.

SAN FRANCESCO - This simple brick and stone church, typical of the Franciscan Gothic style, was built between the late 13th and 14th centuries. Inside is a celebrated fresco cycle, the *Legend of the True Cross*, painted by Piero della Francesca between 1453 and 1464. The right wall of the church, with its Gothic and Renaissance altars, still has part of its 14th-15th century fresco decoration. Other noteworthy features are a *Crucifixion* by Spinello Aretino, an *Annunciation* attributed to Signorelli, and a 13th century crucifix. The lower church, reached by a staircase, dates from the 13th-14th centuries.

SIENA

In the Imperial Age, Siena was a Roman dominion under the name *Sena Julia.* In 1147, a burgeoning center of commerce, it abandoned the feudal form of government, becoming a free commune. This marked the beginning of its period of greatest splendor, but also of greatest torment. Throughout the 12th and 13th centuries bitter power struggles went on both on the inside (among local factions) and on the outside (Ghibelline Siena vs. Guelph Florence). Then, in the mid-1300s, more troubles arose in the wake of the terrible plague epidemic, the Black Death, which struck in 1348, decimating the population. Around the end of the century Siena became a dominion of the Viscontis and then part of the *Signoria* of Pandolfo Petrucci. In 1555, it succumbed to Florence,

never really regaining its political independence in the centuries that followed. During the Middle Ages, Siena flourished artistically as well as politically. For two centuries (13th and 14th) the Sienese school, represented by Duccio di Buoninsegna, Simone Martini, and the Lorenzetti brothers, rivaled the Florentine masters as the most important in Italy. Twice a year (on July 2 and August 16), the *Palio* is run in Piazza del Campo. More than just a horse race (an unbelievably intense couple of minutes often punctualed by violent falls of horses and/or jockeys), the event involves a year of preparation and a month of festivities.

PIAZZA DEL CAMPO - Just «*Il Campo*» to the Sienese, the great fanshaped square slopes down in the direction of Palazzo Pubblico. In

the center of the brick paving is *Fonte Gaia,* adorned with sculpted reliefs by Jacopo della Quercia ranked among the masterpieces of 15th century art. Although the palaces and buildings bordering the square date from different periods (12th through 16th centuries), they nevertheless blend perfectly to form a harmonious whole.

PALAZZO PUBBLICO - Built, like Florence's Palazzo Vecchio, around the late 1200s, Palazzo Pubblico conveys an effect of major airiness for a variety of reasons: curvature of the facade, more color contrast, wide use of Gothic windows, and the vertical emphasis of the tower. The original architect is not known (Agostino di Giovanni or Agnolo di Ventura are two names advanced), although much of the design is

actually due to later alterations and additions. The building is not only Siena's city hall but also a museum. On the left side of the building is the *Torre del Mangia* designed by Lippo Memmi and built by Agostino di Giovanni around 1340. On top of the brick tower is a stone bell chamber where a certain Giovanni di Duccio nicknamed *Il Mangia* would sound the hours sometime in the 14th century. Il Mangia's job was later taken over by a mechanized figure (up to the 18th century), but the name stuck. Below the tower is the *Cappella di Piazza,* built between 1352 and 1376 in thanksgiving for deliverance from a plague epidemic. On the second floor is the entrance to the *Museo Civico.* On the right in the *Sala del Mappamondo* are two of Simone Martini's masterpieces: frescoes of the *Maestà* dated 1315 and *Guidoriccio da Fogliano* (depicted during the siege of Montemassi) dated 1328. Executed with a remarkable eye for pattern and line, they are among the outstanding example of the notably refined Sienese style of the

14th century. On the right is the *Sala della Pace* featuring a famous fresco cycle painted by Ambrogio Lorenzetti around 1340, with scenes showing *Good Government,* the *Effects of Good Government* and the *Effects of Bad Government.*

PALAZZO PICCOLOMINI - One of the most elegant examples of Renaissance civic architecture extant, the palace was begun under the supervision of Pietro Paolo del Pottino in 1469. The original design is ascribed to Bernardo Rossellino.

PINACOTECA NAZIONALE - The museum building (*Palazzo Buonsignori*) is an elegant Gothic-style 15th century brick palace. The collection, focusing mainly on Sienese art between the 12th and 17th centuries, was begun in the late 1700s by an abbot, Giuseppe Ciaccheri. Among the most important works are: the delightful *Madonna*

Palazzo Pubblico. Preceding page: exterior. Right: Guidoriccio da Fogliano, by Simone Martini. Below: detail of Ambrogio Lorenzetti's Allegory of Good Government.

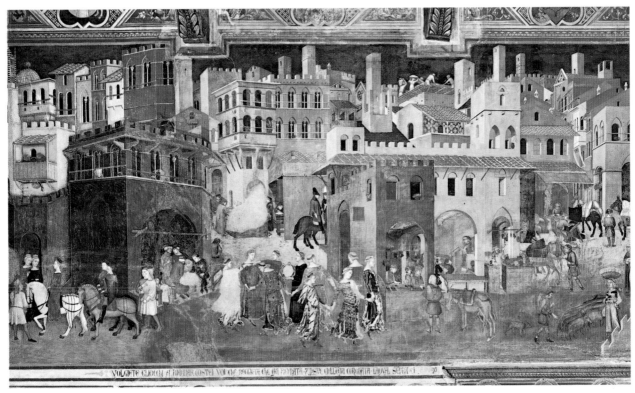

Siena's Cathedral, wholly faced in a striped marble pattern.

dei Francescani, by Duccio a celebrated *Virgin and Child* by Simone Martini; a sampling of works by Ambrogio Lorenzetti, e.g., *Annunciation* (1344), plus two panel paintings, one of a *castle by a lake* and the other of a *city near the sea-shore*, the earliest known Italian landscapes.

DUOMO - The Duomo rose in the mid-1100s on the site of a pre-existing 9th-10th century church. In 1339, when the project was nearing completion, it was decided to enlarge the original plan: the existing building would be just the transept of a «*Duomo Nuovo*» (new cathedral). Plague and economic political setbacks caused the gigantic project to be abandoned (and ensuing return to the original plans). Work was finished in the late 1300s. The lower section of the *facade* is by Giovanni

Pisano (1284-1296), except for the reliefs of the central portal architrave which are by Tino di Camaino. The *interior* is quite impressive: striped marble pillars set off the nave from the single aisles and the *floor* is alive with stupendous mosaics of *biblical scenes*. The church is a treasure-house of art masterpieces. At the left transept crossing is one of the masterpieces of Italian Gothic sculpture, the *pulpit* carved by Nicola Pisano in 1268. From the left aisle enter the *Libreria Piccolomini*, built between the late 15th-early 16th centuries as the personal library of the Piccolomini pope, Pius II, with Pinturicchio frescoes, illuminated manuscripts, and the celebrated *Three Graces*, a Roman copy of a Greek original.

MUSEO DELL'OPERA METRO-POLITANA - Founded in 1870, the collection features works originally part of the Duomo or Baptistry decoration, such as the ten *statues* by Giovanni Pisano (once part of the Duomo's facade) in the ground floor sculpture hall. Duccio's *Maestà*, painted in 1311 for the main altar of the church, is displayed in a special room on the second floor. One of the great paintings of Western art, it is a complex work consisting of a great *Virgin Enthroned* panel (originally the front) plus 26 smaller panels (originally the back) depicting *scenes of the Passion*. In addition, the Maestà Room contains another *Virgin* by Duccio and the *Birth of the Virgin*, one of Pietro Lorenzetti's finest works (1342).

UMBRIA

Umbria is situated right in the middle of the Italian boot, lying along the Apennine mountain range. The remarkable Umbrian towns of today look very much the same as they did during the Middle Ages, their period of great splendor. Also, despite the inevitable changes wrought by industry and modern times, the region is still heavily wooded, mostly with oak forests.

HISTORY - The name Umbria derives from the name of the Italic people, the Umbri, who settled along the left (east) bank of the Tiber long before the arrival of the Romans. The right bank (west) was instead the domain of two major Etruscan cities, Perugia and Orvieto, that by the 3rd century B.C. were already known as flourishing centers. Shortly after, however, the Romans defeated both Umbri and Etruscans, and annexed the whole territory to their dominions. For centuries, Umbria's destiny was closely linked to the Roman Empire's and, like Rome, it was invaded, looted, razed, and subjugated by the Goths in the 6th century A.D. The Byzantines proceeded to drive off the Goths, only to be ousted a few years later by the Longobards. In 571, the Longobards founded the Duchy of Spoleto, which remained independent up to the 8th century when the Duchy and the territories bordering it became property of the Catholic Church. By the outset of the 11th century, trade and commerce had developed to such an extent that the population's prosperity soon fostered the rebirth of cities and towns. By the 12th century, when St. Francis was born in the Umbrian city of Assisi, the region was a cluster of free and independent city-states. After the 15th century transition period when many of the free city-states were gradually stripped of their "free" status (i.e., they succumbed to the power of the local lords, the Sig-

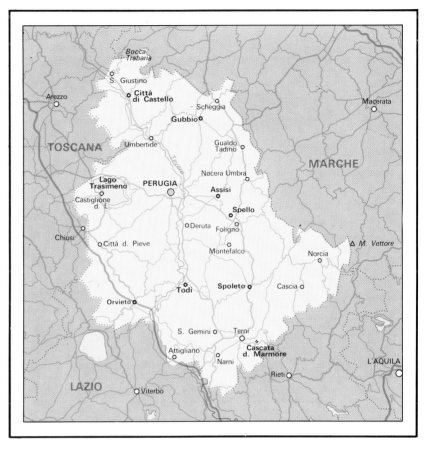

noria), the Papal State wrested control of the region, and the next centuries were uneventful from a historical viewpoint.

ART - Although few traces of Umbri culture have survived, numerous Etruscan remains (mostly around Perugia and Orvieto) and Roman ruins (scattered) have come down to us in various states of preservation. Many cities are still encircled by Roman walls, some with gates (Spello), while in others there are notable remains of Roman theaters (Gubbio, Spoleto) and temples (Assisi, the facade of the Temple of Minerva). Starting from the Romanesque period, and continuing throughout the whole Middle Ages up to the Gothic period, countless churches and monasteries were built

all over the region. The Franciscan movement was a key factor in sparking the boom, especially in the 12th-13th centuries when the first great Franciscan building, the Basilica of Assisi, was erected. In painting, the influence of Tuscan painters especially Giotto (Florentine school) and Simone Martini (Sienese school) was overriding up through the 14th century. Tuscan influence continued well into the 1400s, actually until the turn of the 15th century, when an Umbrian school of painting grew up around two masters, Perugino (Raphael's teacher) and Pinturicchio. During the following centuries, no major artistic breakthroughs came out of Umbria, although it could always vaunt remarkably-skilled craftsmen, such as the potters of Deruta.

PERUGIA

Settled by the Etruscans around the 7th-6th century B.C., probably over an even earlier settlement, by the 4th century A.D., it had burgeoned into a sizable walled city of huge gates and elaborate tombs. When Perugia fell to the Romans, it relinquished its dominion over the other Umbrian towns, regaining supremacy only at the outset of the city-state period (11th-12th centuries). As a free city-state Perugia expanded and prospered. This period of splendor lasted well into the 16th century, until it was occupied by the papal army in 1540.

By the 15th century, the Umbrian school painters ranked among the foremost in Italy and were kept busy filling commissions for the numerous princes and dukes whose rivalry extended from battlefields to art collections. The most prominent were Pinturicchio and Perugino, whose pupil Raphael trained in Urbino before being summoned to Rome.

FONTANA MAGGIORE - The fountain has come to symbolize the city of Perugia itself. It was built in 1275, probably based on a design by Fra' Bevignate da Perugia. The sculptural decoration, among the great masterpieces of Western art, is one of the last works by Nicola Pisano. Nicola was aided by his son Giovanni, also a sculptor of great renown.

PALAZZO DEI PRIORI - Once headquarters of the Free City-State of Perugia, this superb palace was begun in 1293 and finished in 1443. Two architects, natives of Perugia, are believed to have designed it: Giacomo di Servadio and Giovannello di Benvenuto. Despite the fact

Left: Fontana Maggiore. Above left: Palazzo dei Priori. Above right: Etruscan Arch.

that its construction spanned a century and a half, its typically medieval features, i.e., three-part windows, crenelation, and belltower, are harmoniously integrated in a striking whole. On the third floor is the *Galleria Nazionale dell'Umbria*, a prominent art museum featuring Umbrian painting and sculpture from the 13th through 18th centuries. Among the many outstanding works displayed in its thirty-three halls, we shall list only the highlights: *Virgin and Child with Angels*, by Duccio di Buoninsegna, *Virgin and Child*, one of Fra' Angelico's most important pictures (1437), the *St. Anthony Altarpiece*, an outstanding work by Piero della Francesca, as well as an *Adoration of the Magi*, and a *Dead Christ* by Pietro Perugino.

COLLEGIO DEL CAMBIO - The ground floor of the Palazzo dei Priori, originally the headquarters of the Moneychangers' Guild, was built in the mid-15th century. A Baroque-style antechamber leads to the *Sala dell'Udienza del Cambio* (Audience Hall), which is one of the finest examples of 15th century Renaissance interior decoration extant. The room is elaborately appointed: wood paneling with inlay designs around the bottom and superb frescoes on both the upper section and vaulted ceiling painted by Perugino and his pupils — Raphael might just have been one — from 1498 to 1500.

ETRUSCAN ARCH - The majesty of the archway, built by the Etruscans as a city gate in the 2nd-1st century B.C., conveys an idea of what the economic and political power of Etruria must have been at the time. The loggia on the left side of the tower is an attractive 16th century addition.

CATHEDRAL - Although the building, which rises on the site of a pre-existing Romanesque church, was begun in 1345, work continued for decades. (The facade, for example, despite its late Baroque portal, was never wholly finished.) The patterned facing of colored marbles along the left side is especially attractive. Next to the 16th century portal (by Galeazzo Alessi) is a seated statue of Pope Julius III, by Vincenzo Danti. The church plan is simple: a Latin cross with aisles as high as the nave. The first bays are closed off by wrought-iron gates, which form two chapels. On the altar of the righthand one, the Chapel of St. Bernardino, is a *Deposition*, by Federico Barocci. Painted in 1569, it ranks as one of the master's finest works.

SAN BERNARDINO - The church, erected in the 15th century, is a masterpiece of Renaissance art. The architect, Agostino di Duccio, was plainly influenced by the work of his contemporary and fellow Florentine, the great Leon Battista Alberti. The patterned marble facade is accented with reliefs and sculpture. The scene in the lunette over the double portal represents *St. Bernardino in Paradise*. The stark interior contains an interesting altar, which was once a 4th century Early Christian sarcophagus.

SANT'ANGELO - Originally an Early Christian church (5th-6th century A.D.), it underwent much modification and restoration over the centuries, especially in the 1300s. Although its original plan

163

was a Greek cross, today it is a round building with a raised interior and a barrel-shaped roof — a picturesque sight in its country setting among the olives trees. The highlights of the interior are the sixteen Roman columns sustaining the drum, an altar made of antique marbles, and 14th century frescoes.

SAN DOMENICO - The original 14th century Gothic-style building was entirely rebuilt in the 17th century by a Swiss-Italian architect, Carlo Maderno, then active chiefly in Rome. The right side, with pointed arches and buttresses, belongs to the original building. The portal dates from the late 16th century.

ARCHEOLOGICAL MUSEUM - The museum is right next to the church of San Domenico, occupying what was once its monastery. It comprises two sections, Prehistoric and Etrusco-Roman, and features works chiefly excavated in the region. The notable Etruscan sarcophagi, urns, vases, and weapons on display come from excavations of Umbrian necropolises.

SAN PIETRO - The church was founded in the 10th century on the site of Perugia's first cathedral. The charming 17th century courtyard preceding the entrance also leads to the monastery. The belltower, designed by Bernardo Rossellino, dates from the 15th century. The single aisles are set off from the nave by Roman Ionic columns. Most of the paintings along the aisles are by masters of the Mannerist school, foremost of whom Guido Reni, Guercino, and Giorgio Vasari. Four superb panels by Perugino are displayed in the Sacristy at the far end of the right aisle. Another fine Perugino, a *Pietà*, hangs in the left aisle, between the first and second altars. The inlaid choir stalls in the apse are renowned for their superb craftsmanship. They were carved by Bernardino Antonibi and Stefano Zambelli in the mid-1500s.

Above: Sant'Angelo. Below: Renaissance facade of the church of San Bernardino.

164

ASSISI

As soon as Assisi appears nestled on the slopes of Mt. Subasio, you can make out the unusual structure of the Basilica, rising majestic on its massive arch supports. Founded by the Umbri, Assisi achieved some importance during the Roman period, but the event that had the greatest impact on its history, art, and entire being was the birth of St. Francis. Born in the year 1181 into a family of wealthy Assisi merchants, in 1206 he left behind the carefree existence of his youth for a life of self-imposed poverty and meditation. This experience led him to found the monastic orders of the *Frati Minori* (for males) and *Clarisse* (for females), and carry his mission all over the Italian peninsula and abroad. His beatification dates from

1228, two years after his death. During the long years the church dedicated to St. Francis was in the process of being built (13th-14th centuries), the foremost artists of the day were summoned to contribute to its embellishment.

SAN FRANCESCO - The Basilica was begun in 1228, the year St. Francis was beatified, through the efforts of his disciple, Fra Elia — who is also believed to be its architect. The Basilica actually consists of two separate buildings, an upper and lower church, plus several monastic structures. LOWER CHURCH: The entrance, preceded by a Renaissance portico, is a 13th century double portal on the left side of the church. The mortal remains of St.

Panoramic view of the city. The Duomo (left) and Santa Chiara (right) are clearly visible.

Francis have been preserved in the crypt since 1230. Although the architecture of the Lower Church reveals strong influxes of the elaborate Gothic style which was spreading down from Northern Europe at that time, it is mitigated, as in many Italian buildings, by the effect of simple Romanesque monumentality. The plan is simple: an aisleless Latin cross lined with chapels. Of the numerous masterpieces of art adorning the building, we shall mention only the highlights. The nave frescoes (*Life of St. Francis* on the

lefthand wall, *Life of Christ* on the right), painted in the 1340s or slightly after, are ascribed to an unknown artist dubbed the Maestro di San Francesco. In the Cappella della Maddalena (third chapel on the right), are murals recounting the *Lives of Mary Magdalene, Christ, and the Saints*, attributed to Giotto and his pupils. Opposite is the *Tribune*, a 13th century masterpiece executed by craftsmen belonging to the renowned Cosmati school of marble inlayers. The adjacent Cappella di San Martino was frescoed around 1325 by the great Sienese master, Simone Martini. The frescoes, revealing his typical ex-

Above: complex of the Basilica of San Francesco. Right: Virgin Enthroned, Cimabue's 13th century fresco in the right transept of the Lower Church.

ceedingly refined style of painting, recount the *Life of St. Martin*. The *crypt* in which the mortal remains of St. Francis are preserved is reached from the right side of the nave. The celebrated frescoes on the crypt vault, *Allegories of Poverty, Chastity, and Obedience*, and the *Apotheosis of St. Francis*, were originally attributed to Giotto, though recently they have been ascribed to an unknown master who has been called *Maestro delle Vele*. The left transept is entirely frescoed with a cycle on the *Life of Christ*, the work of the Sienese great, Pietro Lorenzetti. On the right side of the righthand transept is a fresco by Giotto's master, Cimabue, depicting the *Virgin Enthroned with St. Francis*. Frescoes by followers of Giotto complete the decorative scheme. Among the fig-

ures of saints, that of *St. Claire* is a fine example of Simone Martini's inimitable style. UPPER CHURCH: The Upper Church, airier and with greater emphasis on the vertical, is more Gothic in style. The simple facade has a huge rose window with the four *Evangelist symbols*; on the left rises an impressive square-shaped belltower. Aisleless, the interior consists of a single hall with a gallery on high pierced by enormous windows. The lower section of the walls was frescoed by Giotto with twenty-eight scenes of the *Life of St. Francis*, rated among the great masterpieces of Western art. Especially noteworthy are the scenes showing *St. Francis giving his cloak to a poor man*, *St. Francis renouncing his earthly possessions*, *St. Francis driving the devils from Arezzo*, the

Nativity of Greccio, *St. Francis preaching to the birds* (one of the best-loved art works in existence), and the *Death of the Knight of Celano*. The transepts contain masterpieces by Cimabue — the dramatic *Crucifixion* in the left one and the *Life of St. Peter* in the right one.

PIAZZA DEL COMUNE - Right in the heart of medieval Assisi, the square contains several medieval buildings. Next to the 13th century *Palazzo Capitano del Popolo* rises the stately *Torre del Popolo*. The belltower was completed in the early 1300s, while the bell was donated in 1926 by the Italian cities to Assisi on occasion of the twelfth centennial of St. Francis' death. On the opposite side is the *Palazzo dei Priori*, seat of the city-state government, and the

Left: St. Francis expelling the devils from the city of Arezzo, by Giotto, in the Upper Church of San Francesco. Above: Santa Chiara.

Pinacoteca Civica, a collection of paintings of the Umbrian and Giottesque schools. Unlike the other buildings on the square, the *Temple of Minerva* is not medieval, but a fine example of Roman architecture dating from the outset of the Imperial Age. Although the interior has been used as a church since the 16th century, the six-sided pronaos with fluted Corinthian columns has remained intact.

DUOMO - Erected on the site of an earlier 8th century church, the Cathedral was rebuilt in honor of St. Rufino starting in 1140. The facade is an outstanding example of Umbrian Romanesque, with carved portals and rose windows harmoniously set in a three-register design. The massive Romanesque belltower is also noteworthy. The interior was remodeled in the 1500s by Alessi.

SANTA CHIARA - The church was erected in 1265 in honor of St. Claire, who was one of St. Francis' earliest and staunchest supporters. Aside from the striped marble facing, the exterior much resembles the Upper Church of the Basilica. The massive buttresses flanking it are of different styles: open on the left side of the facade and filled in on the right (forming part of the Convent of St. Claire's). The Gothic interior, aisleless, is a striking showplace for its outstanding artworks. Off the nave of the right aisle, in the Cappella del Crocifisso, is the celebrated 12th century *Crucifix*, which, the legend goes, spoke to St. Francis in the church of San Damiano. The stairs in the middle of the nave lead down to the crypt where the mortal remains of St. Claire are preserved. The charming 13th century panel in the right transept recounts episodes from the *Life of St. Claire* by an unknown master, the so-called Maestro di Santa Chiara.

SANTA MARIA DEGLI ANGELI - This complex, comprising numerous buildings set around a basilica de-

Left: Piazza del Comune, with the Torre del Popolo rising between Assisi's medieval town hall and the Roman temple of Minerva. Above: Romanesque facade of the Duomo consecrated to St. Rufino.

signed by Alessi (mid-1500s), rises on a vast plain extending from the lower reaches of Mt. Subasio. In this area, St. Francis founded his first monastery. The interior of the state-ly basilica is magnificently adorned. Beneath the dome is the 10th century *Cappella della Porziuncola*, around which St. Francis built the cells for his monks.

ORVIETO

Orvieto stands atop a huge tufa boulder overlooking the Valle del Paglia. The irregular-shaped streets of the old city center with their tufa and basalt buildings radiate out from the Duomo, whereas the modern (industrial) section has grown up in the plain at the foot of the boulder. Between the 7th and 3rd centuries B.C. Orvieto ranked as a major Etruscan center about which much can be learned from a study of its extensive necropolis. Decline set in when the city fell to the Romans. Only in the 10th-11th centuries, when the city-state of Orvieto was formed, did propserity return once more. (Indeed much of present-day

Orvieto dates from this medieval period of splendor.) Orvieto is famous for still another reason — its superb white wine that comes in two versions, dry and tart.

DUOMO - A superb example of Italian Gothic architecture, the Duomo rises on the site of a pre-existing cathedral. Work on the building, supposedly designed by Arnolfo di Cambio, was started in 1290. The facade (1305-1330) was designed by Lorenzo Maitani, who is also the sculptor of the renowned reliefs adorning it (Last Judgment, and other religious subjects). The elegant rose window and main portal,

Above: panoramic view of the city.
Right: Gothic facade of the Duomo.

the work of Orcagna, date from the mid-1300s. The bronze portal sculptures on the theme of Charity are by a contemporary Italian master, Emilio Greco (1964), while the mosaics were executed in the 17th-18th centuries. The interior of the single-aisled church is truly impressive. Inside the *Cappella Nuova*, off the right transept, is one of the great masterpieces of Renaissance painting: the fresco cycle that Luca Sig-

172

norelli painted from 1499 to 1504 depicting scenes of the *Coming of the Antichrist* and the *Last Judgment*. Opposite, in the Cappella del Corporale, is the much-venerated *Reliquary of the Corporale*. (The relics was supposedly miraculously spotted with blood stains from a host during a mass celebrated in Bolsena in 1261.) The two museums in Piazza del Duomo are the *Museo Civico* (*Palazzo Faina*) and the *Museo dell'Opera del Duomo*, containing works by Simone Martini, Luca Signorelli, and Nino Pisano.

CASCATA DELLE MARMORE - (70 km). This is Italy's biggest waterfall (a drop of 165 meters and flow of 60 cubic meters per second). A breathtaking sight, the harsh roaring waters often produce delicate rainbows of incredible effect. The interesting thing about the Marmore Falls is that they are virtually man-made: the Roman general, Curius Dentatus, famous for having vanquished the Sabines, ordered digging of a channel to deviate the Velino River over a precipice into the Nar River, for the purpose of preventing floods along the Rieti plain. This early land reclamation project was enacted in 271 A.D. Two other channels were

Marmore Falls viewed from the scenic roadway, Strada Valnerina.

later added (one in 1400 and one in 1785). The falls may be viewed both from below (Valnerina Road) and from above (road for Rieti).

174

MARCHE

The name Marche derives from the German mark which, during the Middle Ages, stood for the border regions of the Holy Roman Empire, i.e., the mountainous lands occupying the north central zone of the Adriatic coast. There are no particularly extensive waterways, but here and there you can see spectacular falls such as the Gola del Furlo, Gola della Rossa, and Gola dell'Infernaccio, to name the most prominent. Also, there are numerous grottoes, some of which truly breathtaking, among them Acquasanta, Sant'Eustachio, and the most remarkable of all, the Grottoes of Frasassi.

HISTORY - The first documented civilization, however, is that of the Piceni who settled the area south of the Esino River in the 10th century B.C. Then, in the 3rd century, the Romans arrived to subjugate the region, naturally not without bloodshed. Roman rule also meant a bloodless revolution; the region was split into several administrative districts. When the Roman Empire started to fall apart, Marche was drawn into two different spheres of influence, Longobard (south of Ancona) and Byzantine (the so-called Pentapolis, i.e. the Five Town Maritime League). By the time Southern Marche was annexed to the Papal State in the 13th century, the newly-founded duchies in the rest of the region had begun to attain political and economic power. Of these, the most important, both politically and culturally speaking, were the Duchies of Urbino (the Montefeltros), Pesaro (the Malatestas), and Camerino (the Varanos). By the 17th century, the whole region had come under the rule of the Papal State. The French occupation of 1796 brought about repression, insurrection, and periodic uprisings, which ceased only when Marche adhered to the Kingdom of Italy in 1860.

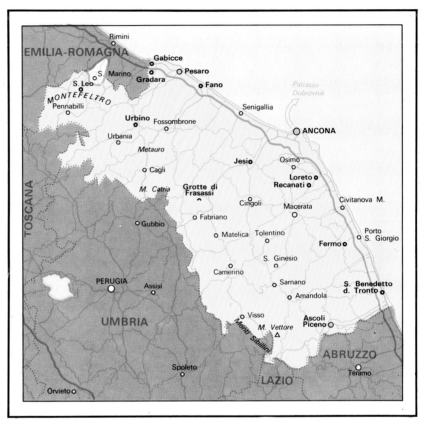

ART - There are hardly any remains of the Piceno civilization (mostly utensils and ornaments unearthed from burial grounds). Roman ruins, on the other hand, are plentiful and of great artistic and historical interest. Among these are two virtually intact archways (Ancona and Fano), an excavated city (Helvia Ricina, not far from Macerata) and Urbs Salvia (present-day Urbisaglia), as well as sarcophagi and statuary (Ancona and Osimo). Many remarkable Romanesque and Gothic buildings have come down to us, and these are more or less evenly spread over the whole territory. One of the foremost masters of the International style, Gentile da Fabriano, was a native of the region, although his art took him all over Italy. The golden period of art, however, was the Renaissance, when the Duchy of Urbino was one of the most splendid courts in Europe. It is hardly surprising that of the "name" artists and writers of the day, few failed to work under the patronage of the mighty dukes of Urbino. With the building of the Santuario della Santa Casa (Sanctuary of the Holy Dwelling), Loreto too became an important artistic center, while all around princely palaces and massive fortresses were being erected for the local lords. Despite the fact that both Raphael, the great painter, and Bramante, the great architect, were born in the region in the 15th century, they, like their predecessor Gentile da Fabriano, were mainly active elsewhere. Two prominent Venetian masters, on the other hand, Carlo Crivelli and Lorenzo Lotto, moved south to Marche. And, in fact, both had great impact on mid-15th century local painters.

ANCONA

Settled by a colony of exiles from Syracuse in the 4th century B.C. Ancona belonged to the Pentapolis before becoming a city state. Unfortunately, however, the appearance of the city has undergone extensive changes in recent times due to both human-wrought disasters (two world wars) and natural ones (earthquakes).

DUOMO - Ancona's superb cathedral rises atop Mt. Guasco dominating the whole city. Begun in the Early Christian era, the basilica was later remodeled during the 11th to 13th centuries in the Romanesque style with notable Byzantine influxes. The *facade* is set off by a superb *porch* with crouching lions framing a carved portal. The recently-restored *interior* has a Greek cross plan.

Each arm of the cross is divided into a nave and single aisles, while the two lateral arms are raised over crypts. (The lefthand crypt is actually all that is still extant of the original 6th century building.)

ARCH OF TRAJAN - The single-opening archway, which has come down to us in excellent state of preservation, was erected in the 2nd century A.D. in honor of the Emperor Trajan who had sponsored the improvement and enlargement of the port. The majestic arch is ascribed to the greatest architect and sculptor of the times, Apollodorus of Damascus.

MUSEO NAZIONALE DELLE MARCHE - The museum building (*Palazzo Ferretti*), a fine example of

Above: Passetto, the section of the city overlooking the port.

16th century civic architecture has been attributed to Pellegrino Tibaldi. Its collections include prehistoric artifacts from the Piceno necropolises, Hellenistic and Roman sculpture, and a remarkable group of Imperial Age bronzes from Cartoceto di Pergola. The *Pinacoteca Civica* (Via Pizzecolli 17) displays paintings by Crivelli, Lotto, and Titian.

SANTA MARIA NELLA PIAZZA - This gem of 13th century Romanesque architecture has a striking marble facade adorned with blind arcading, a fine sculpted portal by Maestro Filippo, and a striking — very plain — interior.

Unusual Romanesque facade of the church of Santa Maria della Piazza adorned with a myriad of blind arches and elaborate carvings.

PASSETTO - This attractive modern district overlying the Adriatic lies at the end of Viale della Vittoria, beyond the old city center. The beach is reached by descending a flight of stairs or by elevator.

URBINO

Urbino is undoubtedly one of the most beautiful cities in Central Italy. Its Palazzo Ducale alone ranks among the foremost examples of Italian Renaissance civic architecture. Probably founded by the Romans, Urbino was loyal to the emperor throughout the Middle Ages until it was ceded to the Counts of Montefeltro from Carpegna. The Montefeltros, who retained their political hold up to 1508, ruled over one of the most splendid courts in all of Italy, especially during the time of Duke Federico II. When Federico's son Guidobaldo died without leaving any direct heirs, the

duchy passed into the hands of Francesco Della Rovere. The Della Roveres ruled until 1631, the year the duchy was annexed to the Papal State. Urbino was the birthplace of a host of famous artists, including Girolamo Genga, Federico Barocci, Bramante, and, Raphael.

PALAZZO DUCALE - Baldassarre Castiglione defined the Montefeltros' palace as "*città in forma di palazzo*" (a palace like a city). Having sojourned here at length in the 1500s, he was well-acquainted with the superb palace which is indeed remarkable for both vastness and

complexity. The original building was first enlarged when Federico II wed Battista Sforza in 1460. The stupendous *main facade* (*Facciata dei Torricini*, facing west) was designed by Luciano Laurana. The architect created the building as a majestic extension of the hill it rises upon, so that it has come to be the very symbol of the city of Urbino itself: a visitor approaching it from Tuscany or Rome perceives it from far off as such. The east side (facing into the town) takes up two adjoining squares: an elongated rectangle on *Piazza Rinascimento* opposite the 14th century church of *San*

Domenico, and two protruding wings, designed by Francesco di Giorgio Martini occupying *Piazza Duca Federico*. Inside is the superb Renaissance *courtyard* designed by Laurana, the great Dalmatian architect responsible for the overall plan of the building.

GALLERIA NAZIONALE DELLE MARCHE

The museum is a treasure house of paintings dating from the golden period of Urbinate painting (15th-16th centuries), when Italy's greatest masters were summoned to work under the patronage of the dukes of Urbino. The highlights: *Profanation of the Host* (predella), by Paolo Uccello; *Communion of the Apostles* by the Flemish master Justus van Ghent; *Portrait of Duke Federico and his son Guidobaldo*, by the Spanish painter Berruguete; two masterpieces by Piero della Francesca: the *Flagellation of Christ* and the *Virgin of Senigallia*; two paintings by Raphael: the celebrated *Portrait of a Lady* (known as *La Muta*, painted in Florence) and an early predella with *scenes from* the *life of the Virgin*, probably executed in conjunction with Perugino, Raphael's master; and two processional banners by Titian (*Last Supper* and *Resurrection of Christ*). The remarkable inlaid wood paneling in the *Studiolo del Duca Federico* (the duke's study) is attributed to Botticelli.

CASA DI RAFFAELLO (Raphael's House)

This 15th century building originally belonged to the painter Giovanni Sanzio, Raphael's father, and it was here that the great Renaissance painter spent his youth. Today a museum, it is hung with 16th century paintings and copies of Raphael's famous works. The fresco of the *Virgin and Child* in the room where Raphael was born is traditionally believed to be one of his first works.

Preceding page: Palazzo Ducale dominating the whole townscape. Above right: Palazzo Ducale's courtyard designed by Luciano Laurana. Below right: Torricini facade, also designed by Laurana. Following page: Raphael's La Muta, one of the masterpieces in the Galleria Nazionale.

LAZIO

Lazio's landscape is varied, ranging from the mountains of the Central Apennine range (whose tallest peak, Mt. Terminillo, reaches the respectable height of 2213 meters) to approximately 260 kilometers of sandy shoreline. Its sole sizable plain, Agro Pontino, originated as a great marshland, until an extensive reclamation project was undertaken in the 1930s. Lazio's principal river is the Tiber which crosses the entire region. Lakes, mostly of volcanic origin, dot the territory; the most important ones are Bolsena (fifth largest in Italy), Bracciano, Vico, Nemi, and Albano. A tiny cluster of islands, the Ponziano Archipelago, lies off the coast.

HISTORY - Around the year 1000 B.C., the region was inhabited by three peoples: Etruscans, Sabines, and Latins, who joined together in a political-religious league. Originally their capital was Alba Longa, but it was not long before Rome, settled around the 8th century B.C., began to emerge. The well-known story about the founding of Rome recounted by Ovid and Virgil (among others) dates back to the 4th-3rd centuries. According to the legend, Eneas, fleeing Troy, settled in Latium (present-day Lazio) where his son Ascanius founded Alba Longa. One of Ascanius' descendants, Rea Silvia, the daughter of King Numitore, gave birth to twins, Remus and Romulus, fathered by the god Mars. The brothers, whose mother was forced to abandon them to save them from certain death, were raised by a she-wolf. Romulus, the first of the so-called Seven Kings, traditionally founded Rome in 753 B.C. (a date arbitrarily set sometime in the 1st century B.C.). During the monarchy, the city supposedly occupied seven hills, i.e., the Palatine (believed to be the site of Romulus' original settlement), Capitoline, Quirinal, Celium, Viminal, Esquiline, and Aventine.

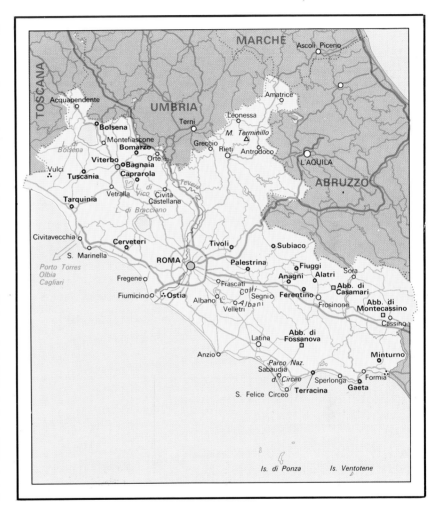

Around the end of the 6th century, Rome became a republic. Dominion over the other Italic peoples was assured when Taranto, the capital of Southern Italy, succumbed in 242 B.C. This was the starting point for the great Roman expansion in the Mediterranean basin. Victories in the Punic Wars (3rd-2nd centuries B.C.) brought Sicily, Sardinia, Corsica, Spain, and North Africa, followed by the great conquests of the 2nd and 1st centuries B.C. which expanded Rome's boundaries even further (Grecian and other Oriental territories). Growing social problems, however, began to lacerate from within. The reforms enacted by the Gracchus brothers (Tribunes of the People) provoked a counter-reaction whose end result was civil war (Marius vs. Silla) and rebellion (revolt of the slaves led by Spartacus). The crisis did not dissolve under the rule of the first triumvirate composed of Caesar, Pompey, and Crassus. Caesar, returning from his brilliant conquest of Gaul (58-52 B.C.), managed to defeat his fellow triumviri and have himself proclaimed dictator. His plans to reform the state were just getting underway when he was murdered in 44 B.C. The outcome of the ensuing civil wars was the end of the republic. Octavian, who put an end to the conflict, was acclaimed Augustus (i.e., he who is worthy of veneration) and the Roman Empire was born. Augustus ruled from 27 B.C. to 14 A.D. The dynasty he founded, the Julian-Claudians, continued with Tiberius, Caligula, Claudius, and Nero, and was succeeded by the Flavians (Vespasian, Titus, and Domitian). The great age of the empire came in the 2nd century with a succession of able rulers (Nerva, Trajan, Hadrian, and Marcus Aurelius). By the 3rd century however, the first signs of decline were already well in view. In the meantime, one of the new religions, Christianity, was steadily gaining ground among the populace, despite the violent persecutions of emperors such as Diocletian aimed at stamping it out. The farsighted emperor Constantine thought otherwise. Convinced that Christianity would prove a cohesive force in preserving the empire, he issued the Edict of Milan, granting freedom of religion, in 313. Toward the end of the 4th century, warring from within (factions) and without (barbarian invasions) caused a schism into the Roman Empire of the East (capital: Constantinople) and the Roman Empire of the West (capital: Rome). The latter was shortlived: in 455 the Huns, led by Attila, and the Vandals sacked Rome and in 476 the last of the Roman emperors, Romulus Augustulus, was deposed. In the 6th century not only Rome, but all of Italy, could be considered simply provinces of the Byzantine Empire. During this period of disintegration, new forces were emerging, and soon the most important of these, the papacy, managed to wrest temporal control of the region. Nevertheless, up until the 11th century, Lazio was in the throes of economic troubles and natural disasters (primarily plague epidemics). Recovery was considerable in the 12th and 13th centuries, but when the papacy was moved to Avignon, France, in the early 1300s, Rome was affected to the extent that the city no longer ranked as either a political, economic, or religious capital. The situation changed radically in the 15th century with the return of the papacy and subsequent rise of the papal state. Not unsurprisingly, Humanist-inspired popes were among the greatest of the Renaissance art patrons. Once the rifts following the bloody looting of Rome in 1527 had healed, the papacy, acting on a renewed policy of political neutrality, promoted stability within its own state (whose territory covered the present-day central Italian regions of Lazio, Umbria, Marche, and Romagna) that allowed it to attain widespread economic wellbeing. In the 19th century, Lazio joined the Kingdom of Italy. At the outset (from 1860-1870), the papal state was reduced to the sole region of Lazio. In 1870, however, the Italian army entered Rome by way of a breach in one of the city gates, Porta Pia, and a year later Rome was proclaimed capital of Italy.

ART - The foremost examples of pre-Roman art are the Etruscan tombs in the necropolises of Tarquinia, Cerveteri, and Vulci. In addition, some important temple sculpture has survived (e.g., the so-called Capitoline Wolf, the Veius Apollo, and the Winged Horses of Tarquinia). Starting from the 2nd century B.C., Greece became the main cultural reference point for Roman art: Greek architectural styles were used in Roman buildings, celebrated Greek sculptures were copied by Roman craftsmen, and Greek temples and theaters were adapted to Roman tastes and requirements. Rome's outstanding contribution to art (and engineering) is represented by the great building projects undertaken by Roman architects and designers. These embrace everything from stadiums, temples, and basilicas to civil works such as aqueducts, sewer systems (Cloaca Maxima), and public baths, not to mention paved roads and bridges — often of gigantic scale. The golden age of Roman art was followed, in the 3rd-4th centuries, by the Early Christian period. The works produced (mainly mosaics and sarcophagi) reveal an overriding dependence on late Roman prototypes, Thereafter, Roman influence gave way to Byzantine which lasted a good three hundred years (6th through 9th centuries). The 10th to 12th centuries was a period of intensive churchbuilding, as several Romanesque churches (e.g., San Clemente, Santa Maria in Trastevere, and Santa Maria in Cosmedin in Rome) attest. Skilled marble inlayers (collectively known as Cosmati) were commissioned to decorate them. The region produced outstanding artists in the Gothic period, including painters (Jacopo Torriti and Pietro Cavallini, both of Rome) and architects (the designers of the Fossanova and Casamari abbeys and Viterbo's Palazzo Papale). Among the most notable Early Renaissance works are Filarete's Vatican portal, Palazzo Venezia, the Sistine Chapel wall frescoes, Palazzo della Cancelleria, and Bramante's Tempietto di San Pietro in Montorio. Michelangelo and Raphael dominated the Roman (and European) art scene of the 16th century, which was also a time of great architectural undertakings such as Palazzo Farnese in Rome and Villa d'Este in Tivoli, Villa Lante of Bagnaia, the Bomarzo park, and Palazzo Farnese of Caprarola outside Rome. The 17th century was another great artistic period. Painters such as the Carracci and Caravaggio were active, while the great architect-sculptor Bernini (and his worthy rivals, Alessandro Algardi, sculptor, and Francesco Borromini, architect) were carrying out impressive projects that changed the face of Rome. In addition, this was the century when the great private collections of Rome's patrician families were being founded and enriched. The century that followed produced no especially prominent figures. The main artistic activity in the 18th century mainly involved architecture (e.g., the Trevi Fountain, Spanish Steps, facade of Santa Maria Maggiore and facade of San Giovanni in Laterano). Two outstanding artists, the sculptor Antonio Canova and the architect Giuseppe Valadier, dominated the neo-Classical years of the early 19th century. Aside from a handful of monuments such as the Vittoriano, Palazzo di Giustizia, and the Gianicolo Monument to Garibaldi the 19th century failed to produce any significant architectural achievements.

ROME

The eternal city, *caput mundi* (capital of the world), *Urbe* (City) — these are some of the names people use to describe Italy's capital and largest city. A unique artistic-historical-religious center of over two thousand years duration, Rome has oft times been likened to Athens (the other great cradle of Western civilization). Nevertheless, it differs from the Greek city in one very important respect, for the visible remains of Rome's past are not confined to a single «historical section,» but rather spread throughout her entire metropolitan area in a vital overlapping of periods and styles. Modern-day Rome, sprawling over a huge territory twenty miles from the Mediterranean, encompasses a million faces, some of which old (Roman ruins, medieval churches, as well as Renaissance and Baroque palaces), and some of which new (concrete and glass office buildings, housing developments, and midday traffic jams). Each district has its keynote: shopping and eating out (Via Veneto, Via Condotti), antiques (Via del Babuino), art galleries (Via Margutta), genuine Roman spirit (Trastevere) — the list could go on and on. Rome is also a vital cultural center, vaunting international universities and research centers, archives of unequalled value, a renowned opera house (Teatro dell'Opera) and conservatory (Accademia Musicale di Santa Cecilia), as well as the prestigious Università di Roma. As a political capital, its history goes back two thousand years, first of Antique Rome, then of the Holy Roman Empire of the West, then of the United Kingdom of Italy, and finally of the Italian Republic. As a religious capital, it is Christendom's major

View down the Tiber River with Ponte Sant'Angelo leading to Castel Sant'Angelo visible on the left of the photo.

pilgrimage center, especially when a Holy Year has been proclaimed by the Pontiff.

ROMAN FORUM - Situated at the junction of the Palatine, Capitoline, and Esquiline hills, the Roman Forum was for centuries the site of the city's most important public buildings (and thus of the city's major public events). The major sights include: the *Arch of Septimius Severus*, erected in 203 B.C. (the reliefs on its triple arch represent Rome's victories over Oriental tribes), the *Rostri*, named after their (lost) decoration of captured ship beaks, but actually a celebrated orator's

podium, the *Curia*, the brick Senate building, and the *Basilica Aemilia*, an immense Republican period building that rose alongside the Senate of which only little remains. On the Capitoline side: *Temple of Saturn* (eight granite columns and entablature) built in 497 B.C., the *Temple of Vespasian* (three corner Corinthian columns), and the *Portico degli Dei Consenti* (in honor of Olympus' twelve major deities) built in the 4th century A.D. and thus probably the last pagan monument in Rome. On the Palatine side: *Temple of Castor and Pollux* (three Corinthian columns) built in 484 B.C. in honor of the *Dioscuri*; the *Temple of Vesta*, a section of what

was originally a circular colonnade of Corinthian colums; the *House of the Vestal Virgins* (of which several statues have survived; the Vestal priestesses were responsible for seeing that the sacred fire dedicated to the goddess Vesta never went out); the *Temple of Antonine and Faustina* built in the 2nd century A.D. by the Senate in honor of Emperor Antonine Pius and his wife Faustina (the building's original pronaos of six Corinthian columns has survived as the porch of the church of *San Lorenzo in Miranda*); the *Basilica of Maxentius*, an immense building begun by Maxentius and completed by Constantine (of the 35-meter-tall aisled building, two of

Roman Forum. Above: partial view. Facing page, above: Arch of Septimius Severus and the Garden in the House of the Vestal Virgins (below).

the huge nave pillars have survived); and the *Arch of Titus* at the highest point of the *Via Sacra* that crossed the whole Forum, a single-opening triumphal arch built to commemorate Titus' late 1st century A.D. defeat of the Jews. There are also some interesting churches by the Forum, including *Santi Luca e Martina* (Curia area) designed by Pietro da Cortona in the mid-1600s, *Santa Maria Nova* also known as

Santa Francesca Romana (Basilica of Maxentius area), an 18th century church vaunting a fine 12th century mosaic, *Santa Maria Antiqua* (slopes of the Palatine), an unusual Early Christian remodeling of an Imperial Age building, and *Santi Cosma e Damiano.*

IMPERIAL FORUMS - The first of the Imperial Forums, Caesar's, was built in 54 B.C. when the Roman Forum proved too small for the capital's ever-growing public activities. Trajan's, the last to be built chronologically, ranks as the largest. An entire medieval district was torn down to make way for the *Via dei Fori Imperiali* built in 1933 to traverse Rome's greatest archeological zone. Starting from Piazza Venezia, the first forum you encounter is *Trajan's Forum* built under the supervision of Apollodorus of Damascus, the renowned architect in the emperor's service from 107 to 114 A.D. The 35-meter-tall *Trajan's Column* was built in 113 A.D. to commemorate the emperor's victory over the Dacians, probably by Apollodorus himself. It is adorned with a continuous relief that spirals approximately 200 meters around the column recounting episodes from the war (and utilizing over 2500 figures to do so). The statue of St. Peter on the top was added in the 17th century (in place of one of Trajan). *Trajan's Market*, three stories of shops and stores, once sprawled over the slopes of the Quirinal Hill (entrance from Via IV Novembre). Facing the marketplace was another of the Imperial Forums, Caesar's, which on three sides was surrounded by shops *(tabernae)*, today little more than a heap of ruins. A section of entablature sustained by three Corinthian columns is all that remains of the *Temple of Venus Genetrix*, commissioned by Caesar in fulfillment of a vow made before the Battle of Pharsalus fought in 48 B.C. *Augustus' Forum*, situated alongside the marketplace, was girthed by a massive stone wall serving to isolate it from the frequent fires which broke out in the neighboring working-class district of *Suburra*. The *Temple of Mars Ultor* (of which the base, some columns,

Left: Trajan's Column, with the Vittoriano Memorial in the background. Above: Colosseum. Following pages: bird's eye view of the Colosseum.

and sections of cella wall are extant) was built to commemorate the Roman victory in the Battle of Philippi. Of *Nerva's Forum*, only fragments have survived. These include the so-called *Colonnacce* sustaining a remarkable frieze with a relief of women laboring, originally part of a temple built in honor of Minerva, the protectress of the hearth.

COLOSSEUM - The Colosseum (actually the *Flavian Amphitheater*) ranks as Rome's greatest monument and the one which has come to be identified with the Eternal City itself. The enormous project was begun by Vespasian in 72 A.D. and inaugurated by Titus eight years later. It has

been attributed to Rabirius, the architect of Domitian's Palace. Its vital statistics are: elliptical in shape, it measures 188 × 156 meters, and is 57 meters tall. The four-story structure is wholly faced in travertine. The exterior consisted of three floors of eighty round arches in the Classical progression (Doric topped by Ionic topped by Corinthian) and an upper floor composed of a stone wall divided by pilaster strips with alternating windows. The opening was memorable (100 days of parties and shows), as was the celebration held for the 1000th anniversary of the founding of Rome in 249 A.D. (hundreds of animals, including elephants, lions, tigers, hippos, zebras, and giraffes, as well as 2000 gladiators met their death). The shows comprised mock sea battles, tournaments, and games of all kinds (despite the fact that no documentary evidence exists to back up the story of Christians being fed to the lions)

and were open to all Roman citizens. Seating was on the basis of sex and social class. The spectacles continued well into the Christian era. (Gladiator fights were outlawed by Honorius in 404 A.D., although animal combats continued for another century.) Throughout the Middle Ages, the Colosseum was used as a handy quarry. In addition, all the metal clamps between the facing blocks were removed over the centuries, leaving unsightly holes. The subterranean chambers where the animals were caged before the games may still be viewed inside.

ARCH OF CONSTANTINE - One of the best preserved of the Roman triumphal arches, this celebrated monument embodies Rome's final artistic outpouring which took place in the early 4th century A.D. It was built in 315 to commemorate Constantine's victory over Maxentius in

187

the Battle of Pons Milvius in 312. The 21-meter-tall, 25-meter-long triple arch contains statues and reliefs from pre-existing buildings, framed by immense Corinthian pillars: the eight *statues of Dacians* over the columns originally adorned Trajan's Forum, the *medallion* with hunting and sacrifice scenes date from the early 2nd century A.D., while the uppermost *reliefs of battle scenes and imperial triumphs* belonged to a building erected to commemorate Marcus Aurelius. Nearby was the *Meta Sudans*, a cone-shaped fountain built in the 1st century A.D. (of which only the base has been restored).

PALATINE - The hill believed by the Romans to be the site of Romulus' mythical founding of the city is actually, according to modern scholars, where the earliest settlements (9th-8th centuries B.C.) rose. Later it became an exclusive residential district (with a sumptuous imperial palace and numerous patrician villas). During the Renaissance period (16th century) most of it was transformed into the Farnese family estate, i.e., the so-called *Orti Farnesiani*. Remains of the *Palazzo Imperiale*, erected by Domitian in the late 1st century A.D. over pre-existing buildings, have survived. These include: the 160-meter-long *Stadium; Domus Flavia*, and *Domus Augustana*, the majestic palace overlooking the Circus Maximus built as Augustus's private residence. Other sights on the Palatine include the *Temple of Cybel*, built in 204 B.C. in honor of *Magna Mater* (= Mother Earth), the *House of Livia* (Augustus' wife), in which several interesting frescoes are extant, and the Circus Maximus: the biggest of the Roman circuses.

SANTA MARIA D'ARACOELI – The church rises on the spot where the Sibyl supposedly prophesized the coming of the Son of God to the Emperor Augustus. A stairway leads up to the plain 14th century facade. Inside are some fine 15th century works, including frescoes by Pinturicchio and tombs by Donatello and Andrea Bregno.

CAMPIDOGLIO – On the Campidoglio (or Capitoline Hill), the acropolis of ancient Rome, rose the temples of Capitoline Jupiter and Juno Moneta facing in the direction of the Roman Forum. Remodeled by Michelangelo in the 16th century, the square has since served as the city's political center (and today hosts Rome's city hall). The great ramp leads up to the remarkable *Piazza del Campidoglio*. On the far end is *Palazzo Senatorio* which rises on the site of the *Tabularium* (Roman state archives). Apart from its fine external staircase (designed by Michelangelo himself), the palace was executed between 1582 and 1605 by Giacomo Della Porta and Girolamo Rainaldi. The twin buildings opposite it, *Palazzo dei Con-*

Left: Arch of Constantine. Above right: Roman stadium. Below: Santa Maria d'Aracoeli.

servatori on the right and *Palazzo Nuovo* on the left, were both designed by Michelangelo. Today they are museum buildings (Musei Capitolini). In the center of the square is Michelangelo's base for the *equestrian statue of Marcus Aurelius*, the celebrated 2nd century A.D. gilded bronze that for centuries served as the prototype for equestrian monuments.

MUSEI CAPITOLINI - Started around a bequest by Pope Sixtus IV in 1471 (and thus the oldest public collection in existence), it has been divided into three separate museums. The *Museo dei Conservatori*, one of the world's finest collections of Greek and Roman art, features sculpture, ceramics, mosaics, sarcophagi, etc. Its highlights include: *Apollo with a Bow*, a 5th century Greek original, a colossal statue of *Athena*, a copy of a 430 B.C. original by Cresilas, the so-called 1st century B.C. *Esquiline Venus*, and fragments of a *colossal statue of Constantine* (courtyard). The collection in the *Pinacoteca Capitolina* focuses mainly on 16th-18th century painting. Among the most noteworthy: Titian (*Baptism of Christ*, dated 1512, Lorenzo Lotto (*Portrait of a Soldier*, c. 1522), Rubens (*Romulus and Remus Nurtured by the She-Wolf*), and Caravaggio (*St. John* and the *Fortune-Teller*, both youthful works). Several notable works adorn the rest of Palazzo dei Conservatori. In settings of frescoes, tapestries, and carved wooden ceilings are statues of *Urban VIII* by Bernini and *Innocent X* by Algardi, *Boy Removing a Thorn* (1st century B.C. bronze), and the celebrated Etruscan *Lupa Capitolina* (6th-5th century B.C.), a bronze statue of a she-wolf that for centuries was the symbol of Rome. (The figures of the twins were added on by Antonio del Pollaiolo in the 15th century.) The *Museo Capitolino* hosts another extraordinary collection of Greek and Roman art. It contains some celebrated works such as the *Capitoline Venus*, a copy of a Hellenistic work, the *Dying Gaul*, marble version of a 3rd century B.C. Pergamon school bronze.

Left: Capitoline Venus, Roman copy of a Hellenistic original, in the Musei Capitolini. Above: Fontana del Tritone, Bernini's stupendous fountain.

FONTANA DEL TRITONE - This celebrated fountain, designed by Bernini in 1463, stands in the middle of bustling *Piazza Barberini*. It consists of a triton (sea god) atop an immense oyster in turn sustained by dolphins. On the dolphins' tails is the emblem of Pope Urban VIII Barberini who commissioned the project.

Above left: Trevi Fountain. Below left: Tiberine Isle. Above: Spanish Steps in Piazza di Spagna.

TREVI FOUNTAIN - The most celebrated of the seemingly countless Roman fountains, it takes up practically all of the minute Piazza di Trevi. The fountain was built in 1762 over the terminal point of a Roman aqueduct. Its architect, Nicola Salvi, conceived it as a natural scenario of cliffs and falls framed against an almost triumphal arch background in the neo-Classical style. In the center is an oversize *statue of the god Oceanus drawn by seahorses* sculpted by Pietro Bracci.

PIAZZA DI SPAGNA - The hour glass-shaped square is one of the most popular spots in the city. The fountain in the center of the square, the *Fontana della Barcaccia*, was designed by Pietro Bernini, father of the great Gian Lorenzo, in 1629. The stairs, the celebrated *Spanish Steps*, were built in 1726 by Francesco de Sanctis. At the top is an Egyptian obelisk, the so-called *Obelisco Sallustiano*, as well as a church, *Trinità dei Monti*, with a 16th century facade by Maderno.

PIAZZA DEL POPOLO - The square as we see it today was designed in the early 1800s by Giuseppe Valadier. In the middle is a 12th century B.C. obelisk, the *Obelisco Flaminio*, which was moved here from the Circus Maximus in 1589. On the Corso side of the square are twin churches, *Santa Maria di Montesanto* and *Santa Maria dei Miracoli*, designed by Carlo Rainaldi (and completed by Bernini) in the 17th century. Across the way Valadier built two twin buildings, one of which conceals a Renaissance church, *Santa Maria del Popolo*, a veritable treasure house of art works. A list of the church highlights includes: *frescoes* by Pinturicchio, *Renaissance tombs* by Andrea Bregno; two masterpieces by Caravaggio, the *Conversion of St. Paul* and the *Martyrdom of St. Peter* (c. 1602); and the *Cappella Chigi* by Raphael.

TIBERINE ISLAND - The islet, dedicated by the Romans to the god of medicine, Aesculapius, was turned into a hospital (Ospedale di San Giovanni di Dio), in the 16th century. The church of *San Bartolomeo* opposite it was built in the 17th century. The nearby bridges are the *Pons Fabricius*, built in 62 B.C., the *Pons Cestius*, built in 46 B.C., and the 16th century *Ponte Rotto*.

Left: Piazza Navona with the 17th century Fontana del Moro in the foreground. Above: Pantheon.

PIAZZA NAVONA - One of the most picturesque in Rome, this Baroque square rises on the site of the Stadium of Domitian repeating its exact dimensions (240 × 65 meters) and shape. It is adorned with three monumental fountains: the *Fontana del Moro* executed in the mid 17th century by Giovanni Antonio Mari (based, however, on a drawing by Bernini), the *Fontana del Nettuno* (19th century), and the *Fontana dei Fiumi* in the center, one of Bernini's greatest works, built in 1651. (The figures around it are personifications of the *Danube, Ganges, Nile*, and *Rio della Plata Rivers*.) Opposite it is

the church of *Sant'Agnese in Agone*, started by Carlo and Girolamo Rainaldi in 1652 and completed by Borromini in 1657.

PANTHEON - This remarkable domed building has survived almost two thousand years of history virtually intact. The original rectangular temple built by Augustus' son-in-law Agrippa in 27 B.C. was turned into the pronaos of the present-day building when, in 120 A.D., Hadrian had it greatly enlarged. The *pronaos* consists of sixteen ten-meter-tall columns, each topped by a Corinthian capital. The *interior* is a circle whose diameter and height are equal (43.3 meters). The five-register lacunar *dome* ends in a central 9-meter-wide aperture. The

building which the ancient Romans dedicated to the Pantheon (= all gods) became the burial place of Italian personages.

PIAZZA DEL QUIRINALE - On the top of the Quirinal, the highest of the seven hills of Rome, is a lovely square, Piazza del Quirinale. One side of the square is taken up by the *Palazzo del Quirinale*, formerly the residence of popes and kings and today the home of the president of the Italian republic. Several architects (e.g., Mascherino, Fontana, Maderno, Bernini, Fuga) worked on the project during its long gestation period (from 1574 to 1735). The richly appointed interior was frescoed by Melozzo da Forlì and Guido Reni.

197

SAN GIOVANNI IN LATERANO -

The oldest church in Christendom, San Giovanni has been the Cathedral of Rome for almost 20 centuries. The striking *main facade* designed by Alessandro Galilei in 1735 marks the midpoint between Roman Baroque and neo-Classical. The *interior* was partially remodeled by Borromini on occasion of the 1650 Holy Year celebrations. He redid the nave and double-aisle section, whereas the transept dating from the century before was left unaltered. The superb *tabernacle* in the transept is a mid-14th century work by Giovanni di Stefano.

SANTA MARIA MAGGIORE -

Of the great basilicas of Rome, Santa Maria has best preserved its original Early Christian structure. Its 75-meter Romanesque *belltower* (dated 1377) is the tallest in the city. The five-arch *facade* was designed in 1750 by Ferdinando Fuga. Inside the loggia are superb mosaics originally part ot the late 13th century facade. The stately single-aisle *interior* is lined with fine Ionic columns. It vaunts notable Cosmati floor mosaics (12th century) and a fine coffered *ceiling*. Its most remarkable feature, however, is its *mosaic decoration*: 36 panels executed in the 5th century (walls and nave arch) and others designed by Jacopo Torriti in 1295 (apse).

SAN PIETRO IN VINCOLI -

Founded in the 5th century to house a precious relic, i.e., the chains (= *vincoli*) that supposedly bound St. Peter when he was imprisoned by the Romans, the church has a plain facade preceded by a portico (1475). Its most noteworthy feature is Michelangelo's *Moses* located in the right transept. The statue was supposed to be part of a gigantic undertaking, Julius II's elaborate tomb in the Vatican, to which Michelagelo devoted three years of his life (1513-1516). However, Leo X, Julius' successor, never allowed him to complete the project.

Above left: San Giovanni in Laterano. Below: Santa Maria Maggiore. Right: Michelangelo's Moses, in San Pietro in Vincoli.

SAN PAOLO FUORI LE MURA -
The second largest basilica in Rome was founded in the 4th century on the site of St. Paul's tomb. Remodeled over the centuries, it was completely destroyed in 1823 and subsequently rebuilt. The huge building (132 × 65 meters) is preceded by a great quadriporticus. The double-aisle *interior* is adorned with a frieze of *mosaic portraits of popes*. A notable *ciborium* crafted by Arnolfo di Cambio in 1285 and *apse mosaic* attest to the artistic quality of the lost medieval church. The remarkable *cloister* is by Vassalletto (1214).

SAN PIETRO IN MONTORIO -
Inside the Renaissance church are two notable tombs sculpted by Bartolomeo Ammannati around 1550 and an outstanding *Flagellation* painted by Sebastiano del Piombo in 1518. In the church courtyard is one of the most celebrated examples of High Renaissance architecture, Bramante's *Tempietto*, a round building encircled by Doric columns and crowned by a dome.

Above: nave of San Paolo Fuori le Mura. Left: Bramante's Tempietto in San Pietro in Montorio.

SANTA MARIA IN COSMEDIN -
The Romanesque church was founded in the 6th century (and rebuilt in the 12th). Inside are notable Cosmati school works: the floor, a baldacchino, and a *schola cantorum*. In the portico is the stone mask known as the *Bocca della Verità* (literally, mouth of truth) since, the story goes, any liar who dares put his hand inside will have it bitten off.

SAN CARLO ALLE QUATTRO FONTANE -
This tiny elliptical-shaped building represents Borromini's first work (the plan: 1638) and his last (the *facade*: 1667). Interestingly, its plan was derived from that of a single pillar of St. Peter's dome.

SANTA CECILIA IN TRASTEVERE -
The original church was founded before the 5th century on the site of a Roman dwelling (perhaps the home of Cecilia, a 2nd century Roman martyr). Remodeled by Paschal I in the 9th century, it has since undergone several restoration campaigns. In the vestibule is the 15th century *Tomb of Cardinal Forteguerri* by Mino da Fiesole, while in the choir are two celebrated sculptures: Arnolfo di Cambio's *Ciborium* (1283) and Stefano Maderno's *St. Cecilia*.

SANTA MARIA IN TRASTEVERE -
The first church in Rome to be dedicated to the Virgin Mary, Santa Maria was built by Calixtus in the 3rd century and remodeled many times over the centuries.

CATACOMBS -
The catacombs, actually the early Christians' subterranean burial chambers, are mostly clustered around the Appian Way. They consist of networks of underground tunnels, often on several levels, out of which *loculi* (the simplest tombs) are dug or else fashioned into cubicles or crypts to hold sarcophagi. The best known are the *Catacombs of St. Calixtus, St. Sebastian*, and *Domitilla*.

Above: Santa Maria in Cosmedin.
Right: San Carlo alle Quattro Fontane.

GALLERIA BORGHESE - This unique private collection, housed in a charming 17th century building, the *Casino Borghese*, became property of the Italian state in 1902. Ground floor (sculpture): *Paolina Borghese* (Napoleon's sister) portrayed as Venus Victrix, Canova's celebrated sculpture of 1805); *David*, by Bernini (the face is a self-portrait of the master, 1624); *Apollo and Daphne* (1624) and *Rape of Proserpine*, another youthful work by Bernini (1622). Upstairs: painting by Raphael (Deposition, dated 1507), Caravaggio (*Boy with a Basket, David with the Head of Goliath, St. Jerome*, and the celebrated *Madonna dei Palafrenieri* painted in 1605-1606), Titian (including the celebrated *Sacred and Profane Love*, dated 1516), and Antonello da Messina (*Portrait of a Gentleman*, dated 1473).

Galleria Borghese. Above: Canova's Paolina Borghese. Below: Raphael's Deposition.

MUSEO NAZIONALE DI VILLA GIULIA

The collection focuses on pre-Roman art in Lazio. The highlights include: a reconstructed *tomb from Cerveteri* (6th century B.C.), *Apollo* and *Heracles*, late 6th century B.C. Etruscan statues from Veii, and the *Sarcofago degli Sposi*, a remarkable Etruscan terracotta dating from the 6th century B.C. unearthed at Cerveteri. In addition there are dozens of bronze figurines and ceramic vases, including a 5th and 4th century B.C. vase, a 7th century B.C. *oinochoe*, several *ciste* (typical of the Palestrina area) among which the superb 4th century B.C. *Ficoroni Cista*, and jewelry, including two exquisite Oriental-style *pectorals*. Lastly, the collection includes *ivories* and *bronzes* from Palestrina.

GALLERIA DORIA-PAMPHILJ

One of the world's major private collections, it was started in the 17th century by Pope Innocent X Pamphilj, continued by his descendants, and, when the Pamphilj line died out, by the Doria family. It is housed in a grandiose Rococo mansion, *Palazzo Doria*, with a Renaissance courtyard. Most of the works are still hanging in the places selected by the original collectors; many are famous masterpieces. Among the Italians: Titian (*Spain Coming to the Aid of Religion* and *Herodiad*), Tintoretto, Correggio, Raphael *(Double Portrait)*, Caravaggio (*Mary Magdalene, St. John,* and *Rest on the Flight into Egypt,* a youthful work still a long way from the shockingly realistic treatment of his mature works), Carracci, Savoldo, Mattia Preti, Parmigianino, and Salvator Rosa. Among the foreign masters, the most important are Velazquez (*Portrait of Innocent X*, dated 1650), Claude Lorrain (five *mythological landscapes*), Rubens *(Portrait of a Franciscan Monk)*, Metsys, and Breughel. There is also noteworthy sculpture, including three *busts of Innocent X* (two by Bernini and one by Algardi).

Galleria Borghese. Above: Caravaggio's St. Jerome. Right: Bernini's Daphne and Apollo.

gustus, one of the finest Roman sculptures extant, *Sleeping Hermaphrodite*, copy of a Hellenistic original, as well as the celebrated *frescoes* from Livia's house at Prima Porta (1st century B.C.).

MUSEO DI PALAZZO VENEZIA - Despite its crenelation and massive forms making it resemble a medieval castle, this building dated c. 1455 is the earliest example of Renaissance architecture in Rome. The collections comprise ceramics, furnishings, tapestries, silver, as well as *paintings* (Gozzoli, school of Giorgione, Paolo Veneziano) and *sculpture* (Arnolfo di Cambio, Mino da Fiesole, Tino di Camaino, Nicola Pisano).

PALAZZO BARBERINI - The grandiose palace was commissioned by Urban VIII (in 1624), begun by Carlo Maderno, continued by Borromini, and completed by Bernini (in 1633). It houses the 13th to 18th century section of the *Galleria Nazionale d'Arte Antica*. The painters represented include: Simone Martini, Fra Angelico, Filippo Lippi (youthful *Virgin and Child, Annunciation*), Lorenzo Lotto, Agnolo Bronzino, Raphael (*La Fornarina*, dated 1516), El Greco, Tintoretto, Titian, Hans Holbein the younger (*portrait of Henry VIII*), Caravaggio (*Judith and Holfernes*), Guardi (*Giudecca Canal, Landscape with Ruins*), and Bellotto.

ARA PACIS AUGUSTAE - The temple was commissioned by the Senate of Rome to commemorate the *Pax Augustae* (Peace of Augustus) proclaimed by Augustus throughout the empire in 14 B.C. It consists of a sacrificial altar around which is an enclosure adorned with ornamental friezes surmounted by stupendous reliefs of processions.

MUSEO NAZIONALE ROMANO - The museum building was once a monastery. It contains some of the greatest Greek and Roman masterpieces. Among the most important works are: the *Athena Parthenos*, a Roman copy of Phidias' original 5th century B.C. Parthenon statue, *Gaul about to commit suicide after having killed his wife*, a copy of a Pergamum bronze (3rd century B.C.), the so-called *Ludovisi Throne*, an extraordinary 5th century B.C. work, the *Tiber Apollo*, a Roman copy of a 5th century Greek original, attributed to Phidias, the *Discobolos Lancellotti, Niobe's Daughter from the Horti Sallustiani*, copy of a Greek mid-5th century B.C. original, *Boxer at Rest*, an original Hellenistic bronze signed by Apollonius, the *Sacrifice of Au-

CASTEL SANT'ANGELO - This massive building, looking like a medieval castle, rises on the site of *Hadrian's Mausoleum*. Most of the original floorplan and sections of the original building have survived. Built in 130 A.D. as the emperor's tomb, it had an immense square base on top of which was a circular drum structure. Then, in 271, Aurelian had it remodeled as a fort. Its name, literally, Castle of the Holy Angel, dates from 590 when an angel foretelling the end of a terrible plague epidemic reputedly appeared on its summit. Throughout the Middle Ages, it served as the popes' stronghold-prison, providing convenient shelter in the case of enemy attack. In the 15th century the great corner bastions were added on and the drum, devoid of its marble facing, was raised. A statue of the angel was set up in place of one of the emperor on top of the building. (The present-day angel is an 18th century work.) The vast five story *interior* is composed of an intricate web of rooms and corridors

dating from various periods. Among the most interesting sights are the *spiral staircase* leading to the emperors' burial chamber preserved virtually intact, the *Cortile dell'Angelo*, a picturesque medieval courtyard still containing medieval ammunitions, and the *Armory*, containing an extensive collection of weapons from various places and periods. Another interesting section is the *Papal Suite*, which was remodeled and sumptuously refurbished by Baccio da Montelupo, Perin del Vaga, and other 16th century masters who received the commission from Pope Paul III.

VATICAN CITY - The importance of the 108-acre Vatican is inversely proportional to its size. It ranks as the smallest independent state in the world, as any self-respecting stamp collector knows. Vatican City covers the Vatican Hill lying between Monte Mario and the Janiculum. In the 1st century B.C. it was the site of Caligula's circus - where Nero had hundreds of Christians martyred

Above: Castel Sant'Angelo. Right: bird's eye view of Vatican City.

some years after. The church rises on the spot where one of Nero's victims, St. Peter, was buried. Over the years other buildings grew up around it. The Vatican, independent starting from the 8th century, was of primary importance throughout the Middle Ages. The Papal State expanded to such an extent that, until the unity of Italy when it was wiped off the Italian political scene, it covered practically all of Central Italy. It only regained an independent political status in 1929 (as a state with less than a half a square kilometer of territory).

ST. PETER'S SQUARE - Bernini created a striking scenic effect by enclosing the square inside a gigantic, four-pillar-deep colonnade. The uninspiring boulevard leading to the square, *Via della Conciliazione*, was built in 1937. Bernini worked on the

colonnade which girths two sides of the perfectly elliptical shaped, 240-meter-wide open space between 1656 and 1667. It is composed of 284 pillars surmounted by 140 *statues of saints and martyrs*. On either side are grandiose *fountains* de-signed by Carlo Maderno. The Egyptian *obelisk* in the center, brought to Rome from Heliopolis by Caligula to adorn his circus, was set up on its present site in 1586 — an undertaking so arduous that, according to the records, it took over

Above: St. Peter's. Right: nave of St. Peter's with Bernini's Baldacchino visible at the crossing.

four months and required the efforts of over one thousand men and beasts of burden.

ST. PETER'S BASILICA - The greatest church in Christendom originated in 324 as a shrine for the mortal remains of St. Peter. The building we see today took hundreds of years to complete. The earliest version of the basilica had a double aisle plan with a facade characterized by a portico and mosaic decoration. In the 15th century, when landslides threatened the building's stability, Nicholas V had it torn down, at the same time commissioning Bernardo Rossellino to design a new one. When Nicholas died, work was suspended and the project was not resumed until 1506 when Bramante, commissioned by Julius II, began working on his design entailing a Greek-cross plan. Bramante — who never completed his project — was succeeded by Raphael, Antonio da Sangallo, Peruzzi, and Michelangelo. Michelangelo designed the *dome*, the biggest ever built, in 1574, basing himself partially on Bramante's own plans and partially on Brunelleschi's dome on the Florence cathedral. (It was finished, however, sixteen years

later by Domenico Fontana and Giacomo Della Porta.) In the 17th century, Carlo Maderno was commissioned to enlarge the church, which he did by extending the nave — thereby turning it into a Latin cross. Maderno's imposing *facade* was erected in 1614. A portico decorated with statues of popes precedes the church proper, which has five entrance portals. The one on the far right, the *Porta Santa*, is opened only on occasion of Holy Year celebrations, the middle one, the *Porta del Filarete*, vaults superb bronze reliefs cast by Filarete in 1433, while the one on the far left, *Porta della Morte*, is the work of a contemporary Italian master, Giacomo Manzù (1964). The *interior* conveys an impression of remarkable harmony despite truly gigantic dimensions (length: 210 m, width at the transepts: 137 m, height at the nave: 44 m, and dome height: 136 m). Eight pairs of immense pillars line the nave. By the last one on the righthand side is a celebrated bronze effigy of *St. Peter*. The much-venerated statue, dated around the mid-

dle of the 13th century, has been attributed to Arnolfo di Cambio. In the left aisle is the *Tomb of Innocent VIII* by Antonio del Pollaiolo (1498), while opposite, in the first chapel on the right aisle is Michelangelo's stupendous *Pietà*. Sculpted when the master was only twenty-five years old for a French prelate, it is the sole work that bears his signature. Beneath the *dome* (which can be climbed) are the *Pope's Altar* and *Confession*, i.e., a semicircle area marked by a railing where ninety-nine perpetual lights are kept burning over *St. Peter's Tomb*. Above the altar is the impressive bronze *Baldacchino* that Bernini conceived as a processional canopy (in lieu of the more traditional ciborium) sustained by oversize twisted columns (1624-1633). In the tribune is another of Bernini's striking Baroque creations, the gilded bronze *Throne of St. Peter* (1656-1665), flanked by two superb tombs. On the left is the *Tomb of Paul III* crafted by Guglielmo Della Porta in 1575, while on the right is Bernini's *Tomb of Urban VIII* dated 1646. Four

colossal statues adorn the dome pillars. (The *St. Longinus* holding a spear is also by Bernini.) In the right transept is the *Tomb of Clement XIII* sculpted by Canova in 1792, while in the left one is a late work by Bernini, the *Tomb of Alexander VII*, dated 1678. In the adjoining chapel is a fine marble altarpiece depicting *St. Leo's encounter with Attila* sculpted by Algardi in 1650. Other notable works are preserved in the *Museo-Tesoro di San Pietro*. The most significant include: a *ciborium* by Donatello (1432), the *Tomb of Sixtus IV*, a masterpiece of Renaissance sculpture executed by Antonio del Pollaiolo in 1493, and a celebrated Early Christian sculputre, the *sarcophagus of Junius Bassus*, (4th century). In the underground chambers, the so-called *Grotte Vaticane*, are tombs of popes, sarcophagi, and other monuments.

VATICAN MUSEUMS - The incredible Vatican collections — among which the world's greatest collection of Classical art — occupy a complex of buildings comprising over 1400 rooms and 20 courtyards. MUSEO PIO CLEMENTINO. The high-lights of the Vatican's Greek and Roman collection include: the celebrated *Belvedere Torso*, perhaps representing Hercules, a late 1st century B.C. work by Apollonius of Nestor which was unearthed in the 15th century and much admired by Michelangelo, *Meleagrus*, a Roman copy of a 4th century B.C. sculpture by Scopas, *Apollo killing a lizard, Satyr at rest*, and *Venus of Knidus*, all Roman copies of Praxiteles 4th century B.C. originals, *Sleeping Arianna* a refined 2nd century B.C. Hellenistic work, the *Wounded Amazon*, Roman copy of a Phidias original (5th century B.C.9, the *Laöcoon*, a celebrated marble group dating from the late Hellenistic period which came to light in the Domus Aurea (1st century B.C.), the extraordinary *Belvedere Apollo*, a Roman copy of a 4th century original by Leocares,

and *Athlete grooming himself*, a Roman copy of a 4th century B.C. Lysippus. MUSEO CHIARAMONTI. Two great masterpieces, the *Prima Porta Augustus*, a late 1st century B.C. Roman work, and the *Spear-Holder* a Roman copy of a

5th century B.C. Polycletus. PINACOTECA VATICANA. The collection includes: Giotto's *Stefaneschi Altarpiece*, commissioned in 1300 for the main altar of the old basilica of St. Peter's, a painting by Fra Angelico (*scenes from the life of*

Vatican Museums. Above: Raphael's Adoration of the Magi. Below: Laöcoon. Right: Caravaggio's Deposition.

St. Nicholas, predella), Melozzo da Forlì (*Sixtus IV and Platina,* detached fresco, and the celebrated *Music-Making Angels*); paintings by Raphael (the *Virgin of Foligno,* 1513, commissioned as an ex-voto offering by a prelate in the entourage of Julius II, the *Transfiguration,* Raphael's last work and by some judged his finest dated 1520, and the *Coronation of the Virgin*); Leonardo's unfinished *St. Jerome* that is nevertheless a remarkably effective painting; Giovanni Bellini's *Pietà* (c. 1474) which is the upper section of the Pesaro Altarpiece. Works by Veronese, Titian (*Virgin and Child with saints*), Paris Bordone (*St. George and the Dragon*), Annibale and Ludovico Carracci, Federico Barocci, Guercino, Domenichino (*Communion of St. Jerome,* dated 1614), Guido Reni (*Crucifixion of St. Peter*), Caravaggio (the moving *Deposition* of 1604, formerly in Santa Maria in Vallicella), Orazio Gentileschi, van Dyck, Pietro da Cortona, Rubens, Poussin.

Sistine Chapel. Left: view from the entrance. Above: detail of Michelangelo's ceiling frescoes: God creating the sun and the moon.

RAPHAEL'S STANZE

RAPHAEL'S STANZE - The decoration of the Vatican rooms known as the «Stanze» was carried out by Raphael and his helpers in the early 16th century under a commission by Julius II. Their subjects are: the *Disputa,* the *School of Athens* (which shows the greatest philosophers of all times portrayed around Plato and Aristotle), and *Parnassus* in the *Stanza della Segnatura*; the *Mass of Bolsena* the *Expulsion of Heliodorus from the Temple,* and the *Deliverance of St. Peter* in the *Stanza di Eliodoro.* Nearby is the remarkable *Loggia of Raphael,* a long gallery composed of thirteen bays, adorned with paintings by Raphael's pupils.

SISTINE CHAPEL

SISTINE CHAPEL - The conclave of cardinals meets to elect the new pope beneath Michelangelo's stirring frescoes. The earliest frescoes, those along the walls, date from 1481. They recount the *life of Moses* (left) and *Christ* (right) in twelve panels painted by some of the major figures of 15th century painting: Perugino, Pinturicchio, Botticelli, Cosimo Rosselli, and Ghirlandaio. Michelangelo, commissioned by Julius II to decorate the ceiling, carried out the job — without any help — in only four years (1508-1512). The iconographic scheme is vast, starting with the *Creation* and continuing up to the *Redemption of Mankind.* Dozens of figures are artfully set into the architecture, painted and not. These include: seven *Prophets* and five *Sibyls* (spandrals), twenty-two *forerunners of Christ* (lunettes over the windows), *saviors of the Hebrew people* (Esther, Judith, David), as well as several *nude figures* on the arcades bordering the Old Testament scenes whose meaning is unknown. The subjects of the scenes in the nine rectangles in the center of the ceiling are: *Separation of Light and Darkness, Creation of the Universe, Separation of Land and Sea* and *Creation of the Animals, Creation of Adam, Creation of Eve, Fall of Man* and *Expulsion from Paradise, Noah's Sacrifice, the Flood* and the *Drunkenness of Noah.* On the end wall is Michelangelo's dramatic *Last Judgment,* painted on a commission from Paul III, more than twenty years later (1536-1541). The complex composition involving 391 figures is wholly dominated by the stern figure of *Christ the Judge,* above which are angels and martyrs bearing symbols of their martyrdom

215

and below which are angels with trumpets, with the elect going to heaven on the left and the damned being hauled off to hell on the right. At Christ's feet is the figure of St. Bartolomew who met his martyrdom by being flayed alive. The caricatured face in the folds of the skin held by the saint is supposedly a self-portrait of Michelangelo.

Paintings by Michelangelo in the Sistine Chapel. Above: Temptation and Adam and Eve being expelled from Paradise. Below: section of the ceiling. Right: Michelangelo's Last Judgment on the far wall.

TIVOLI

Tivoli is situated on a hillside by the banks of the Aniene River. Among the Roman personages who sojourned in the splendid villas built as the patricians' country homes were Julius Caesar, Augustus, and Trajan. Hadrian's Villa, located in the environs, was the most celebrated in ancient Rome. Roman Tivoli was also renowned as the site of numerous temples, although little remains even of the largest which was consecrated to Hercules.

VILLA D'ESTE - The villa was originally a monastery that Cardinal Ippolito I D'Este commissioned Pirro Ligorio to remodel as his personal residence. The project (1550), took the Neapolitan architect almost twenty years to complete. Roman school painters such as Zuccari, Agresti, and Muziano, to name the most prominent, were commissioned with the fresco decoration. The park, with its over five hundred fountains, is considered one of the finest example of the so-called «giardino all'Italiana.»

HADRIAN'S VILLA - (6 km). The villa commissioned by Hadrian, among the most cultured of the Roman emperors, was built between 118 and 134 A.D. Of note are the *Pecile*, an immense quadriporticus (232 × 97 meters) around a pool and the *Island Nympheum*, encircled by a portico of Ionic columns and a kind of moat. The tiny villa which once stood on the island (today a heap of ruins) is believed to have been Hadrian's personal residence. The most interesting remains of the maze-like *Imperial Palace* belong to the huge peristyle known as *Piazza d'Oro* and an elegant hall known as the *Sala dei Pilastri Dorici.* The *Canopus*, a pool in the middle of a natural valley, was named after the place near Alexandria in Egypt that inspired it.

Above: Fontana dell'Ovato, in the garden of Villa d'Este. Below: Canopus Pool of Hadrian's Villa.

VITERBO

Settled by the Etruscans, Viterbo only became a prominent center in the Middle Ages, during which time, however, it was the scene of fierce power struggles. Two local families, the Gatti and Di Vico, alternated in ruling the city whose sympathies correspondingly seesawed from Guelph to Ghibelline. Between 1145 and 1280 Viterbo was often the residence of the popes. During this time (and thereafter as well), the majority of its medieval palaces and churches were built.

CATHEDRAL - Viterbo's cathedral is situated in charming *Piazza San Lorenzo* surrounded by fine medieval buildings such as the Palazzo Papale and an elegant 13th century dwelling. Consecrated in the 13th century, the church sports a Renaissance *facade* (1570). Alongside is its fine 14th century *belltower*. The *interior* with its fine monolithic columns surmounted by elegant carved capitals and Cosmati floor has been restored to its original Romanesque appearance.

PALAZZO PAPALE - This striking Gothic building, once the residence of the popes and today that of the archbishop of Viterbo, dates from around the middle of the 13th century. The palace, reached by way of a staircase, is flanked by a delightful *Gothic loggia* composed of paired columns. Inside is a historical hall, the *Salone dei Conclavi*.

MEDIEVAL DISTRICT - Viterbo's picturesque medieval district still looks like a 13th century city. Its main thoroughfare, *Via San Pellegrino*, is lined with remarkable old buildings, many of which sport so-called *profferli* (i.e., outside stairs ending in a balcony). Another charming sight is *Piazza San Pellegrino*, hardly changed since the 13th century.

Above: Cathedral. Right: Palazzo Papale, the Gothic residence of the popes.

TARQUINIA

This attractive town located not far from the Tyrrhenian coast vaunts numerous sights, including notable documentation of its Etruscan past. The *Museo Nazionale Tarquiniese*, with collections mainly devoted to Etruscology, is housed in a *Palazzo Vitelleschi*, a Renaissance style building with marked Late Gothic influxes completed in 1439. The exhibits comprise painted *Etruscan sarcophagi*, locally-crafted and imported (mainly from Greece and Egypt) pottery, and the celebrated *Winged Horses*, 3rd century terracotta reliefs. In addition there are several *frescoes* detached from nearby tombs, the most noteworthy

of which come from the 5th century B.C. *Tomba del Triclinio*. The palace antechapel and chapel are adorned with 15th century frescoes and paintings, among which a Filippo Lippi. Other notable Tarquinia monuments are the *Duomo* and the church of *San Francesco*. Inside the fine 12th century Romanesque basilica of *Santa Maria di Castello* are remains of Cosmati *mosaics*, a Roman sarcophagus turned into a medieval *baptismal font*, a pulpit, and a *ciborium*. The *Etruscan necropolis*, contains tombs dating from the 7th to 3rd centuries B.C. (of which approximately sixty with their paint decoration extant). Among the most

noteworthy: *Tomba della Caccia e della Pesca* (6th century), *Tomba dei Giocolieri* (6th-5th centuries), *Tomba dei Tori* (the oldest, dating from the 7th century), *Tomba dei Leopardi* (5th century), *Tomba dell'Orco* (4th-3rd centuries) which features a noteworthy portrait of a woman, *Tomba Cardarelli*, *Tomba della Leonessa*, both of which adorned with scenes of dancers, and the *Tomba del Tifone*, one of the largest and latest (2nd century). The finest of all, the late 6th century B.C. *Tomba del Barone*, sports scenes of horseback riders, a flute-player, as well as allegorical animal figures.

ABRUZZO

Abruzzo is mostly mountainous, although in the middle of the region there is a sizable area of rolling plains. There are three mountains of notable height (Laga, Maiella, and Grand Sasso), the 2912-meter-tall Corno Grande del Gran Sasso, being the highest peak of the Apennine Range. The local fauna and flora are well protected in the Parco Nazionale d'Abruzzo, one of Italy's most beautiful national parks.

HISTORY - Recent archeological finds in several grottoes in the Marsica and Gran Sasso areas show that Abruzzo was settled by the prehistoric era (Paleolithic and Neolithic). Even more interesting excavations have documented the later settlers of the regions, i.e., the numerous Italic tribes who inhabited the valleys, plateau lands, and coast starting from the 11th-10th century B.C. When Rome rose to power, however, the tribes were no match for her military superiority and rapidly succumbed (3rd-1st century B.C.). Thereafter, they shared the vicissitudes of the Empire up to the time of the Barbarian invasions. Under the Longobards (6th-8th centuries), Abruzzo was split up between the duchies of Spoleto and Benevento. In 843 it was granted the status of a free county. Under the Normans and then Swabians (after the 12th century), it came under the imperial sphere of influence. Abruzzo's borders with the Papal State were drawn up at the River Tronto, and these remained unaltered for centuries. In 1268, the defeat of Corradino of Swabia at Tagliacozzo left the way open for the Anjous. Thereafter, Abruzzo became part of the Kingdom of Naples until October 1860.

Preceding page, left: flute player, fresco in the Tomba del Triclinio in Tarquinia. Right: genre scenes frescoed in the Tomba della Caccia e Pesca.

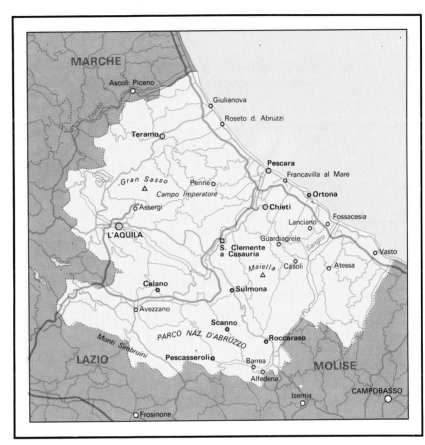

ART - The most important documentation of Italic art is the celebrated Warrior of Capestrano, today in the Museum of Chieti, although there are other outstanding Italic and Roman pieces spread throughout the region. These include statuary, remains of temples (e.g., Iuvanum, Mt. Morrone), theaters (Chieti, Teramo), and excavations of settlements. Although documentary evidence points to Sulmona as the major Roman center in Abruzzo, the most important excavations have been made in the area of Avezzano where the Roman city of Alba Fucens has been brought to light. Few remains of the Longobard and Byzantine periods have survived. Starting, however, from the 12th century, the influence of the monasteries and the interest shown by Emperor Federik II for the region (which entailed the founding of L'Aquila in 1254) contributed to producing a notable artistic-cultural boom that endured three hundred years. During this period — Abruzzo's time of glory — dozens of remarkable churches and abbeys were erected. Among the latter, the finest are San Clemente at Casauria, San Giovanni in Venere at Fossacesia, and Santa Maria Arabona. Abruzzo's outstanding church building is Santa Maria di Collemaggio in L'Aquila. Although Abruzzese painting never really reached great heights, the region produced some excellent sculpture, especially gold and silver artifacts, mainly between the 14th and 17th centuries. Major goldsmith centers were Sulmona, Teramo, and Guardiagrele.

221

L'AQUILA

To commemorate the 99 castles that once rose in the area of the 13th century city of L'Aquila (the valley of the Aterno and the surrounding hills), the bell in the tower of L'Aquila's Courthouse Building is sounded 99 times every night. L'Aquila still has its original townplan and considerable stretches of medieval walls. Its period of glory spanned the 14th and 15th centuries — during the time of the Kingdom of Naples it was second only to the capital. Thereafter, however, internecine squabbling and natural disasters (mainly earthquakes) contributed to its decline.

SANTA MARIA DI COLLEMAGGIO - Built in 1287, this is one of the finest Romanesque churches in Italy. The striking pink and white patterned facade is divided into three vertical zones by three portals (the middle one is especially impressive) above which are three splendid rose windows. The octagonal tower to the right of the facade is all that remains of the original, demolished

in the 19th century. The single aisles of the recently restored interior are set off from the nave by octagonal pillars. Thirteen canvases depicting *scenes from the life of pape Celestino V*, 18th century works by Carl Ruthart, and frescoes adorn the walls. In the righthand apse is the *Tomb of Celestino V*, a remarkable example of the Lombard Renaissance style by Girolamo da Vicenza. Before becoming pope, Celestino lived as a hermit on Mt. Marrone. Chosen pope after two years of Conclaves (1294), he abdicated only five months later. He was canonized as St. Piero Celestino in 1313.

SAN BERNARDINO - The basilica was founded in 1454 (ten years after St. Bernardino died in L'Aquila) and completed in 1472. The superb *facade* was designed by Cola dell'Amatrice in the 16th century. It is divided horizontally into three registers in the Doric, Ionic, and Corinthian styles. The lunette in the charming center portal is by Silvestro dell'Aquila. The Baroque *in-*

Above: striking facade of Santa Maria di Collemaggio. Right: detail of the Fontana delle 99 Cannelle.

terior (with a fine carved ceiling) vaunts other outstanding sculpture by Silvestro, e.g., the *Tomb of St. Bernardino* right aisle) and the fine *Tomb of Maria Pereira* (by the main altar).

CASTELLO - This massive square fortress, today the *Museo Nazionale d'Abruzzo*, was built between the 16th and 17th centuries under the Spaniards. It is protected by a moat and surmounted by huge triangular bastions. The collections span the Italic-Roman period (archeological finds) up through medieval and modern art. In addition to painting and sculpture, there are fine examples of religious objects in gold and silver dating from the 12th to 18th centuries.

FONTANA DELLE 99 CAN-NELLE - Ninety-nine spouts spraying into an underlying basin make up this unusual fountain. (Each spout stands for one of the castles supposedly forming the original city of L'Aquila). The fountain was built in 1272, although it was later restored and remodeled several times.

GRAN SASSO D'ITALIA - The highest peak of the Apennines, the Gran Sasso has typically alpine characteristics — steep walls, year-round snow, and a tiny glacier (the only one in Central-Southern Italy). The area is a favorite with mountain-climbers and hikers. Skiers find excellent facilities, including ski lifts and kilometers of trails. From the L'Aquila side (14 km from the city,

at *Assergi*) you can take the *Gran Sasso Cableway*, which climbs 2130 meters to reach *Campo Imperatore*, a superb plateau replete with facilities for winter sports. On the Teramo side are the excellent ski trails of the *Prati di Tivo* (37 km from Teramo and 65 from L'Aquila).

CELANO - (50 km). The *Castello di Celano*, one of the most important in Abruzzo, is beautifully situated in this hilltown. Begun in 1392, it was completed in 1463 by Count Piccolomini. The square fortress, with towers on each corner, is enclosed within massive walls.

PARCO NAZIONALE D'ABRUZ-ZO - The Abruzzo National Park extends over a huge territory (400 km²) that includes both inhabited and non-inhabited areas. Visitors must at all times respect the environment (flora and fauna). Within the park area are mountains (the southern tip of the Marsicano Range, the Meta Range, and part of the Mainarde Range) and towns (*Pescasseroli, Opi, Villetta Barrea, Civitella Alfedena*). Popular excursions are hikes through the *Val di Fondillo* and the *Camosciara*. There are many rare plants and animals in the protected area making up the park. Most of the flora is to be found in woodlands. The most common trees are beechwood and a local pine known as the «*pino di Villetta Barrea.*» The array of fauna is vast. (In fact, the park area was once the private hunting-grounds of the Italian royal family.) The best-known animals are: the famous Abruzzese bear (*orso bruno marsicano*); once faced with extinction, they now number about a hundred and are expected to steadily increase over the next few years; the Abruzzese chamois, as well as wolves, foxes, beechmartens, woodchucks, wild cats, buzzards, hawks, and eagles.

Above: castle and town of Celano.
Below: Gran Sasso d'Italia.

MOLISE

Molise greatly resembles its neighbor Abruzzo in terms of morphology, history, and cultural heritage, and, in fact, the two shared a regional government until 1963. Physically, the tiny region is mountainous, crisscrossed by the Mainarde, Sannio, and Matese Apennine ranges and a myriad of low-lying hills. The tallest peak is Mt. Miletto (2050 m) of the Matese Range. The main river is the Biferno which originates at Bojano in the Matese area and crosses the whole region to empty into the Adriatic. The only port along its 38-kilometer-long coast is Termoli. The tiny beach zone is low-lying and sandy. Molise lives mainly on agriculture (farming and cattle-raising), despite recent attempts to establish industries in the region.

HISTORY AND ART - Molise was settled by the Samnites, a belligerent Italic tribe, in Antiquity. The Samnites proceeded to conquer great chunks of Abruzzo and Campania before being vanquished by Rome — although Rome did not have an easy time of it. Remains of the Samnite period are to be found in Pietrabbondante, while Roman ruins are visible in extensive excavations at Larino, Venafro, and Saepinum. A governing body, the Comitatus Molisii, was set up during the Middle Ages when the region was ruled first by the Longobards and then by the Normans. The name Molisii probably derives from that of a family of Bojano counts, then prominent. Thereafter, it shared the fate of its neighbor Abruzzo, finally succumbing to the Kingdom of Naples, in whose power it remained for long centuries. Sev-

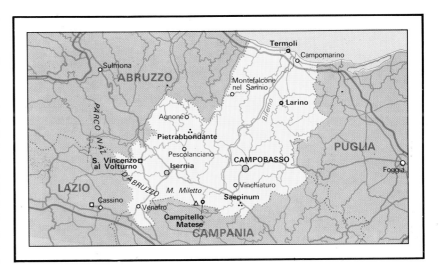

eral important monuments have survived from the Middle Ages, including the abbey of San Vincenzo al Volturno decorated with 9th century frescoes, the Romanesque abbeys of Santa Maria di Canneto and Santa Maria della Strada, the cathedrals of Larino and Termoli, and the church of San Giorgio at Petrella Tifernina. Some major economic activities are bellcasting and metalworking (copper and wrought iron) in Agnone, lacework in Isernia, and steel-making in Campobasso.

Right: Castello Monforte overlying Campobasso.

CAMPOBASSO

Despite its small size, Campobasso has always been considered an important center in a region where large-size cities have never grown up. Pleasantly situated on a hillside, it is quite picturesque, especially the old downtown with its myriad of ascending-descending little streets. Dominating the city from above (974 m) is the Castello of Monforte. Other outstanding monuments include the churches of San Giorgio, Sant Antonio (containing several interesting 17th century paintings), and San Bartolomeo.

SAN GIORGIO - This 12th century Romanesque church is the oldest in Campobasso. The facade, ex-tremely simple, is adorned with a striking carved lunette depicting the *Mystic Lamb* (above the entrance portal). The aisles date from a re-modeling of the church. Inside is a fine 17th century altarpiece with a painting of *St. George and the Dragon*.

CASTELLO MONFORTE - Cylin-drical towers once stood at the corners of this huge square building whose austere appearance is light-ened only by the presence of a row of battlements. Built by the Long-obards around the year 1000, it was later completely remodeled by Cola di Monforte, Count of Molise (1549). Today, after being restored

Romanesque church of San Giorgio, Campobasso.

twice in the 20th century, it houses a monument to the Italian war dead and a weather station.

TERMOLI - (67 km). This pictures-que city of tiny, winding streets and lanes is set atop a promontory along the coast. It vaunts two remarkable medieval monuments: the Castle, built by Frederick II in 1247, and the Cathedral, built in 1153, with a beautiful Pugliese-Romanesque fac-ade. Termoli is a popular beach resort and the main embarkation point for the *Tremiti Island*.

226

CAMPANIA

Campania is a region of varied landscapes with long stretches of plain along the coast and pre-Apennine and Apennine mountain ranges inland. Naples is situated right in the middle of a volcanic zone comprising the islands of Ischia and Procida, Campi Flegrei, Roccamonfina (inactive volcano), and Vesuvius (active volcano). In the vicinity of the two promontories embracing the Gulf of Naples are three good-sized islands: Ischia and Procida (in the north) and Capri (in the south). The climate along the coast is exceptionally mild, with little rainfall throughout the year. In the mountain areas it gets rather cold and, especially in the Matese and Irpina regions, there is often snow.

HISTORY - Throughout the five-hundred-year period that the Italic tribes inhabited Campania (10th-5th centuries B.C.), they sought increasingly intense contacts with the Greek coastal cities and the Etruscans. The Etruscans, in fact, driven south by the Celts, soon prevailed over the local population, but this dominion lasted only to 474 B.C. when the Etruscan army was soundly beaten at sea by the Siracusans in the Battle of Cuna and on land by the Samnites who attacked from the mainland. The Samnites ruled Campania until the 3rd century B.C. when their whole territory became a Roman possession (273 B.C.). The Romans brought peace and prosperity to the region, which soon ranked as the favorite vacation land of the upper classes. In the 6th century most of Campania was ruled by the Byzantines, except for the area occupied by the Longobards, who made Benevento the capital of a vast duchy (while the Byzantines installed their capital in Naples). In the meantime, Salerno and Capua managed to regain their independence. During the following centuries, Naples, well out of the reach of the central

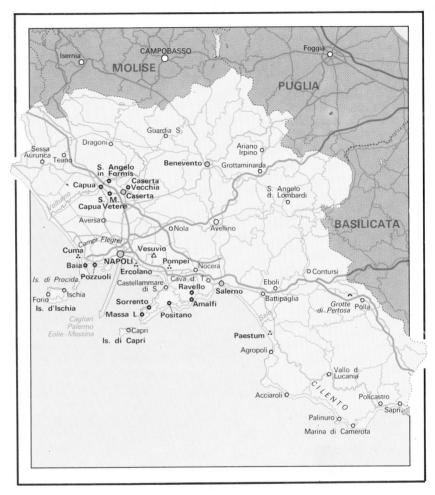

Byzantine rulers, continued to extend her power, and it was not long before the major coastal cities (i.e., Sorrento and Amalfi) could proclaim their independence. The fact that the region was split up into numerous little city-states favored the expansionist schemes of the Normans who by the 11th century had handily subjugated most of the important Campania centers and become masters of all of Southern Italy. In the 13th century, Emperor Frederick II revitalized and reformed the state, but his son Manfredi was defeated by Charles d'Anjou who, backed by the pope, became the new ruler of Campania with Naples as his splendid capital. In the 15th

century the Anjous were succeeded by the Aragonese. Under the Spaniards, whose main interest in the region lay in tax collecting, decline set in everywhere except Naples. The capital, on the other hand, continued to be embellished with princely palaces and government buildings, but it too suffered from grave problems, most insidious of which overpopulation and frequent epidemics. The situation hardly changed in the 18th century with the advent of the Bourbons, who remained firmly ensconced until Garibaldi's army drove them out in 1860. The unification of Italy failed to bring great benefits — with the exclusion of a few sporadic interven-

227

tions, the region continued to remain cut off from the mainstream of the industrialization process then extensively underway in the north, and soon became a land of emigration. World War II aggravated matters. Rebuilding of the heavily-bombed cities was carried out hapazardly, without following an overall plan, with the result that the region is still plagued by strident socio-economic imbalances and contradictions. Campania's economic activities today, as in the past, are centered around agriculture. Major industries, mostly clustered in the Naples area, include food processing (canning and pasta production), steel mills (Bagnoli), and automobiles (Pomigliano d'Arco). Naples is also an important commercial port. Tourism is another important economic resource: Campania is favored with a marvelous climate, important artistic momuments, and an exceptionally beautiful coastline.

ART - Some of the world's greatest Greek and Roman artworks are to be found in Campania. The Paestum temples, for example, are among the foremost Doric buildings extant, while two Roman towns,

Pompeii and Herculaneum, were preserved intact with all their paintings and sculpture when Vesuvius erupted in 79 A.D. burying them beneath a protective mantle of volcanic ash. Art and architecture of the same period may also be viewed in other Campania cities such as Pozzuoli, Cuma, Baia, and Capua. In addition, there are extraordinary pieces preserved in the Museo Nazionale in Naples. Works from the Longobard period are to be found mainly in the Benevento and Capua areas. During the Middle Ages, when the region prospered under the rule of the Normans, Swabians, and then Anjous, great building projects were undertaken. The churches of Amalfi, Salerno, Caserta, Caserta Vecchia, Ravello, and Naples dating from this period are a remarkable blend of Byzantine, Classical, and Romanesque elements, to which French Gothic influxes were added in the 13th century. In painting, the 11th century was dominated by Byzantine influence strikingly revealed in the frescoes decorating the church of Sant'Angelo in Formis, as well as in the miniatures painted in the Monastery of Cassino. Tuscan influence in painting, mainly due to Giotto and Simone Martini, began to make itself felt in the 13th-14th centuries, when Campania's artistic activity was practically all confined to Naples, the royal capital. Another Tuscan, Tino di Camaino, who sojourned in the capital in the 14th century, had great impact on local sculpture schools, while Tuscan architects were commissioned with many of the Aragonese building projects undertaken in the 15th century. In the 17th century, Naples produced an outstanding group of painters including Battistello Caracciolo, Mattia Preti, Luca Giordano, and Salvator Rosa. The foremost painter of the 18th century was Solimena, although the major monuments of the period were grandiose palaces commissioned by the court, such as the Reggia of Caserta designed by Vanvitelli. No important artists (except for Giacinto Gigante) emerged in the 19th century, when the prevailing school was academic neo-Classicism.

NAPLES

Naples' strong points, i.e., historical monuments, beautiful architecture, art masterpieces, top quality food, mild climate, and picturesque sights, outweigh her weak ones, i.e., pollution, chaotic traffic, and all the problems related to a long history of poverty. The city was founded around the 7th century B.C. by the Greeks who first called it *Parthenope* after a mythical siren, and then *Neapolis* (New City). During the Roman era when it became a popular vacation spot, it retained many of the characteristics of a

Left: Dancing Faun, from Pompeii, displayed in Naples' Museo Archeologico. Above: Gulf of Naples.

cultured Greek center (e.g., theaters). It was inhabited by prominent Romans such as Nero, Lucullus, and Virgil (who is buried here). In the 6th century it became a Byzantine domain. Although the city was actually fully autonomous, it nominally remained under Byzantine rule until 1139 when it was taken over by the Normans. From then on, it became the foremost city of the region, and as such exerted an overriding influence on Campania's history. Under Frederick II of Swabia who succeeded the Norman emperor in the 13th century, Naples became an important artistic and cultural center. The Anjous did much to further local development in the 13th and 14th centuries: under

their rule, the Maschio and Castel Sant'Elmo were built, artists such as Simone Martini, Pietro Cavallini, and Tino di Camaino were summoned to work in the city, and writers such as Boccaccio sojourned here. In the 15th century as an Aragonese possession and in the 16th as a Spanish domain ruled by a viceroy, Naples was impoverished both culturally and economically. In 1647, the people, led by the fiery Masaniello, rose up, but their revolt was suppressed. Nine years later, in 1656, 400,000 Neapolitans perished in a terrible plague epidemic. Under the Bourbons in the 18th century, Naples once more became a cultural-artistic center. The Reggia of Capodimonte and its porcelain

works of worldwide renown were built, great music was written by composers such as Cimarosa and Pergolesi, and important works were produced by philosphers such as Giovan Battista Vico. In the 19th century, after a brief period under Napoleon's envoy, Murat, Naples returned to the Bourbons, regaining her independence only in 1860 when Garibaldi's army arrived in Campania.

DUOMO - Built in the 13th century and later remodeled, the Duomo has a 19th century facade with three Gothic portals (1407) adorned with reliefs by Baboccio. Inside is a masterpiece of the early-17th century Baroque style, the *Cappella di San Gennaro* (entrance from right aisle), frescoed by Domenichino and Lanfranco. The reliquaries containing the blood of the patron saint of Naples (which miraculously liquifies in May and September) are preserved in the chapel. In one of the transept chapels is Perugino's *Assumption of the Virgin*. Two other chapels are of considerable interest: the 13th century *Cappella Minutolo and the underground Cappella Car-* afa with a 16th century *statue of Cardinal Carafa in prayer*. There are also subterranean remains of an Early Christian church, *Santa Restituta*, and a *baptistry* adorned with 5th century mosaics.

SAN LORENZO MAGGIORE - This 13th-14th century Franciscan church is one of the finest examples of Neapolitan Gothic. The church was the site of Boccaccio's historic encounter with Fiammetta in 1334, and the next-door monastery is where Petrarch sojourned in 1345. The aisleless interior is lined with

Left: Maschio Angioino. Above: Galleria Umberto I.

chapels containing some important works of art such as a 14th century wood *crucifix*, the *Tomb of Caterina d'Austria* by Tino di Camaino (c. 1325), and the *Tomb of Robert d'Artois and Giovanna di Durazzo* (1399). Outside the building are the 18th century cloister and ruins of the Greek and Roman buildings that originally occupied the site.

MASCHIO ANGIOINO - The castle (also called *Castel Nuovo*) was built in the 1280s by the Anjous and then restructured in the 15th century. Its present configuration, a massive stone structure with great round towers, is the result of an Aragonese rebuilding campaign — and also of a restoration effected in the early 19th century. It served as a royal palace, first for the Anjous, then for the Aragonese, and lastly for the Spanish viceroy. The entrance is a majestic *triumphal arch*. Various architects worked on the arch, which was commissioned by

Alfonso I in 1443. The highlights of the interior are the *Cappella di Santa Barbara* and the *Sala dei Baroni*.

GALLERIA UMBERTO I - This elegant Belle Epoque arcade, crowned by a glass and iron roof, is one of several built in Italy at the turn of the century. The mall contains a theater, *Teatro Margherita*, as well as shops, cafés, and offices.

PALAZZO REALE - Originally designed by Domenico Fontana in 1602 as the viceroy's royal palace, it

was later Gioacchino Murat's headquarters. On the facade are eight statues of famous monarchs. The 15th century bronze *portal* in the atrium was originally part of the Maschio Angioino. A cannonball mars the esthetic effect of the sculptural decoration. The *Royal Suites* are reached by way of the monumental staircase. The elaborate rooms feature 17th and 18th century Neapolitan furnishings and paintings. Ferdinando Fuga designed the *Court Theater* in 1768. The palace is not only a museum: a section is occupied by the *Naples National Library* and it often hosts exhibitions.

CASTEL DELL'OVO - The castle is situated on a quaint islet, the *Borgo Marinaro*, an old fishing village whose modern-day restaurants overlook the *Santa Lucia Port*. It was built in the 12th century on the site of the villa belonging to Roman

bon vivant Lucullus, which was later transformed into a Basilian monastery. Its name (literally, Castle of the Egg) originated out of a medieval legend recounting how Virgil (then classified among the great magicians) tied the fate of the castle to an enchanted egg - if it broke the castle would be destroyed. Inside are Gothic halls, dungeons, and several cells once part of the old monastery.

CHARTERHOUSE OF SAN MARTINO - The monastery is situated in a splendid position atop Vomero Hill overlooking the whole city. Designed in the 1300s by several architects, among them Tino di Camaino, it was rebuilt in the 17th century by Cosimo Fanzago in the Baroque style. Today it is a museum, the *Museo Nazionale di San Martino*. The *church*, a 15th-16th century design by Dosio and Fanzago, is splendidly adorned with 17th century Neapolitan marbles, sculpture, and paintings. The highlights are: *Deposition* by Stanzione, *Prophets* by Ribera, *Christ Washing the Apostle's Feet* by Battistello Car-

acciolo, a fresco by Luca Giordano in the *Cappella del Tesoro*, as well as works by Vaccaro, Reni, and Solimena. The *Museum* features a collection of fascinating 18th century Neapolitan *crèches*. In the *Pinacoteca* are paintings by Solimena, Salvator Rosa, Caracciolo, Luca Giordano, and other 19th century artists. The *Sculpture Section* features works by Tino di Camaino, Sammartino, and Pietro Bernini, while the *Minor Arts Section* displays Murano glassware and Capodimonte china. The *Chiostro Grande*, a splendid 16th-17th century cloister, was built by Antonio Dosio and Cosimo Fanzago.

SAN DOMENICO MAGGIORE - Despite much remodeling, the church, built in the 13th-14th centuries, ranks as an outstanding example of the Anjou Gothic style. The Baroque spire in the square, the *Guglia di San Domenico*, was commissioned in 1658 in thanksgiving for deliverance from a plague epidemic. The interior contains a 13th century *Crucifix* that, according

to tradition, spoke to St. Thomas of Aquinus (*Cappellone del Crocifisso*) and a fresco by Solimena (1709) in the Sacristy. There are also works by Luca Giordano and followers of Tino di Camaino.

CAPPELLA SANSEVERO - Built by the Sangro family (from 1590 to the mid-18th century), the chapel is adorned with some remarkable sculpture: *Caught in the Net* by Francesco Queirolo, *Modesty* by Antonio Corradini, and *Veiled Christ* by Giuseppe Sammartino. Alongside is a room containing two mummies, examples of experiments on mummification conducted by one of the princes of Sangro.

MUSEO ARCHEOLOGICO NA-ZIONALE - One of the largest and most important archeological museums in the world, the Museo Archeologico was founded in the 18th century by the Bourbons. (The present-day museum building is a 16th century palace.) Its extensive collection comprises Greco-Roman art, especially from digs in the Pompeii, Herculaneum, and Stabia areas. *Marble sculpture* is displayed on the ground floor. The highlights include: The Assassins of the Tyrant, a Roman copy of a 5th century Greek work by Kritos and Nesiotes; a relief depicting *Hermes, Orpheus, and Eurydice* (Greek, 5th century B.C.); *Athena*, copy of a Phidias;

the *Doryphorus* (from Pompeii), one of the finest copies extant of the Greek original by Polycletus; the *Ephebus* (from Pompeii), a copy of the 5th century Greek original; *Venus Callipigia*, from a Hellenistic original; the *Farnese Bull*, a copy of a Hellenistic work, excavated in Rome; and the *Sosandra Aphrodite* from Stabia. On the mezzanine are *Pompeian mosaics*, including the *Battle of Darius and Alexander the Great*, *Seascape*, *Street Musicians*, *Sorcerers*, and the *School of Plato*. On the second floor are statues, paintings, and celebrated *papyri* with Greek inscriptions discovered in the *Villa dei Papiri* in Herculaneum. The *Painting Collection*

Museo Archeologico Nazionale. Left: detail of the Pompeian mosaic depicting the Battle of Darius and Alexander the Great. Above: fresco portrait of a girl, also from Pompeii.

features a *portrait of Paquius Proculus and his wife* (from Pompeii), *Diana the Huntress*, the so-called *Spring*, Stabian paintings, a grisaille picture from Herculaneum depicting *Women shooting dice; Theseus and the Minotaur* (from Pompeii) and *Hercules and Telephus* (from Herculaneum). The other sections comprise the *Jewel Collection*, the so-called *"Gabinetto Segreto"* (a collection of erotica not open to the general public), and the fascinating *Technology Section*.

Above: Royal Palace of Capodimonte. Below: Caravaggio's Flagellation of Christ in the Galleria Nazionale. Right: Vesuvius.

CAPODIMONTE – Capodimonte's *Royal Palace* was designed in 1738 by Medrano for Charles, the Bourbon king. On the grounds (an enormous *Park* that was once the king's private hunting reserve) is the *Fabbrica di Porcellane*, the porcelain works. The fine porcelain produced here in the 18th century rivaled the famous china of Sèvres and Saxonia. There are two museums in the Royal Palace, the *Galleria Nazionale* and the *Historic Suite*. The Galleria Nazionale occupies 45 rooms on the third floor. It is hung with 13th-18th century paintings of different schools and periods. We shall list only the highlights. Room II: seven 16th century Flemish *tapestries* illustrating *episodes from the Battle of Pavia*. Room IV: *St. Louis of Toulouse Crowning Robert d'Anjou* by Simone Martini (1317). Room V: *Virgin and Child* by Bernardo Daddi, the *Foundation of Santa Maria a Nives* and the *Assumption of the Virgin* by Masolino da Panicale (14th century). Room VI: *Crucifixion* by Masaccio (c. 1427), part of a dismantled altarpiece. Room VII: *Virgin and Child* by Sandro Botticelli and the *Annunciation* by Filippo Lippi. Room VIII: *St. Jerome and the Lion and St. Francis handing down the Rule to the Franciscan monks and nuns* by Colantonio, one of the foremost 15th century Neapolitan school painters. Room X: *Holy Family* by Sebastiano del Piombo. Room IV: the *Gypsy Girl, Mystic Marriage of St. Catherine,* and *St. Joseph* by Correggio. Room XVII: *Transfiguration* by Giovanni Bellini and *Portrait of Bernardo de' Rossi* by Lotto (1505). Room XIX: two *portraits of Pope Paul III* and *Danae* by Titian. Room XX: *Parabola of the Blind Leading the Blind* and *The Misanthrope* by Brueghel, and *Pietà* by Roger van der Weyden. Room XXIX: *Flagellation* by Caravaggio (formerly in the church of San Domenico Maggiore). Room XXX: *Flight into*

Egypt by Caracciolo. Room XXXV: *St. Cecilia* by Cavallino (1645). Room XL: works by Mattia Preti. Rooms XLII: *The Secret Letter* by Gaspare Traversi. The *Galleria dell'Ottocento* on the second floor features works by 19th century Neapolitan artists. The delightful *Salottino di Porcellana*, moved here from the Bourbon royal palace in Portici, is superb creation of the Capodimonte china works (1759).

VESUVIUS - Vesuvius' cone is one of the symbols of Naples and its gulf. Still an active volcano, it rises 1227 meters alongside a no-longer active volcano, *Mt. Somma* (1132 m). Vesuvius' first recorded eruption, preceded by an earthquake some years before, took place in 79 A.D. It buried the nearby cities of Pompeii, Herculaneum, and Stabia

under a blanket of volcanic ash and lapilli. The inquisitive Roman historian Pliny the Elder was eyewitness — and victim — of the event, while his son, Pliny the Younger, then an 18-year old, was chronicler of the ensuing tragedy of the inhabitants of the disaster zone. After the Roman era, several eruptions were recorded (the last having occurred in 1944). The Vesuvian area has been renowned since Antiquity for the fertility of its lava-impregnated soils, the quality of *Lacryma Christi*, the locally-produced wine, and the charm of the 18th century villas situated in the vicinity of the volcano. The hike to the crater is doubly interesting: first, for the incredible spectacle of smoke coming out of the huge hole, and second, for the breathtaking view of Naples and its environs it affords.

POMPEII

Pompeii was settled by the Osci, colonized by the Greeks (6th century B.C.), conquered by the Samnites, and lastly subjugated by the Romans. After having been partly destroyed in the 62 A.D. earthquake, it was wholly buried under the ashes and lapilli that Vesuvius spewed forth in 79 A.D. The volcanic matter, in which numerous inhabitants of the city perished, solidified over the centuries, thus preserving animate and inanimate Pompeii in a several-meters-thick layer of earth. The area remained unpopulated for centuries; the first digs only date from the 1800s. Today Pompeii ranks as the best-preserved example of a typical Roman city that has come down to us. A tour of it allows us to get a glimpse into the life of 1st century Rome, to see what the houses, inns, warehouses, and bordellos of the time were like, and to appreciate its

art and architecture in situ. Not far from the excavations is the modern city of Pompeii which is famous for its sanctuary, the *Santuario della Madonna del Rosario*.

PORTA MARINA - This two-arch gate was part of the Samnite city walls. (The left arch was reserved for pedestrians and the right one for vehicle traffic.) Nearby are remains of barns and storehouses.

ANTIQUARIUM - In the museum are numerous excavated objects such as tools, artifacts, sculptures, architectural fragments, paintings, vases, and plaster casts of people and animals caught in the great eruption. (The shapes of their bodies were preserved by the solidifid volcanic ash.) The major artworks discovered in Pompeii have been taken to the Museo Archeologico in Naples.

BASILICA - Built around the end of the 2nd century B.C., the Basilica (a combination of business center and courthouse) was the earliest civic building in Pompeii. It had single aisles set off from a nave by 28 Corinthian columns. At the far end was a platform framed by two orders of columns.

FORUM - The center of Pompeii's civic life, the Forum comprised government, religious, and business buildings around an enormous square. No vehicular traffic was allowed. During both the Samnite and Roman periods it was bordered by a colonnade of tufa and travertine columns. The buildings on the Forum are: the Basilica (short side), the *Temple of Apollo*, built by the Samnites and adorned with superb statuary (now replaced by copies); the *Temple of Jupiter* (on a high base in the middle of the north side), built in

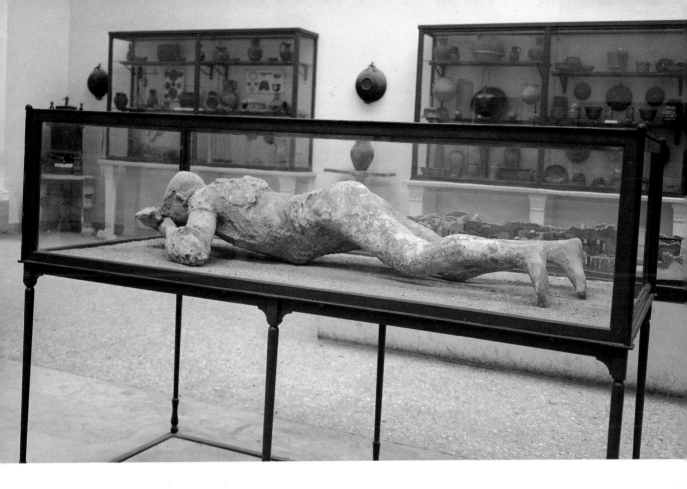

*Preceding page: Porta Marina.
Above: cast of one of the volcano's
victims. Right: the 2nd century B.C.
Basilica.*

the 2nd century B.C. and dedicated
to the *Capitoline Triad*, i.e., Jupiter,
Juno, and Minerva; the *Macellum*
(roofed marketplace); the *Temple of
Vespasian* with a carved sacrificial
altar; and the *Eumachia Building*
built by the priestess Eumachia for
the weavers' guild, with a magnifi-
cently-crafted portal.

STABIAN BATHS - The huge
building, in excellent state of preservation, was the first public bath in
Pompeii. There were two sections
(men and women), a gymnasium, a
swimming pool, and locker rooms.
The domed rooms sport elegant
stucco decoration and niches for
street clothes.

MAJOR THEATER - The five-
section cavea of Pompeii's main
theater could hold up to 5000 people. Built in the 2nd century B.C. it
is still being used.

MINOR THEATER - Built in the 1st century B.C., this indoor theater, i.e., *Odeon*, had a capacity of 1000. It served mainly for concerts and pantomime shows.

HOUSE OF LOREIUS TIBURTINUS - This elegant mansion is one of Pompeii's most interesting sights. On either side of the entranceway are shops connected to the interior. In the middle of the courtyard is an *impluvium*, i.e., a basin for collecting rainwater. Beyond the atrium is the peristyle, with a garden leading to a trellis-covered terrace traversed by a little canal down the middle and adorned with statuary and fountains. This was the starting point of the mansions's great park.

AMPHITHEATER - This building, dated 80 B.C., ranks as the oldest surviving Roman amphitheater. It had four sections of seats, for a total capacity of 20,000. There was no problem if it rained — the stadium could be quickly covered with a canvas *velarium*. Spectacles such as gladiator combats and animal hunts were held here. In 59 A.D. a fight broke out between the fans from Pompeii and the nearby city of Nocera - with the result that the Roman Senate prohibited spectacles in the amphitheater. The episode is documented in a painting in the Naples Archeological Museum.

FORUM BATHS - The well-preserved Forum Baths were built in the 1st century B.C. All the rooms have stucco ornamentation and in the *tepidarium* there are terracotta telemon figures (sustaining a shelf). The heating system was thoroughly modern, i.e., hot air circulated beneath the floor.

HOUSE OF THE FAUN - Built in the 2nd century B.C. (Samnite period), this is a superb example of an upper-class Roman *domus*. Its

owner was probably a wealthy politician. There are two atriums: the main one in the Tuscan style and a secondary one with four columns (which served as a passageway). The *impluvium* of the main atrium is adorned with a statuette of a *dancing faun* (a copy; the original is preserved in Naples) which gave the house its name. Several of the finest mosaics displayed in the Naples Archeological Museum come from this house, including the celebrated *Battle of Darius and Alexander the Great*.

HOUSE OF THE VETTII –

Among the best preserved and artistically interesting of the houses in Pompeii, this mansion belonged to two wealthy merchants. It offers a unique reconstruction of everyday life in Pompeii and provides superb examples of the late-Pompeian

House of the Vettii. Above: Peristyle. Above right: section of the Cupid frieze. Below: mythological scenes and architecture motifs frescoed in one of the rooms.

painting style. In the vestibule is a fresco of *Priapus* the god of fertility (similar figuresand numerous phallic symbols believed to ward off the evil eye are visible all over Pompeii). In the atrium are two safes. In a room

242

VILLA OF THE MYSTERIES –
This magnificent estate was built in the 2nd century B.C. and later remodeled. After the 62 A.D. earthquake, its owners had decided to turn it into a farm, but the project was never completed due to the eruption of Vesuvius 17 years later. Some of the most famous Pompeian frescoes are preserved in situ here. A semicircular veranda of columns once faced the sea. (The present-day entrance is on this side, whereas originally it was on the other end.) In the great meeting hall, the *tablinum*, are Egyptian-style designs frescoed on a dark ground. On the right is the *Sala del Grande Dipinto*. The room is

to the left of the atrium are frescoes of *Cyparissus in pain, Pan and Cupid*, as well as fantasy architectural motifs. Beyond is a peristyle with fountains (still in working condition), statues, frescoes, and a colonnade-enclosed garden. In a room to the right side of the peristyle are some fine frescoes whose subjects are *Dedalus and Pasiphae, torture of Ixio*, and *Dionysus and Arianna*. There are also noteworthy frescoes in the suite of the *Gyneceum* and in the enormous *triclinium* (living room) Of especial note is the frieze of *Cupids* potrayed as goldsmiths, florists, farmers, and perfume distillers adorning the *triclinium*.

Detail of the Villa dei Misteri frescoes depicting a follower reading the Dionysiac Ritual.

adorned with renowned 1st century B.C. frescoes, whose subject is *initiation into the cult of the Dionysian mysteries*. Measuring 17 × 3 meters, the scenes, painted against a striking red background, show the initiation of a young woman. The stages of the rite comprise uncovering of a phallus (i.e., fertility symbol), flagellation by a winged female goddess, and the ritual dance. The other rooms are decorated with architectural motifs.

HERCULANEUM

According to legend founded by Hercules (*Ercole*, in Italian), Herculaneum originated as a Greek settlement. Made a Roman *Muncipium* in 89 B.C., it was preserved for posterity by the 79 A.D. eruption of Vesuvius. Although excavations have been going on since the 18th century, much remains to be unearthed (especially beneath the modern section). Herculaneum was a typical 1st century A.D. Roman town. Its main features were a *Decumanus Maximus* (major thoroughfare intersected by *cardines* running perpendicular to it), low dwellings adorned with loggias and set in gardens, baths, and various civic buildings. We shall mention only the chief sights. *Cardo IV: House of the Mosaic-Adorned Atrium* and the *House of the Wooden Divider* (which sports a carbonized wood partition wall). Intersection of *Decumanus Inferior: Samnite House*, one of the oldest buildings in the city (right) and the *Cardo IV.*

superbly decorated *Baths*, divided into two sections, one for women and one for men (left). *Cardo IV*: *House of Neptune and Amphitrite* named for the mosaic decoration of its nympheum. *Decumanus Maximus*: *House of the Bicentennial*. Returning by way of *Cardo V* we pass the *Gymnasium*, with its lovely fountain, on the lefthand side. At the end of the street are the *House of the Telephus Relief*, the *House of the Gem*, and, opposite them, the *House of the Deer* which features two sculpture groups of *deer being attacked by dogs* and an elegant terrace overlooking the sea. Nearby are the so-called "Suburban Baths."

Left: House of the Deer. Below: Suburban Baths.

SORRENTO

This charming little town rising on a promontory overlooking the gulf was already famous as a resort in Roman times. In the Middle Ages, it was a Byzantine possession, then an independent duchy, a Norman possession, and throughout a staunch defender of the coast from the attacks of the Saracen pirates. The great poet, Torquato Tasso, was born here in the 16th century. The region is renowned as a citrus-fruit producer and for its luxurious silk and embroidered fabrics. The *Cathedral* stands at the intersection of Corso Italia and Via Tasso. Extensively remodeled in recent years, it features a 16th century *Bishop's Throne* and *pulpit*, plus a 15th century painting of the *Adoration*. Another noteworthy church is the basilica of *Sant'Antonino*, a medieval building remodeled in the Baroque period. The present-day basilica was built incorporating a pre-existing 14th century oratory next to the *Tomb of the Saint* which is now visible in the crypt. Other interesting sights are the *Sedile Dominova*, an elegant 15th century loggia, the church of *San Francesco* with its charming *cloister* adorned with 14th century Arab-style arches, and the *Museo Correale di Terranova* housed in the 18th century palace that once belonged to the counts of

Panoramic view of Sorrento.

Terranova. The museum vaunts an extraordinary collection of minor art masterpieces ranging from maiolicas, Neapolitan Baroque furnishings, and antique watches, to Capodimonte porcelain. It is also hung with Campania school paintings. At *Punta del Capo* in the environs of Sorrento are remains of a Roman villa, the *Villa di Pollius Felix*, which, perched atop a tiny bay and enclosed in sheer rock walls, is reached by a passageway cut through the stone.

CAPRI

Capri is one of the great tourist attractions of Italy all year round. Its setting is enchanting — the island, covered with Mediterranean vegetation, rises out of a turquoise sea. Slightly over 6 km long and a bit short of 3 km wide, it was settled in prehistoric times, later became a Greek colony, and was celebrated all through the Roman era. The *Grotta Azzurra* — A tiny opening precedes the actual grotto. Inside, the light effects make the water an incredible shade of blue, while objects underwater appear a glowing silver. *Capri* — This quaint little town is the main center of the island. The quiet lanes and streets become particularly animated in summer and on New Year's, when a local festival is held. The town center is a picturesque square, *Piazza Umberto I*. On it stand the 17th century church of *Santo Stefano*. *Marina Piccola* — This tiny port on the south shore of the island is where boats leave for tours of the huge rock formations known as *Faraglioni*.

Above: Faraglioni. Below: Marina Grande. Right: Isle of Ischia dominated by its castle.

248

ISCHIA

Ischia's volcanic origin is clearly evident in the kind of rock it is composed of and the mineral springs dotting it. Renowned for its spas, scenic beauty, and exceptionally mild climate, the island was colonized by the Greeks in the 7th century B.C. who named it Pithecusa. The Neapolitans and Romans who came after them turned it into a vacation resort. Later it was a Norman, Anjou, and finally Aragonese possession. Throughout its long history it was plundered by the Saracens many times (which is the reason there are numerous watchtowers along the coast). The exceptional fertility of the Ischian soil has always favored agriculture (citrus fruit and grapes). *Ischia* — The chief town of the island is divided into two sections, i.e., *Ischia Porto* (the elegant resort area surrounding the harbor) and *Ischia Ponte* (the neighborhood by *Ponte Aragonese*, the bridge built in 1438 by the Aragonese, to join the island fishing village to the islet where their *Castle* rose). In addition to the castle, there are remains of the *Cathedral*, the church of the *Immacolata*, and the *Convent of the Clarisse* (with a macabre nuns' cemetery).

CASERTA

ROYAL PALACE - One of the world's greatest royal palaces, the Reggia is the masterpiece of Luigi Vanvitelli who, commissioned by the Bourbon king, Charles, worked on the project between 1752 and 1774. The landscape architect was Francesco Collecini. In addition to regular crews of laborers and craftsmen, prisoners of the Islamic wars were put to work. When the Bourbons were ousted, the Reggia was taken over by the Savoys, and it is now the property of the State. The facade overlooking Piazza Carlo III sports 243 windows! Entering the atrium by way of the main entrance brings you to a vestibule from which four courtyards radiate. (The second leads to the charming *Court Theater*.) From the vestibule you can go directly to the garden or, climbing the *Monumental Staircase*, start your tour of the sumptuous *Royal Suites*. We shall mention only the highlights. In the 19th century *Appartamento Nuovo*: the *Throne Room* with a ceiling fresco depicting *Charles of Bourbon breaking ground for the palace*. In the *Appartamento del Re* (also 19th century): the *Bedrooms of Francis II and Murat* (Empire style). In the *Appartamento Vecchio* (the first to be decorated): living rooms, a *dining room*, the queen's quarters, the *library*, and a room featuring an enormous 18th century Neapolitan *crèche*. 19th century works and portraits of members of the Bourbon family are displayed in the *Pinacoteca* and *Quadreria*.The three-kilometer-long *grounds* offer spectacular scenic effects. A long path leading to the hillside skirts woods, meadows, fountains, pools, and cascades, interspersed with statuary. The most noteworthy of the decorative *fountains* are those named for *Eolo, Ceres*, and *Venus and Adonis*. The *Great Waterfall* features a 70-meter drop. To the right of the fall is a typically late-18th century *English garden*, replete with woods, streams, and mock Roman ruins.

Below: Fountain of Ceres on the landscaped grounds of Caserta's Royal Palace. Right: Duomo of Amalfi.

AMALFI

The Amalfi coast, i.e., the area lying between Sorrento and Salerno along the Peninsula of Sorrento, is celebrated worldover for its scenic beauty. The winding road which skirts it right along the water's edge, called the Amalfi Drive, is a remarkable procession of breathtaking views. On the way (66 kilometers from Sorrento to Salerno) there are numerous fine restaurants and hotels. Amalfi is one of the most popular Italian resorts thanks to its natural and artistic beauty. Settled by the Romans, it achieved its greatest splendor in the Middle Ages when it proclaimed itself the first Free Sea Republic of Italy. Renowned as one of the mightiest of the Mediterranean sea powers, Amalfi also made two great contributions to navigation history: one, the *Tavole Amalfitane*, i.e., a code of marittime legislation, and two, Flavio Gioia's perfection of the compass. Its decline started in the 12th century when it was defeated and plundered by the Pisans. Sailors from Amalfi annually take part in the *Regatta of the Sea Republics*. Amalfi's major monument is the *Duomo*, founded prior to the 9th century and remodeled several times between the 13th and 18th centuries. The facade of the church, strikingly visible at the top of a great staircase, has a two-tone marble facing that was put up in the 19th century. The gable mosaic also dates from the same period. The upper section of the 12th-13th century belltower with its maiolica facing is typically Arab style. The remarkable *bronze door* of the main entrance was crafted in Constantinople in the 11th century. The interior is Baroque, although there are some interesting pre-Baroque pieces, such as two Romanesque pulpits, the baptismal font, and the relics of St. Andrew the Apostle (in the crypt). The *Chiostro del Paradiso*, the charming cloister alongside the Duomo, was built in 1268 in pure Arab style. Set around the cloister are Romanesque and medieval sculptures.

PAESTUM

Paestum was settled in the 7th century by the Greeks who called it *Poseidona*. In 273, it became a Roman colony, one of the most prosperous and faithful in the Latin world. By the early Middle Ages, however, it was no longer a major center, for the area had become increasingly swampy due to land slippage, and it was soon reduced to a malaria-infested marshland. The last diehards abandoned it in the 9th century when Saracen attacks became particularly incessant. It remained abandoned for centuries. The earliest excavations date from the 18th century, although they are still underway today. The arch-eological area comprises dwellings, theaters, baths, and superb Doric-style temples. The excavated material not left in situ is on display in the museum. Actually dedicated to Athena, the *Temple of Ceres* was built in the 6th century B.C. The shorter ends still bear their original pediments and architraves. Inside is the cella, preceded by a pronaos of which only the column bases have survived. The three tombs on the cella wall date from the Middle Ages when the temple served as a church. Built around the middle of the 5th century B.C. and dedicated to Hera Argiva, the *Temple of Neptune* is one of the finest and best-

Temple of Neptune, a superb example of Doric architecture remarkably preserved.

preserved of the Doric temples. The huge building, preceded by six columns, measures 59.9 meters long and 24.3 meters wide. The greatly-tapered columns showing marked éntasis are a beautiful golden tone which makes a stirring sight, especially at sundown. The *Basilica*, one of the oldest temples in Paestum, was built around the middle of the 6th century B.C. and dedicated to Hera. Inside, fifty sturdy archaic columns run the length of the interior.

APULIA

Apulia is the long, narrow territory at the southeastern tip of the Italian boot, i.e., the heel «pointed» toward Albania (from which it is separated by the Otranto Channel). The region, the flattest in southern Italy, is characterized by scarcity of waterways and the presence of geological phenomena such as dolinas and grottoes. Roughly speaking, we may distinguish four geographical divisions. Gargano, the promontory constituting the «spur» of the boot, Tavoliere, a huge, intensely cultivated plain that was once marshland, Murge, a low-lying rocky plateau, and Salento, a narrow, elongated peninsula that is absolutely flat.

HISTORY - Among the numerous remains testifying to the region's prehistoric past are the dolmen, i.e., stone markers, the largest and most interesting of which is to be found in the Bisceglie area. Other important finds have been made in Salento and Gargano. The Greeks settled the cities of Otranto, Gallipoli, and Taranto which by the 5th century B.C. ranked as one of the foremost capitals of the whole Magna Grecia area. Romanization of the region started in 272 B.C. with the fall of Taranto and the ensuing rise of Brindisi, which in no time became Roman Apulia's main port. In 216 B.C. one of the most famous battles of Antiquity was fought on Apulian territory (specifically, the Canne area): the Romans were soundly beaten by Hannibal at the head of the Carthaginian army. As soon as Rome fell, the region became an appetizing land of conquest in the fierce power struggles of the Middle Ages: Goths and Byzantines (6th century), Longobards (7th-8th centuries), Byzantines again (9th-10th centuries), Normans (11th-12th) centuries), and Swabians (13th century) took turns in subjugating it, while at the same time the coastal cities were constantly kept busy fending off the

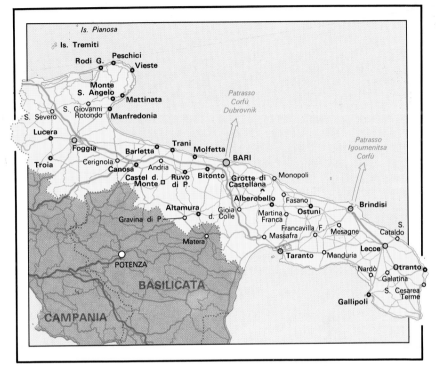

Saracens. Prosperity came with the onset of the Crusades, culminating in the 36-year reign of the Swabian emperor Frederick II (1214-1250). Thereafter, five centuries of unceasing feudalism drained the region of its economic vitality, a situation which did not improve until the late 19th century and the unification of Italy.

ART - The Greeks left their imprint in the region's art and architecture as well as townplanning. The objects excavated in tombs (artifacts, masks, jewels, pottery, etc.) make up an important part of Taranto's art museum. Extensive remains of the Roman period are visible throughout: theaters (Lucera), statues and the celebrated terminal columns marking the end of the Appian Way opposite the Port of Brindisi. The major monument of the Early Middle Ages is the Sanctuary of San Michele Arcangelo in Monte Sant'Angelo (Gargano) dating from the 5th-6th centuries. The foremost

manifestations of Apulian art, however, date from later periods, i.e., the Norman and Swabian 12th and 13th centuries. During these years, the incomparable cathedrals of Bari, Bitonto, Bitetto, Ruvo di Puglia, Trani, Altamura, and Troia were erected in the style known as Pugliese Romanesque, while at the same time Frederick II commissioned building of scores of castles, including the superb Castel del Monte. These centuries, also a time of great economic prosperity, were exceedingly active artistically (especially for the coastal cities of Terra di Bari). Thereafter, while the center of the art world was steadily moving more and more toward Naples, a new architectural and decorative style was gaining momentum in Salento. This unusual style, the so-called «Leccese Baroque» which predominated in Lecce and the other towns of the Terra d'Otranto region from the 16th-18th centuries, left a distinctive imprint on their overall appearance.

BARI

Settled by a tribe known as the Peucezi, it began to develop only under the Romans who were quick to realize that its location was strategic for trade with the Orient. During the medieval period, it was contended by Longobards, Byzantines, and Saracens. It became an important religious center around the year 1100 when the basilica in honor of the city's patron saint, Nicholas, was erected. The long period of the Crusades and subsequent reign of Frederick II brought prosperity to Bari. The following centuries, however, did not live up to their early promise. Lack of interest on the part of the people who governed the region did much to hasten its long decline which lasted until 1813 when Gioacchino Murat, King of Naples, sponsored its renovation.

CASTELLO - Rebuilt time and time again, the castle is a reflection of the different cultures and periods that affected it over the centuries. Settled by the Normans around the year 1000, it was totally rebuilt by Frederik II in 1233 in the form of a rectangle with corner watch towers. In the 16th century the two duch-

esses who used it as their official residence, Isabella d'Aragona and Bona Sforza, added fortified bastions on three sides.

CATHEDRAL - Built between 1170 and 1178 on the site of a pre-existing church, Bari's cathedral (dedicated to St. Sabinus) was extensively altered in the Baroque period. Recently stripped of its Baroque overstructures, it has been brought back to its original appearance: that of a plain Romanesque basilica. The three-part *facade* is characterized by a great rose window and a Romanesque arch two-part window. The round structure protruding from the left end, now the sacristy, was originally the baptistry. On the rear of the building is a fine Romanesque *window* revealing clear Oriental influence. Inside, the nave is set off from single aisles by fine Corinthian pillars which in turn sustain a second row of slighter columns.

SAN NICOLA - The majestic Basilica rises on a tiny square right in the heart of the old city center. San Nicola, founded in 1087, soon became a model for practically all the

Above: panoramic view of the city and port. Above right: Swabian Castle. Below: San Nicola.

Apulian Romanesque churches. The keynote of the *facade* is simplicity. Pilaster strips serve a dual purpose: a decorative motif, they also denote the single-aisle plan of the interior. Of the four towers that originally stood at the corners of the building, only two, the cropped front ones, are extant. The noteworthy *central portal* consists of two octagonal columns resting on bulls. On top of the beautifully sculpted cusped arch is an unusual motif, a *sphinx*. The nave of the grandiose interior is set off from its single aisles by columns surmounted by carved Romanesque *capitals*, the finest of which are those adorning the choir partition. The remarkable *ciborium* on the main altar (dated 1150) has carved capitals with figures of angels. Behind the altar is a 12th century *bishop's throne*. Sculpted in marble, it is sustained by grotesque figures that recall motifs typical of Northern European sculpture. The *Tomb of St. Nicholas* is beneath the altar in the *crypt*.

CASTEL DEL MONTE - (54 km). Probably the most famous castle in Italy, it was built for Frederick II in the mid-1200s. The castle served as a fort, but also as a hunting lodge and site of sumptuous wedding banquets. The eight-sided building has eight-sided towers at each corner. The *main portal* is an example of the Gothic style with marked Classical influxes, while the decorative elements are Gothic, at times revealing Oriental influences.

ALBEROBELLO - (60 km). Alberobello, right in the heart of the region denominated *Murgia dei Trulli*, is famous for its numerous *trulli* buildings. *Trulli* have massive walls built of stone blocks and are covered with cone-shaped roofs obtained by putting stones of diminishing diameters one on top of another. There is even a *trullo* church, *Sant'Antonio*, which dominates the whole town from a nearby hilltop.

Above: Castel del Monte. Below: view of the characteristic Alberobello trulli.

BRINDISI

Brindisi, rising on a promontory gripped in the embrace of the two lobster-like claws of the Adriatic Sea, was, from the time it was settled by the Italic tribe of the Messapi, a sheltered natural port. The most trafficked passageway to the Orient for centuries, the modern town is still an important embarkation station (for both passengers and freight) to points east such as Greece and Turkey.

ROMAN COLUMNS - Erected around the 1st-2nd century B.C., the columns were the terminal markers of the Appian Way (which from Rome traversed all of Italy southward to Brindisi). In the 16th century, one of them toppled from its base and was donated the city of Lecce whereas the other is crowned by a remarkable marble *capital* with sculpted figures of *Jupiter*, *Mars*, *Pallas*, and *Neptune*.

MUSEO ARCHEOLOGICO - The highlights of the Brindisi Archeological Museum include notable Greek and Hellenistic *statues*, Attic and Messapi *ceramics*, as well as Roman reliefs and capitals.

SAN BENEDETTO - This Romanesque church (started in 1080) was extensively altered in the 16th century. It has a fine sculpted lateral *portal*, *capitals*, and a delighful 11th century *cloister*.

SANTA MARIA DEL CASALE - This striking Romanesque-Gothic church was commissioned in the 13th century by an Anjou prince from Taranto. Its striking two-tone facade is adorned with unusual geometric designs; on the portal is an overhead porch. The aisleless interior vaunts early 14th century *frescoes* of notable artistic worth. The finest is a huge *Last Judgment*, the only known work by the painter named Rinaldo da Taranto.

Above: Roman terminus columns marking the end of the Appian Way. Below: Santa Maria del Casale.

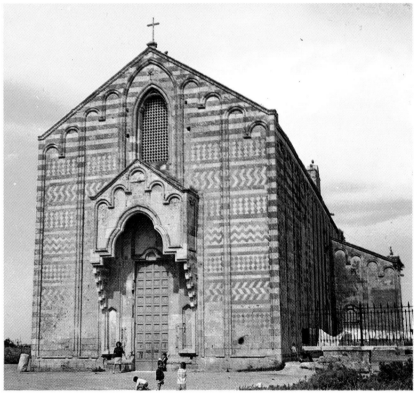

LECCE

It prospered as a Roman city (especially in the 2nd century A.D.). The Middle Ages were spent in fighting for control of the surrounding territory, the city's worst enemy being its neighbor, Otranto. A long period of economic stability (16th through 18th centuries) brought renewed prosperity and the city was adorned with scores of churches, palaces, and civic buildings, decorated in an elaborate style. The artists responsible for this architectural-sculptural movement, unique in Baroque art for originality and homogeneity, were all natives of Lecce.

DUOMO - The Duomo, a 12th century building remodeled in 1659 by Giuseppe Zimbalo, has two *facades*, the main one quite plain, while the lateral one is adorned with statuary and friezes, the whole culminating in a triumphal arch with a statue of Sant'Oronzo in the middle. Alongside is the 68-meter-tall

five-story *belltower*, another of Zimbalo's superb creations. The most notable feature of the interior is the incredibly elaborate decoration of the altars carved in the most imaginative designs.

SANTA CROCE - This church is the masterpiece of Lecce Baroque architecture, a remarkable fusion of the creativity and imagination of its designers, architects, sculptors, and inlayers. Alongside is the *Palazzo del Governo* (1659) designed by Zimbalo, which is a fitting counterpart to the church building. Begun in 1549 by Gabriele Riccardi who designed its interior and remarkable *facade* (up to the level of the relief frieze), it was thereafter continued by Francesco Antonio Zimbalo (responsible for the *portal*) and Giuseppe Zimbalo who in 1646 designed the upper part (which, however, was executed by Cesare Penna). The section above the elaborate *rose window* was the last to be

completed (late 17th century). The single-aisle *interior* is noteworthy for its *sculptural decoration* (capitals, ceiling, dome). The most spectacular of the altars is the one dedicated to San Francesco di Paola, the Baroque masterpiece of Francesco Antonio Zimbalo.

SS. NICCOLÒ E CATALDO - This interesting Norman building erected in the late 1100s was remodeld in 1716. Its fine *facade*, attributed to Giuseppe Cino and Mauro Manieri, is an unusual blend of Romanesque elements (the rose window and superb *portal*) and Baroque decorative motifs set off by pilaster strips and adorned with statues of saints. Half-hidden by the facade is an eight-sided *dome* (c. 1180) resembling a minaret.

TARANTO

According to tradition, Taranto was settled by a group of Spartans, who picked it as the most sheltered and safest point of the Gulf of Taranto, in 706 B.C. The location of the town that grew up - a tongue of land sandwiched between a lagoon (*Mar Piccolo*) and a group of islets closing off a bay (*Mar Grande*) - was extremely favorable; in fact it soon became extremely wealthy to the point of dominating all of the surrounding region and, shortly after, the whole Magna Grecia territory. Decline, which lasted throughout the Middle Ages, began with the Roman conquest of 272 B.B. In 1481, a navigable canal was dug, making it an island after which it became increasingly important as a military port. Its military importance continued right through the French period (19th century) and thereafter, with construction of the Mobile Bridge following Italian unification doing much to enhance it.

DUOMO - The church was erected in honor of St. Cataldo, Taranto's patron saint, in the 11th century over a pre-existing building, and was remodeled several times. Its fine Baroque *facade* was designed in 1713 by Mauro Manieri, an architect from Lecce. The *interior* has been partially restored. Marble columns set off the single aisles from the nave; above is a 17th-18th century gilded wood ceiling. Inside is one of the renowned masterpieces of Southern Italian Baroque architecture, the *St. Cataldo Chapel*. Begun in 1657 and finished in the 18th century, it is an elaborate composition of colored marbles and sculpture.

MOBILE BRIDGE - The original 1886 bridge spanning the man-made canal dividing the old city from the mainland was rebuilt in 1958. It is opened several times a day to allow ships to pass in and out of the docks.

Left: Baroque facade of the Duomo. Right: Ponte Girevole, or mobile bridge.

MUSEO NAZIONALE - This museum, founded in 1889, is of fundamental importance for the art lover who desires to fully comprehend the art of Magna Grecia. The major pieces are, in the Greek sculpture section, a 5th century *Head of Athena* and a superb *Head of Aphrodite*, attributed to the 4th century school of Praxiteles. The outstanding ceramics are a set of *Corinthian vases* (several of which fashioned in the shape of mythological animals), one of painted Spartan *goblets*, and a unique collection of 6th century B.C. *Attic vases*, including the superb *Lydos Goblet* depicting *Hercules the Charioteer*. Most of the remarkable jewel collection dates from the 4th-3rd centuries B.C. One of the highlights is a marvelous engraved *tiara*.

BASILICATA

Basilicata occupies a somewhat barren, mostly mountainous territory traversed by the southern tip of the Apennine Range, here called the Lucano Apennines. Its tallest peaks are Mt. Pollino (2248 m), near the Calabrian border, and Mt. Sirino (2005 m). With little industry most of the inhabitants of Basilicata eke out a meager living as farmers.

HISTORY - The name Lucania (another name for Basilicata) refers to the Lyki, a group of refugees from Anatolia who settled the inland mountain areas around the 14th-13th centuries B.C. The Greeks arrived to found their colonies (Metaponto, Siris, Eraclea) along the coast six hundred years later. Soon after they came into conflict with the descendants of the Lyki, re-christened Lucani, who were ensconced in their fortified towns of Serra di Vaglio, Anzi, and Torre di Striano. The Lucani resisted for many years, but were no match for the Romans who first razed their cities to the ground and then annexed their territories to the Roman Empire as the III Regio of Augustus. Thereafter abandoned to itself, Lucania was at the mercy of the barbarians and Saracens, until the Early Middle Ages when founding of Basilian and Benedictine monasteries sparked a short-lived but intense economic and cultural recovery. Thereafter, the region became a Byzantine possession ruled by a governor, the Basilikos (from which name Basilicata is believed to derive). In the 9th century the Norman Reign was established. Its first capital was Melfi (later moved to Palermo). Under the Anjous, the region was once more abandoned to itself. Later on Basilicata was associated with the Kingdom of Naples. In the 19th century the peasants' rebellion against the few, all-powerful land barons eventually led to the ousting of the Bourbons and the adhesion to the Kingdom of Italy.

ART - For several hundred years (8th-3rd centuries B.C.), the art of the region — not only in the coastal colonies of Metaponto, Siris, and Eraclea, but also inland — had a strictly Greek imprint. Local artists had achieved such skill that often Greek and locally-crafted pieces cannot be told apart. In addition to the excavations themselves, the museums of Potenza and Policoro provide a comprehensive picture of the art of Greek Lucania. Contrarily, there are few notable remains of the Roman period. In the Early Middle Ages, the period of the spread of monasteries and domination of the Byzantines, the first "rock churches" appeared among the so-called "Sassi" i.e., dwellings hollowed into rock characterizing the area around Matera. The Norman period (11th century) was artistically quite active: dozens of churches and castles, e.g., Venosa, Acerenza, Potenza, Melfi, Matera, were erected, and thereafter Romanesque and Gothic art had notable influence on art and architecture. In the 15th century, great fortifications were built in cities such as Potenza and Venosa and works were commissioned of important painters such as Bartolomeo Vivarini and Cima da Conegliano of the Venetian school (although in truth they failed to leave any lasting influence on the local painters). Some architectural projects (mainly religious buildings) were undertaken during the Baroque period, but, aside from sporadic outbursts here and there, no major schools or trends in Basilicata art have since emerged.

MATERA

Matera is undoubtedly unique from an urbanistic standpoint. The city is divided into two well-defined zones: on the west is a typical modern-day section spread over a plain, while the old section on the east is the "*Sassi*," a picturesque cluster of dwellings occupying two sides of a sheer cliff. Matera's territory was settled in the prehistoric era. It did not become important until the Middle Ages under the Longobards, Byzantines, and Normans. Industrialization is starting to make headway in the Matera area where up to recently there were only farmlands.

MUSEO NAZIONALE RIDOLA - This collection, put together by a Materese scholar, Domenico Ridola at the turn of the century, presents a comprehensive picture of pre- and post-Roman archeology in the Matera region. The museum was modernized in 1976; the collection is displayed in four sections.

DUOMO - Situated on the rocky spur dominating the Sassi, the Duomo of Matera was built in the Pugliese Romanesque style in 1270. The facade is adorned with a rose window and carved portals. The highlights of the interior comprise several Baroque works, 15th century carved choir stalls, a 16th century altar frontal, a 16th century *crèche* (left aisle), the 16th century *Cappella dell'Annunciazione* with its elaborate decoration, and a 13th century Byzantine-style painting of the Virgin (*Madonna della Bruna*), the patron saint of Matera.

SASSI - The old town of Sassi is divided into two zones, *Sasso Barisano* on the north and *Sasso Caveoso* on the south. The random juxtaposition of old dwellings partly hollowed into the rock and partly built of brick, little streets, courtyards, and Byzantine "rock churches" makes an utterly charming sight. Evacuated not too long ago for hygienic-sanitary reasons, the town will eventually be renovated and repopulated.

POTENZA - (96 km). Potenza is situated on a hilltop along the Basento River. The mountainous area it belongs to was settled in pre-Roman times, subjugated by Rome, and then engulfed by the Longobard duchy of Benevento in the 6th century. Thereafter Potenza was

Panoramic view of the city with the Duomo in the upper lefthand corner.

dominated by the Swabians, Anjous, Neapolitans, and Aragonese. Throughout the Middle Ages, it proved a mighty bulwark against Saracen attacks. Many times razed by earthquakes, the city has been rebuilt over the centuries. Today, it consists of a historic center encircled by a good-sized modern belt. On *Via Pretoria*, Potenza's main street, are two important churches, the 13th century church of *San Francesco* and the *Duomo*, built in the 12th century and remodeled in the 1700s. Outside the historic center, on Via Appia, is an important museum, the *Museo Archeologico*.

MELFI - (140 km). This city, settled in pre-Roman times, achieved importance, mainly in the medieval period. Capital of the Norman state in the 11th century, it later passed under control of the Swabians. Despite frequent restoration and remodeling (due to the damage wrought by earthquakes), the *Duomo* still vaunts many of its Romanesque features. In the *Vescovado* is a tomb, the so-called *Rapolla Sarcophagus*, a fine example of Roman art of the Imperial Era. The *Archeological Museum* is housed in the majestic *Norman castle* which was the residence of Frederick of Swabia in the 13th century.

METAPONTO - (52 km). This active town, a modern agricultural center and Ionian resort, vaunts extensive remains of its glorious Greek past. The Greek city of Metaponto was not, as legend has it, founded by a group of soldiers after the War of Troy. Rather, it was probably settled by Greek tribes from Peloponnesus in the 8th century B.C. Not far from the Antiquarium are the so-called *Tavole Palatine*. Once believed to have been part of the School of Pythagoras, they are actually remains of a colonnade from a 6th century Doric temple. In the archeological zone in the vicinity of the town are two monuments, a *Theater* and the *Sanctuary of Apollo Lycius* (7th century).

Above: Duomo of Melfi. Below: Tavole Palatine in Metaponto.

View of Maratea and the Gulf of Policastro.

VENOSA - (100 km). The town is situated in the middle of a zone settled in the prehistoric epoch. A Roman colony by the 3rd century B.C., it was the birthplace of the celebrated poet Horace. It was also an important center under the Longobards and the Normans. Wars and earthquakes have destroyed Venosa several times, but there is still much to see. Among the major sights are the *Museo Lapidario* housed in the 15th century *Castle*, the 15th century *Cathedral*, and the *Casa di Orazio*, which is not really the poet's house, but remains of the baths of a Roman villa. Of prime importance is the *Abbey of the Trinity*, a superb example of Benedictine monastic architecture dating from the Norman period. The complex comprises the 11th century *Old Church*, built in the 12th century, and the *Palazzo Abbaziale*. Nearby are ruins of a *Roman amphiteater*.

MARATEA - Maratea, the main center of Basilicata's 15-km-long Tyrrhenian coast, is situated on the Gulf of Policastro. Settled in the pre-Roman period, its main sights are 15th and 17th century buildings. The colossal statue of the *Savior* (21 meters tall) dominating the city is the work of a modern master, Bruno Innocenti (1963). The town is a popular summer resort, as are her neighbors, *Fiumicello-Santa Venere, Porto, Acquafredda*, and *Marina*, strung out along the magnificent Tyrrhenian coast.

CALABRIA

Calabria occupies the irregular-shaped tip of the Italian peninsula «pointed» in the direction of the island of Sicily. The region is mostly mountainous. In the north is Mount Pollino, the highest Calabrian peak (2267 m), while the tallest peak of the Aspromonte Range in the south reaches 1955 m.

HISTORY AND ART - The first to inhabit the region were the Bruzii, an Italic people. In the 7th-6th century B.C. the Greeks started to colonize the area. The cities they settled, Reggio, Sibari, Crotone, and Locri, became among the most splendid of Magna Grecia, as is apparent from the archeological remains visible throughout the region. The Greek cities did not, however, bring peace: they not only fought with the Bruzii, but also quarreled incessantly among themselves. After a long period of warring, Calabria fell to the Romans in the 2nd century B.C. This event marked the beginning of the end for the region in terms of economic well-being. During the Middle Ages, a monk, Fra' Cassiodoro founded a center of religious studies, the Vivarium of Squillace, which sparked the widespread penetration of a form of Greek-Oriental monastic cult. Simultaneously, the Byzantines were gaining power in the region, both politically and culturally, and they would leave their imprint on Calabrian art and architecture. The Normans, under the leadership of Roberto il Guiscardo, took over in the 11th century, during which time there was a greater expansion of a more Latin-Western religious culture. A preacher, Gioacchino da Fiore, had great impact in the 12th century. In the 12th century, too, the first Gothic influxes from the North started to make themselves felt in art and architecture. The Normans were followed by the Swabians, Anjous, and Aragonese. During the Renaissance period Cal-

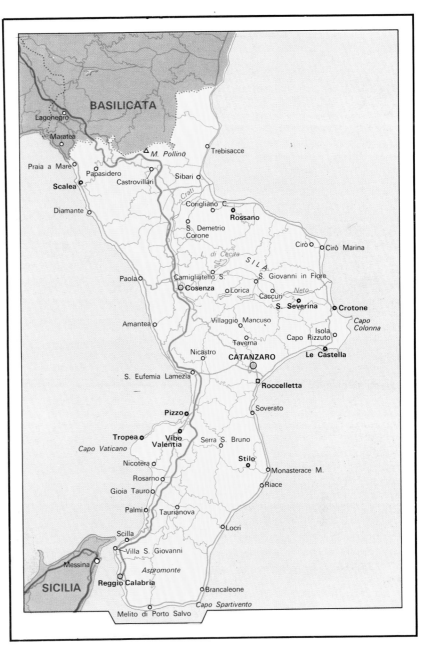

abrian art failed to make any major contributions, and the region became more and more impoverished, with the constant threat of Saracen invasions along the coast adding to the general decline. In the 17th and 18th centuries, a certain artistic rebirth was evidenced, although most of the population was at the mercy of an authoritarian feudalism, which did little to better their general economic situation. The Bourbonic period was hardly an improvement, and Calabria was the scene of numerous uprisings, the best known of which was the victorious struggle of Garibaldi's freedom fighters in 1860.

CATANZARO

Catanzaro is beautifully situated on a rocky plateau. It was settled in the Byzantine period, around the 9th century, by the people originally inhabiting the nearby Ionian coast who were especially anxious to avoid the constant attacks of the Saracen pirates. The picturesque *Grecia* district was the earliest to be settled. Catanzaro prospered during the Norman and Swabian periods, and was made a bishopric as far back as the 12th century. Although the Aragonese conquest (15th-17th centuries) was a period of overall decline, the city managed to preserve her prestige thanks to Catanzaro's great renown as a silk manufacturer. In the 19th century, it was an active participant in the Italian unity struggle against the Bourbons. Epidemics and earthquakes were responsible for destroying it time and time again throughout the centuries, and today its appearance is mostly modern, characterized by such public works as the Fiumarella Viaduct, an engineering feat with its single 400-meter-long, 100-meter-high span.

SAN DOMENICO - Also known as the *Church of the Rosary*, San Domenico was founded in the late-1400s. Its facade, however, is a 19th century work in the neo-Classical style. The interior, adorned with 18th century stuccoes, contains some notable Baroque works.

MUSEO PROVINCIALE - The exhibits in this interesting archeological museum range from prehistoric to Antiquity (5th century B.C. Greek helmet, Attic vases, a statue of *Athena*, and coins). There is also a painting collection. Painters such as Battistello Caracciolo, Salvator Rosa, Antonello de Saliba, Francesco de Mura, and Calabrian masters such as Andrea Cefaly and Gaetan Cosentino (19th century) are represented.

STILO (76 km). What is today a charming little town situated on the slopes of Mt. Consolino was an important monastic center in the Byzantine period, as well as a major iron producer. The *Cathedral* of Stilo, built in the 14th century, still preserves its fine pointed Gothic portal and remains of facade reliefs. The interior was remodeled in the Baroque period. The foremost monument of Stilo, however, is the 10th century *Cattolica*, a square-shaped brick church built by the local monks. Featuring the typical Byzantine architectural style, it has three brick apses and is surmounted by five little domes adorned with a lozange pattern. Inside there are four Antique columns and remains of frescoes.

Left: view of the city. Above:
Saracen fort overlooking the Bay of
Le Castella.

LE CASTELLA - (50 km). The most notable sight in this delightful resort town is the *Aragonese fortress* which rises on an islet in the bay. A sand path connects the island to the mainland. The castle was built in the 16th century to defend the town from attacks by the Saracens who, under the leadership of the pirates Barbarossa and Dragut had completely destroyed it in 1536, 1544, and 1548.

REGGIO CALABRIA

The city was settled in the 8th century B.C. by the Greeks who called it *Rhegion*. Its location on the extreme tip of the Italian boot gave it a dual advantage: economically, in that it was ideal for trade, and politically, in that it was ideal for controlling the Sicilian Channel. In 98 B.C. it became a Roman *municipium* and was rechristened *Rhegium*. Nature is not always kind to Reggio — earthquakes have struck many times over the centuries. When the most recent destroyed the whole city in 1908, reconstruction was carried out according to modern townplanning criteria.

MUSEO NAZIONALE - The museum has one of the most important collections pertaining to prehistoric and Magna Grecia culture in Italy. In the Prehistoric Section is an exceptional collection of pieces excavated all over Calabria. The Greek Colony Section occupies ten rooms. The collection comprises pieces excavated in the area of Locri including: a terracotta group composed of a horse and rider originally part of a 5th century B.C. temple decoration, and the renowned marble group depicting the *Dioscuri*. But the museum's pride and glory is the Underwater Archeology Section where the celebrated *Bronzes from Riace* are displayed. These two oversize statues of warriors were discovered in 1980 in the waters of the Ionian Sea at Riace. Superb examples of 5th century Greek sculpture, their stylistic harmony is so incredible that attributions such as Phidias and Myron have been advanced, even though they are probably the work of local masters of the Magna Grecia school.

CASTELLO - Built in the Early Middle Ages to defend the local population from Saracen attack, the Castle was transformed around the mid-15th century by the Aragonese.

Above: Lungomare Promenade.
Below: Bronzes of Riace.

SICILY

Sicily, the largest of the Mediterranean islands, is surrounded by three seas: the Mediterranean on the south and west, the Tyrrhenian on the north, and the Ionian on the east. A narrow channel (the three-kilometer-wide Strait of Messina) separates it from the Calabria mainland. The coasts of the triangular-shaped island consist mainly of low, sandy beaches (where the rare Sicilian flatland plains, the largest of which is Catania's, have their origin). The rest of the territory is mountainous. There are four major ranges (Madonie, Nebridi, Peloritani, Iblei), as well as plateaus, isolated hills, and a still active vulcano, Mt. Etna, the tallest peak on the island (3323 m). The Simeto, Platani, and Salso are among the numerous Sicilian rivers which, on the whole, are mostly small-sized. Once heavily wooded, the Sicilian countryside is today rather barren, especially moving inland. Great citrus groves are, however, today flourishing where oak and beech forests once thrived. The island's climate is renowned for its mildness. Summer months are hot, but always tempered by pleasant seabreezes, whereas in winter it gets cool but hardly ever really cold. Trains and planes serve the island from the main Italian cities. Ferries to Messina make frequent runs from the Calabrian cities of Reggio Calabria and Villa San Giovanni.

HISTORY - The name Sicilia (from the Siculo and Sicano peoples who first settled here) has been known since Antiquity. The island was also called Trinacria in reference to its triangular shape (from the Greek treis = three and akra = point). In the 8th century B.C. numerous Greek cities started to colonize it. The Greek-founded cities (Nasso, Siracusa, Gela, Selinunte) then proceeded to found others, so that Sicily soon became an important chunk of what would later be designated Magna Grecia (Greater Greece). Thanks to intense Mediterranean traffic, the new colonies grew and prospered, and artistically they even rivaled their mother country. Siracusa won out in the fight for control of the new territories, even managing to defeat the Athenians and Etruscans who were attempting to counter her expansionist policies and put a halt to the Carthaginians' dreams of adding new territories to the colonies they had already founded in western Sicily (Mozia, Panormo, and Solunto). The Sicilian cities relinquished their independence only when the Romans came to power in 212 B.C. Siracusa succumbed and the whole island became a Roman province. In the 5th century A.D. Sicily was invaded by the Vandals, later ruled by the Byzantines, and in the 9th century conquered by the Arabs. Under Arab rule, Sicily enjoyed a long period of peace and prosperity, a time of flowering for all fields of human endeavor. The year 1061 when Roger I the Norman emperor was crowned King of the Two Sicilies in Palermo was the start of a less pacific era which, however, was flourishing from an artistic standpoint. The Swabians and Anjous followed the Normans. 1282 was the year of the Vespri Siciliani when the people of Sicily rose up against the Anjous who, however, were soon after replaced by the Aragonese. The Spanish dominion, which lasted well into the 18th century, meant that for over three hundred years Sicily was kept firmly under the heel of a feudal power, which impoverished it both economically and culturally. The Spaniards were succeeded by others. In 1815 Ferdinando of Bourbon had

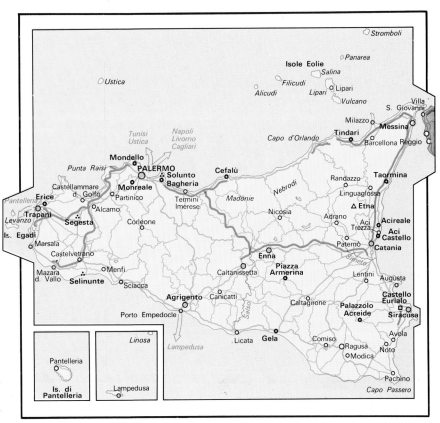

Islamic buildings that were once widespread throughout the island, but the Arabic imprint has left its mark on all of Sicilian architecture, civic and religious. Many other styles and schools gradually came to be mixed with these early ones — the Normans, Swabians, and Anjous brought Northern influxes which are evident in the cathedrals of Cefalù, Monreale, and Palermo, to name the most important. The development of civic architecture reached its apex under the Aragonese who filled the island with magnificent villas, palaces, and castles. In the meantime Byzantine mosaicists arriving in steady streams from Constantinople were busy decorating churches of different periods and styles. By the 15th century Sicily, Spain, and the Italian mainland were closely linked artistically, especially when the great Renaissance painter, Antonello da Messina, made his appearance on the art scene. Antonello was to leave a strong influence on his fellow Sicilians, and on the rest of European art as well. At the same time, the 1400s, sculptors of great renown such as Francesco Laurana and Domenico and Antonello Gagini were active in the artistic capitals of their day, mainly Messina and Palermo. The Baroque period too was a time of great activity in Sicily, as can be seen by the elaborate buildings and monuments adorning Palermo, Catania, Siracusa, and Ragusa, all of which reveal the Baroque impact on their townplans and architecture. Later, in the early 1600s, Caravaggio and van Dyck spent brief periods in Sicily, and their presence had great influence on the local schools of painting. Sicily's artistic production in all fields maintained its excellent quality throughout the 1700s and the neoClassical period during the 1800s.

himself crowned King of the Two Sicilies, a reign encompassing, besides Sicily, Naples and all of Southern Italy. Anti-Bourbon uprisings were common occurrences throughout the early 19th century, but the Bourbons remained ensconced until Giuseppe Garibaldi and his army of a thousand patriots landed in Marsala in 1860 and succeeded in making the island part of the newborn Kingdom of Italy. Gradually, as pressing — mainly economic — problems failed to be adequately dealt with, a separatist movement grew up. (And has not completely died out, even after the birth of the Italian republic.) Today, however, Sicily maintains its own bylaws and separate legislative bodies. Its main economic activites are, in agriculture, cereals, citrus fruit (for which the island is famous), as well as all kinds of produce, and, in industry,

minerals (sulfur and rocksalt), and oil refining.

ART - Sicily has superb monuments dating from the Greek period, including the temples of Agrigento, Selinunte, Segesta, the theater of Siracusa, and exceptional pieces exhibited in archeological museums (Palermo, Agrigento, Siracusa). The Roman period too is amply represented by the amphitheaters of Siracusa and Taormina and the superb Villa del Casale in Piazza Armerina. During the Middle Ages under the Byzantines scores of churches were built and several Greek temples were transformed into Christian places of worship (Agrigento, Siracusa). When the Arabs came to power, the oriental tendencies already inherent in the Byzantine style became more marked. Today little remains of the grandiose

PALERMO

Founded by the Phoenicians, it was later settled by the Carthaginians. In 254 B.C. Palermo was conquered by the Romans who, however, were compelled to defend it several times from the Carthaginians' attempts to win it back. After numerous vicissitudes, the city fell to the Arabs (831), and from then on its history became closely entwined with Sicily's: Palermo soon ranked as the island's main center and one of the most important in the whole Mediterranean. The advent of the Normans and Swabians enhanced its prestige. The court of Frederick II of Swabia was one of the most splendid of the Middle Ages as an intellectual center and in terms of economic wellbeing. The domination of the Anjous and Aragonese put a halt to the growth and development of the city and indeed of the whole island, negatively affecting its artistic-cultural output as well. The

Spaniards were succeeded by the Savoys for a brief period and then by the Bourbons, soon ousted by Garibaldi's troops who entered Palermo on May 27, 1860.

PALAZZO DEI NORMANNI - This imposing building was begun by the Arabs in the 9th century and then in the 12th enlarged by the Normans who turned it into a splendid royal palace. A striking example of a mixed Norman-Arab-Byzantine style is to be found in the *Cappella Palatina*, the chapel on the second floor of the palace. Commissioned by the Norman king Roger II, it was built in 1132. Arab influence dominates in the gilded carved wooden ceiling, whereas the gold-ground mosaics on the walls are Byzantine in both style and iconography. Among the most remarkable of the mosaics, are those of the *Creation*, the *Flood*, and *Christ's Entry into*

Jerusalem. On the third floor are the *Royal Chambers*. The most interesting of these is the *Sala di Re Ruggero* embellished with mosaics of stylized hunting scenes, heraldic animals, and flora.

CATHEDRAL - Huge and sprawling, the Cathedral of Palermo is a complex structure that in the course of its long history has undergone numerous alterations. It originated as a Christian basilica in the Early Middle Ages, only to be turned into a mosque by the Arabs. Later the Normans made their own changes when they turned it back into a church. Further modifications were wrought in the 1700s when the dome was added (architect: Ferdinando Fuga). The right side of the building, revealing a striking composite style, vaults a fine early 15th century portal. The apse zone, is an elegant combination of intertwining

archways, and rounded crenelation. The highlights of the interior include *Royal Tombs*, a *Virgin and Child*, carved by Francesco Laurana in 1469, a 13th century *Bishop's Throne* and the *Cappella di Santa Rosalia*.

LA MARTORANA - Begun by the Normans in 1143, the church was completed in the 17th century. Of the mosaics that decorated the portico once joining the tower to the church proper, only two are extant: the *Coronation of King Roger* and *George of Antioch at the Virgin's Feet,* which are displayed inside the building. Other superb mosaics adorn the interior.

MUSEO NAZIONALE ARCHEO-LOGICO - Founded in the early 19th century, the museum is set out on three floors of what was once a 17th century monastery. It ranks as one of the most important archeological collections featuring Greek and Roman art existing in Italy. Among the most important exhibits are: *fragments of sculpture* that once adorned the temples of Selinunte; these remarkable works rank among the most notable sculpture produced in Magna Grecia; the four metopes from Temple E, the finest of which is a superb scene of the *Holy Marriage of Zeus and Hera*, were executed in the mid-5th century; the *Etruscan Collection* consisting of four rooms of material from digs in Chiusi; works from digs of the Magna Grecia colonies, among which a superb 3rd century B.C. *Pompeiian Ram*, and Roman mosaics floors (the finest of which depicts *Orpheus and animals*).

Above: Palazzo dei Normanni. Right: Cathedral.

GALLERIA NAZIONALE DELLA SICILIA - The museum building is the *Palazzo Abatellis*, a remarkable achievement of 15th century architecture designed by Carnelivari, which features a fine portal, three-part windows, and flanking towers. The most notable works are: a *Bust of Eleonora d'Aragona* by Laurana, *Virgin and Child*, by Antonio Veneziano, paintings by Antonello da Messina including the remarkable *Virgin Annunciate*, and the *Triptych of Malvagna* by the 16th century Flemish painter Mabuse.

PARCO DELLA FAVORITA - This huge park, which spreads out for acres at the foot of Mt. Pel-

272

legrino, was commissioned by Ferdinando III of the Bourbon dynasty
in the late 1700s. Inside is a curious
building, the *Palazzina Cinese*, an
example of neo-Classical exotica.
Ferdinando and his family took up
residence here having been forced
to leave Naples when Napoleon's
troops took over the city. The Museo Etnografico Pitré located on the
grounds features a comprehensive
collection of Sicilian artifacts.

MONREALE

The town overlooks Palermo and the lush plain known as Conca d'Oro from atop a hill. Its main claim to fame, however, is its Duomo, one of the great masterpieces of medieval architecture.

DUOMO - Commissioned by the Norman king, Guglielmo II, and erected in 1174, this remarkable building has managed to preserve virtually all of its original structures intact over eight centuries. The main facade features a superb portal, the work of Bonanno Pisano (1186), which consists of 42 bronze panels with Biblical scenes. Inside, the mosaics covering the upper part of the walls rank as one of the outstanding examples of all times of this art. The work of Venetian and Byzantine master craftsmen, they date from the 12th-13th centuries. The subjects of the nave *mosaics* are *scenes from the Old and New Testaments*, while in the apse is the majestic *Christ Pantocrator* towering above figures of the *Virgin Enthroned, Apostles, and Angels*. The late 12th century *Cloister* is another remarkable sight.

AGRIGENTO

Agrigento, which rises on a rocky plateau running along the southern coast of Sicily, was founded in the 6th century B.C. by the Greeks who had previously settled nearby Gela. It was not long before the city, then known as *Akragas*, became one of the most important of Magna Grecia. In 210 B.C., it fell to the Romans, at which time it lost its Greek name and became *Agrigentum*. Then, during the Middle Ages, a bit of peace and prosperity returned to the city: this was the period when many of its great monuments were built.

MUSEO NAZIONALE ARCHEOLOGICO
This recently-built museum houses one of Sicily's finest archeological collections. The highlights are: Attic redand black figure vases; votive terracottas from the Agrigento temples; a gigantic *caryatid*, one of the thirty-eight which once sustained the trabeation of the Temple of Jupiter; a mosaic depicting a *gazelle* from the Hellenistic area; a 5th century B.C. archaic Greek statue of *Ephebus*.

SAN NICOLA
This Cistercian Gothic church rises in the midst of Greek sanctuaries in the Valle dei Templi. Originally a Greek sanctuary itself, then a Roman one, the building was transformed into a church in the 1200s and successively remodeled several times over the centuries. The facade is clearly divided into two zones by protruding trabeation. Fine reliefs of *Sts. George* and *Peter and Paul* adorn either side. Inside is one of the masterpieces of Classical sculpture: the *Sarcophagus of Phaedra*.

TEMPLE OF THE CONCORDIA
This beautifully-preserved building is one of the finest achievements of Doric-style architecture. Datable around the mid-5th century B.C., it was most likely dedicated to (Castor and Pollux). In the 6th century, the Bishop of Agrigento, St. Gregory, had it turned into a church, at which time many of its sculpted metopes were destroyed.

TEMPLE OF JUNO - This temple rising so majestically on a hill is dated 5th century B.C. Many of its original columns are still in situ.

Pliny narrates that when the *Agrigentini* commissioned the renowned painter Zeusi to decorate the temple with an image of the goddess Juno, he picked fifty young girls, had them disrobe in the temple, and chose the five prettiest to serve as his models. Depicting the most attractive part of each girl's body in a composite figure, he was able to achieve an effect of unbelievable beauty.

Above left: Duomo of Monreale. Below: the cloister. Right: the Temple of the Concordia in Agrigento.

275

SELINUNTE and SEGESTA

SELINUNTE - The majestic ruins of Selinunte rise on two hills on the south coast of Sicily. The city was settled by the Greeks in the 7th century B.C. (It was named after a kind of parsley that grows wild in the area, called *selinon* in Greek.) Twice destroyed by the Carthaginians (in the 5th and 3rd centuries B.C.), it was totally abandoned in the wake of an earthquake which followed. The archeological finds dug up in this area, including remarkable carved metopes, are exhibited in the Museo Archeologico in Palermo. The north hill was the *Acropolis* of the city. Remains of dwellings, roads, fortifications, and temples are still visible. One of the latter, *Temple C* (letters are used to designate the temples as the gods to whom they were dedicated are not known), is the oldest (6th century B.C.). It has 42 Doric pillars in its peristyle, 12 of which still standing on their original bases. Three temples rise on the south hill: *Temples F and G* (6th century), of which very little is extant, and *Temple E* (5th century), of which 38 Doric columns have come down to us. Temple E's metopes are in the Palermo Archeological Museum.

SEGESTA - Scenically located at the bottom of an isolated mountain, Mt. Barbaro, Segesta was settled by the Elimi, a people whose origins are lost in time. It ranks as one of the great archeological sights in Italy. The impressive *Temple* is one of the best preserved in the Greek Doric style. Built in the 5th century B.C., it is remarkably elegant in its simplicity, with 36 unadorned columns sustaining the double tympanum of the peristyle. Not far away is the *Theater* (3rd century B.C.), which consists of a vast semicircular pit carved into the rock.

Above: Temple C in Selinunte. Below: Greek theater of Segesta. Right: Santissima Annunziata dei Catalani in Messina.

276

MESSINA

Originally a settlement named *Zancle*, it was in turn taken over by the Cumans, Greeks, Siracusans, Carthaginians, as well as Romans (and renamed *Messana*). Under the Romans first and then the Byzantines, Messina expanded and flourished. Throughout the Middle Ages, the city was an important port and commercial hub, as well as a flourishing center of art. In the 15th century, it was the birthplace of one of the greatest Renaissance artists, Antonello da Messina. Unfortunately, epidemics and earthquakes too have always played an important role in Messina's history. The last great earthquake was a recent one — in 1908 — which wholly destroyed the city and caused over 60,000 victims.

DUOMO - First built in the 12th century, it was remodeled over the centuries. Three superb Gothic portals (15th-16th century) set off the facade adorned with sculpture, columns, and reliefs, while secondary ones are placed on either side. The *clock* (1923) in the belltower is embellished with mechanized figurines that appear at set hours.

SS. ANNUNZIATA DEI CATALANI - This fine 12th century Norman church was altered in the 13th century following an earthquake. The facade, with three portals and a rose window, dates from the 12th century, but the most interesting part of the exterior is the apse with its blind arches and inlay pattern. The striking interior features a single-aisle plan; the nave has a barrel vault, while the aisles are crossvaulted.

MUSEO NAZIONALE - Among the many fine works in the museum, the outstanding painting is undoubtedly Antonello da Messina's *St. Gregory Altarpiece*, one of the celebrated master's most famous. Other highlights include two superb Caravaggios: the *Resurrection of Lazarus* and the *Adoration of the Shepherds*. The works on display in the Archeological Section include Greek terracottas, figurines, and architectural fragments. The Sculpture Gallery contains a 14th century Sienese school *Virgin and Child* and a 14th century wooden *Crucifix* by a Sicilian master.

SIRACUSA

Siracusa's complicated history begins in 734 B.C. when Archia, leading a group of Corinthian settlers, decided to occupy the *Isle of Ortigia* off the east Sicilian coast. It was not long before the settlement, extended to the mainland. In 485, the city succumbed to the tyrant of Gela, Gelone. Under the leadership of Gelone's brother and successor, Ierone, it embarked on a period of great prosperity, even defeating the Etruscans at Cuma in 474 B.C. A few years later, the Siracusans were able to drive out the dictators and set up a democratic form of government. In a short time their territorial expansions posed a threat to the whole of Sicily, and conflict with the Greeks, the power then dominating the island, loomed inevitable. The war proved a clamorous victory for Siracusa. Soon after, Siracusa found itself once more in the hands of a tyrant, Dionisio the Elder, who nevertheless successfully defended the city from the onslaught of the Carthaginians and lavishly adorned it with monuments. In the late 4th century B.C., under Agatocles, Siracusa reached the height of its politi-cal power, only to fall to the Romans in 212. The city's valiant resistance was made possible by the ingenious defense mechanisms devised by Archimedes, inventor and discoverer of numerous principles of physics, who was killed by a Roman soldier unaware that the slain enemy was one of the greatest minds of the times.

GREEK THEATER - From Antiquity (starting in the 5th century B.C.), this theater has been witness to the Siracusans' deep-rooted love of theater. It was extensively remodeled in the 3rd century B.C. and once again during the Roman era. Semicircular, it could hold up to 15,000 people. The cavea is horizontally split into two sections and vertically into nine. The semi-circular space enclosed by the cavea was the orchestra, beyond which was the stage, so complex in form that it would be virtually impossible to reconstruct today.

ROMAN AMPHITHEATER - Erected in the 3rd century B.C., this huge elliptical structure was partially dug out of bare rock and partially built of stone blocks. In the center of the arena, the site of gladiator and animal combats, is a rectangular basin.

LATOMIA DEL PARADISO - This is the most celebrated of the *latomie*. Originally a kind of gigantic grotto, it was transformed (when a section of the ceiling collapsed) into a huge hole in the ground with limestone rock formations and luxuriant vegetation.

ORECCHIO DI DIONISIO - This 51-meter-long manmade grotto was originally part of an underground cave. Inside, any noise, even the slightest, is amplified many times. It received its unusual name (literally Dionysius' Ear) from Caravaggio, the great Lombard painter, when he visited it in 1586. The name was born from (or, as others say, gave

Above: Greek theater. Following page: Entrance to the Orecchio di Dionisio grotto.

278

birth to) the legend according to which the Siracusan tyrant, Dionisio, had a habit of eavesdropping, through a crevice in the rock, on the conversations of the prisoners he kept locked up in the dungeon-grotto.

MUSEO ARCHEOLOGICO NAZIONALE - Founded in the 18th century, this museum is one of the major Italian collections of prehistoric pieces and Greco-Roman art. The prehistoric collection encompasses tools, bone and stone weapons, painted ceramics, and statuettes from digs all over Sicily.

SANTA LUCIA - The church was built in the 4th century over the spot where St. Lucy was martyred in 303 A.D. Although its present-day appearance is Baroque, it still vaunts a 13th century portal and 14th century rose window. The base of the bell-tower dates from the 13th century. Inside the building is a splendid painting by Caravaggio depicting the *Burial of St. Lucy* (1609).

DUOMO - The present-day Cathedral rises on the site of one of the most important buildings of Greek Siracusa: the Temple of Athena, a 5th century B.C. Doric structure. The spectacular Baroque facade was erected around the mid-1700s. Several of the columns once belonging to the temple are still visible incorporated into the walls of the single-aisle church. Among the highlights of the interior are: an 18th century silver altarpiece dedicated to *St. Lucy* with a late 16th century statue of the saint by Pietro Rizzo, the Chapel of the Crucifixion containing a fine altarpiece with *St. Zosimo* attributed to Antonello da Messina, and the *Virgin of the Snow*, by Antonello Gagini.

MUSEO NAZIONALE - A 13th century palace, *Palazzo Bellomo*, houses the Museo Nazionale, a museum devoted to medieval through modern painting and sculpture. The highlights of the painting gallery include the 15th century *St. Mary Altarpiece* and the *Annunciation* by Antonello da Messina.

TAORMINA

Taormina is situated in a splendid position at the foot of Mt. Tauro looking out on a sparkling blue sea. Its winding shore line is full of spectacular beaches, and wherever the eye turns there are unforgettable views. Its climate is superb — the average temperature in January is 55°F. Its monuments range from Greek to Baroque. Its hotel facilities are excellent. It is no wonder that Taormina is one of the prime tourist attractions in all of Italy. The city originated as a Greek colony called *Tauromenion*. The city's strategic location made it an important center throughout the early medieval period. However, in 907, no longer able to withstand the Saracens' incessant attacks from the sea, it surrendered and was razed to the ground. Reconstruction was undertaken by a caliph, Al-Muezz, who renamed it *Almoetia*, although the city's real economic and artistic rebirth only began in 1079 when it became one of the territories ruled by Count Roger. Extensive remains of its antique splendor may be seen today, the most notable of which are the *Cathedral*, *Palazzo Corvaia*, and the *Greek Theater*.

CATHEDRAL - This splendid church, a 13th century Norman building, underwent considerable alteration in the 18th century. Of the facade portals, one dates from the 17th century, while the other (on the lefthand side) is a fine 15th century work. An *altarpiece* by Antonello da Saliba is on view inside.

PALAZZO CORVAIA - The Sicilian Parliament used this early 15th century castle as its meetingplace. The massive crenelated building with its Gothic portal and windows has a distinctly forbidding air. Inside, however, is a lovely courtyard with an outer staircase and a balcony embellished with reliefs, all that remains of a pre-existing 14th century structure.

GREEK THEATER - Dated approximately 3rd century B.C., the theater was built into a natural slope. It was partially rebuilt during Roman times, when it served for gladiator fights. Its acoustics are excellent and, in fact, it is still used today for summer shows. The nine-sector cavea is 109 meters in diameter. Parts of the stage and orchestra have come down to us in their original form.

Above: Panorama. Below. Greek Theater.

SARDINIA

Sardinia is the second largest Mediterranean island (after Sicily). Its Tyrrhenian coastline is jagged and rocky, full of gulfs and tiny inlets, whereas the west shore, on the Mediterranean, has many more beaches and is dotted with coastal lakes. In the northwest, the coastline once again becomes rocky — a succession of beaches, cliffs, and grottoes. In the north are dozens of islets, and bays along the Bocche di Bonifacio, the narrow tongue of sea that separates Sardinia from Corsica. Inland, the landscape is greatly varied, oft times strikingly lovely, e.g., the gently rolling cultivated plains of the Campidano, typically Mediterranean brush and woods in the midlands, the Barbagia highlands, Mt. Gennargentu (1834 m), and the sheer cliffs and bare boulders of the Gallura.

HISTORY - Monumental remains of Sardinia's remote and mysterious origin are visible in many parts of the island. The earliest domus de janas (elves' houses) date back to 2000-1800 B.C. (copper age). These are tiny tombs cut into the bare rock (sometimes in clusters) which according to popular tradition were once inhabited by elves or witches. The first nuraghi appeared in the 16th century B.C. They are conical in shape and built out of huge blocks of stone. Inside, there is a round vaulted chamber, corridors, and a stairway leading to an upper terrace. There are, however, many variations on this theme, and the nuraghi are found both in village clusters and isolated in the middle of the countryside. Their purpose was most likely connected with defense of the territory, i.e., they served as warning or advance posts. The Nuraghic civilization remained wholly cut off from the rest of the world until the 9th century B.C. when the Phoenicians settled numerous colonies on the island. The Carthaginians, who followed the

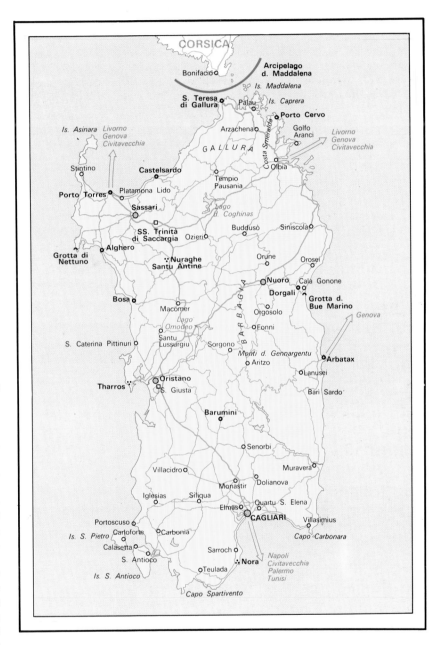

Phoenicians, founded major centers such as Karalis, Tharros, and Nora. Then, in 238 B.C., the Romans set out to conquer the island. It was not long before they succeeded in subjugating the key Carthaginian cities. Thereafter, in the Early Middle Ages, the island fell, in chronological order, to the Vandals, the Byzantines, and the Arabs. Meanwhile, between skirmishes with the Arabs, the Sardinians had managed to establish a somewhat stable system of government. The island was split up into four Giudicati, or duchies, that frequently had trade and political relations with the mighty sea republics of Pisa and Genoa. In

Roman theater of Nora, located at the tip of the peninsula of Capo di Pula. Settled by the Phoenicians, the town was abandoned during the Middle Ages and is now partially submerged by seawater.

the late 1200s, Pope Boniface VIII decreed that Sardinia would be a dominion of the Reign of Aragon, but it was not until the beginning of the 14th century that the Spanish army succeeded in making the decree a reality. The Spanish rule lasted well into the 18th century, so that Sardinia was kept in the throes of a rigid feudal government, while frequent bloody uprisings were of no avail in casting off the Spanish yoke. In 1718, Sardinia was awarded to King Vittorio Amedeo II of the House of Savoy. This marked the end of the feudal system, which was gradually dismantled, and the start of a new era: roads, and schools were built and cultural institutions were founded.

ART - The collections of the Museo Archeologico Nazionale in Cagliari and the Museo Sanna in Sassari contain numerous objects relating to the Nuraghic civilization. These, comprising stone statues, weapons, utensils, and pottery, were discovered in necropolises, nuraghi, and the prehistoric settlements dotting the island. Of considerable interest are the bronze statuettes and painted pottery that link the mysterious Sardinian culture of the begin-

ning of the first millennium B.C. to contemporary Mediterranean civilizations, especially the Etruscans. The few extant traces of Roman culture are confined to Porto Torres, Olbia, and Cagliari, and are of no overriding artistic worth. Only in the 11th century, the era of the Giudicati, did artistic activity of a certain level resume once more. This "renaissance" was mainly a result of the close ties that had meanwhile developed with Pisa and consequently with Lucca. The influence of the Pisan-Lucchese style greatly influenced Sardinian architecture, especially in the 12th century. Many superb Romanesque buildings are visible throughout Sardinia. The apse frescoes in SS. Trinità di Saccargia, bearing evident influence of Tuscan painting, are among the finest extant. The slow penetration of the Spanish style began to make headway in the 14th century, reaching its apex in the 15th. Prominent examples of Spanish-influenced architecture are the Duomo, the church of San Francesco, and the church of the Purissima in Cagliari. During the Spanish-dominated period, many Aragonese and Catalan artists were at work in Sardinia, and their influence on local schools was considerable. After the 16th century, however, Sardinian art declined into little more than an imitation of Spanish prototypes.

CAGLIARI

The city of *Karalis* was founded by Phoenician sailors, and later settled by the Carthaginians. It soon became one of the major seaports of the whole Mediterranean basin, a position it did not relinquish under the Romans. During the early medieval period, Sardinia went into decline without, however, losing her independence — only in 13th century did Cagliari succumb to the Pisans. In the 14th century, the city, along with the rest of Sardinia, became a possession of the Aragonese. Today, Cagliari is a modern city, whose main economic activities are concentrated in the port area and a good-sized industrial belt.

MUSEO ARCHEOLOGICO NAZIONALE

The collection, begun in the early 1800s by King Carlo Felice, includes extraordinary pieces representing Nuraghic, Phoenician, Punic, and Roman art and culture from all over the island. It ranks as one of the finest collections of its kind in Italy.

DUOMO

Begun in the 13th century, it was remodeled in the 1600s as a Baroque building. The pseudo-Romanesque facade was erected in the 19th century, although the architrave above the portal is original. The decoration inside the church is primarily Baroque, especially in the zone around the raised choir. Several Gothic features are still extant, e.g., some of the transept chapels and the beautifully carved *pulpits* on either side of the main portal, which once formed a single pulpit. Originally sculpted for the cathedral of Pisa by a certain Master Guglielmo around the mid-1100s, they were donated to the cathedral of Cagliari by the Pisans who had commissioned Giovanni Pisano to carve a new pulpit for their cathedral in the early 14th century. From the sacristy, we enter the *Museo Capitolare*, an interesting collection of vestments, gold and silver objects, and a 15th century altarpiece attributed to Roger van der Weyden.

TERRAZZA UMBERTO I

Also known as the *San Remy Rampart*, this terrace on the 16th century Spanish bastions offers a superb view over the city, harbor, mountains, and great swamplands of Molentargius and Santa Gilla surrounding Cagliari on the east and west.

SS. COSMA E DAMIANO

One of the most important Early Christian monuments in Sardinia, this church, now in a pleasant landscape setting, was built to house the mortal remains of a martyr, St. Saturninus, in the 5th century. Throughout the next seven centuries it was continuously trans-

Above left: panorama of the city. Above: Nuraghe. Below: beach of Muravera.

formed and enlarged, so that the whole became exceedingly intricate and complex. However, of the original structure in the shape of a Greek cross, only the domed central section (earliest part) and a single wing have survived.

BARUMINI - (61 km). Half a mile from this tiny agricultural center situated at the beginning of the Giara di Gesturi Plateau is the remarkable Nuraghic village of *Su Nuraxi*, one of the outstanding sights in Sardinia. The *nuraghe* rose in the middle of the village, which probably consisted of fifty-odd dwellings. One of the best preserved, the building had five towers on the outside, a courtyard (with a well), and various rooms connected by stairs and narrow hallways inside. The *nuraghe* was built between the 13th and 9th centuries B.C., and later re-used by both Carthaginians and Romans.

SASSARI

Sassari is the second largest city in Sardinia (after Cagliari), in terms of both population and economic importance. Founded in the Middle Ages, it was first a free city-state and then passed under the dominion of the Aragonese.

DUOMO - This huge building rising in the midst of a web of charming old streets is a curious juxtaposition of an 18th century Baroque facade on a medieval building. The aisleless interior is domed at the crossing. On the main altar is a panel painting of the Virgin known as the *Madonna del Bosco* (Virgin of the Forest), painted in the 16th century by a Sardinian master. Beyond the sacristy is the Aula Capitolare, where a fine 16th century *processional banner*, the work of a Spanish artist, is on display.

MUSEO SANNA - It is divided into three sections: Archeology, Pinacoteca, and Ethnography. The first exhibits Nuraghic weapons, artifacts, bronzes, and ornaments. The Pinacoteca collection includes a *Virgin and Child* by Bartolomeo Vivarini, a 14th century Sardinian *Crucifix*, the *Virgin with Grapes* by Jan Gossaert, and *Portrait of a Lady* by Piero di Cosimo.

SS. TRINITÀ DI SACCARGIA - (16 km). The 13th century church of SS. Trinità ranks as one of the finest Romanesque buildings in Italy. It is a clearcut example of the huge influence of the Pisan-Lucchese style on Sardinian architecture. The exterior has an attractive facing of contrasting marbles, in the typical Pisan style. The arch motif on the protruding porch is repeated on the upper sections of the facade and the striking belltower behind. The frescoes on the apse walls are the work of a 13th century Central Italian master.

Romanesque church of Santissima Trinità di Saccargia.

COSTA SMERALDA

The vacation home of the jet set, *Costa Smeralda* was developed in the fifties as an exclusive tourist center. Originally, the area, i.e., the coast lying between the Bay of Arzachena and Cugnana, was unpopulated wilderness. The hotels and villages that now dot it were designed so that they would perfectly blend into the landscape, without marring its remarkable beauty. The main center of the Costa Smeralda is *Porto Cervo*, which has its own little tourist port. Other centers are: *Romazzino*, *Capriccioli*, *Baia Sardinia*, and *Cala di Volpe*.

ARCHIPELAGO OF LA MADDALENA - The archipelago comprises seven islands lying between Sardinia and Corsica. They are a favorite with vacationers because their fine beaches are easily accessible, even by way of the water (bays and gulfs that make perfect landing stations). Aside from some scattered prehistoric encampments, the islands were mostly uninhabited until the 1500s when a group of Corsicans arrived, although not until the 18th century can we speak of permanent settlements. The seven islands are: *La Maddalena* (the largest), *Caprera*, *Spargi*, *Budelli*, *Razzoli*, *Santa Maria*, and *Santo Stefano*. The village of *La Maddalena*, situated on the Isle of La Maddalena, was founded in 1770. Today it is a fully-equipped tourist center (connected to *Palau* in Sardinia by ferry). From La Maddalena you can cross a bridge to *Caprera*, like the others, of remarkable scenic beauty. Here Giuseppe Garibaldi, the heroic figure who contributed more than anyone else to the unification of Italy, spent his free moments — and here he died in 1882.

Gulf of Romazzino along the Costa Smeralda.